KU-766-259

BIG TIME: THE LIFE OF

ADAM
FAITH

To Clemmie, Connie and Georgie

Waltham Forest Libraries £

Please return this item by the last date stamped. The loan may be renewed unless required by another customer.

August 15		
− 9 SEP 2015		

Need to renew your books?
http://www.londonlibraries.gov.uk/walthamforest or
Dial 0115 929 3388 for Callpoint – our 24/7 automated telephone renewal line. You will need your library card number and your PIN. If you do not know your PIN, contact your local library.

WALTHAM FOREST LIBRARIES

904 000 00434244

BIG TIME: THE LIFE OF

ADAM FAITH

DAVID & CAROLINE STAFFORD

OMNIBUS PRESS

London / New York / Paris / Sydney / Copenhagen / Berlin / Madrid / Tokyo

Waltham Forest Libraries

904 000 00434244

Askews & Holts	04-Aug-2015
782.4216 STA	£19.95
4732284	£

Copyright © 2015 Omnibus Press
(A Division of Music Sales Limited)

Cover designed by Fresh Lemon

ISBN: 978.1.78305.552.4
Order No: OP55825

The Author hereby asserts his/her right to be identified as the author of this work in accordance with Sections 77 to 78 of the Copyright, Designs and Patents Act 1988.

All rights reserved. No part of this book may be reproduced in any form or by any electronic or mechanical means, including information storage or retrieval systems, without permission in writing from the publisher, except by a reviewer who may quote brief passages.

Exclusive Distributors
Music Sales Limited,
14/15 Berners Street,
London, W1T 3LJ. UK

Music Sales Corporation
180 Madison Avenue, 24th Floor,
New York,
NY 10016, USA.

Macmillan Distribution Services
56 Parkwest Drive
Derrimut, Vic 3030, Australia.

Every effort has been made to trace the copyright holders of the photographs in this book but one or two were unreachable. We would be grateful if the photographers concerned would contact us.

Typeset by Phoenix Photosetting, Chatham, Kent
Printed in the EU

A catalogue record for this book is available from the British Library.

Visit Omnibus Press on the web at www.omnibuspress.com

Chapter One

"Once you been up there, you know you've been someplace"
Jim Stark, *Rebel Without A Cause.*

Just before Christmas 1957, Terry Nelhams had his hair cut. He went to Eddie Jones', in Acton, the place he'd been going to for a couple of years.

For a long time, Terry had wanted hair like the movie star James Dean. It's a stage that most young men went through in the mid-fifties. Sometimes Dean wore his hair in a long crew-cut that seemed capable of standing up to a height of three or four inches without ever collapsing, and sometimes he wore it a little longer in a quiff that seemed to owe everything to natural curl and nothing to artifice or product.

Terry's hair wouldn't do anything like that. It was blond and floppy. He'd tried using his mother's curling tongs and his sister's rollers, but the only way he'd ever managed to achieve any sense of the vertical at all was by applying liberal quantities of Brylcreem. This gave him the look shared by practically every other spirited 17 year old on the street: the greased three to ten inch quiff or pompadour combed into a DA at the back.

Terry didn't want to look like every other 17 year old on the street.

He wanted to look like James Dean – or failing that at least something different, something distinctive. And besides, as he said later, "I got cheesed off combing it all the time."

Eddie Jones, the barber, sympathised. He understood. He knew hair. Painstakingly, he degreased the barnet and clipped it into what Terry later described as "a funny little crop, tight to the head, with a short fringe".

Other descriptions might have been the beatnik cut, the French cut, the Roman Emperor cut, the pixie cut, the jazz cut. It was ultra-cool, ultra-chic and ahead of its time. It was how, three years later, both Jean-Paul Belmondo and Jean Seberg wore their hair in *À Bout De Souffle,* and how Steve McQueen wore it in *The Magnificent Seven.* By 1963, a longer version of that same style was known to Britain – and by 1964 to the world – as the Beatle cut.

To go with the new haircut, he'd got himself a new name. Adam Faith became his alter ego, his brand, his business – a business that, despite the slings and arrows of market forces and frequent diversification, would do him well for the rest of his life.

The relationship between Terry and Adam would never be easy. From time to time, Adam threatened Terry's equilibrium, rocked his security, drove him to bankruptcy, but Terry let him because, like most other people, he was utterly entranced by Adam Faith.

At the end of *The Wizard Of Oz,* the Great and Mighty Wizard, already exposed as a fraud, tells the Scarecrow that he doesn't need a brain, just a diploma. He tells the Tin Man that he doesn't need a heart, just a 'testimonial' – a heart shaped watch. He tells the Cowardly Lion that he doesn't need courage: a medal will do just fine. In other words he celebrates the triumph of hype over substance.

Adam Faith was never much of a singer, but he had hits. He had his shortcomings as an actor, but he had film, TV and stage credits that most actors would kill for. His understanding of high finance was never more than superficial, but he advised the rich and the famous, he wrote business columns in national newspapers and launched an entire TV channel devoted to the subject. He left school without O-levels but could spin an argument and drop names enough to convince archbishops and broadsheet journalists that he was an intellectual.

He had flair, he had bottle, he had bullshit enough to bio-fuel the national grid. No lad ever lived who more deserved the prefix Jack-The.

By 1959, the first wave of swaggering, hollering rock'n'roll was over.

A year earlier, Cliff Richard, the reigning King of British pop, had scored with 'Move It'. Though it had been denied the number one spot by Connie Francis' stupid 'Stupid Cupid', it was widely praised as Britain's first 'proper' rock'n'roll song. But by then, it was becoming increasingly apparent that it might also have been Britain's last 'proper' rock'n'roll song – an anomaly, a hiccup. Cliff's attempts to repeat its success with other hard rockers – 'High Class Baby', 'Lovin', Livin' Doll', 'Mean Streak', 'Never Mind' – had all fallen prey to the law of diminishing returns.

Meanwhile, most of the major players in American rock'n'roll had gone either to prison, God, the army or hell in a handcart.

Chuck Berry was doing five years, later commuted to three, for "transporting a minor across the state line for immoral purposes". Little Richard had renounced secular music and was studying for the ministry in Huntsville, Alabama. Elvis, his hair shorn, was a GI in Germany. Jerry Lee Lewis had been kicked out of the UK when it was discovered that his third bride, Myra, was his 13-year-old cousin. And Buddy Holly was dead, killed in a plane crash along with Ritchie Valens and JP 'The Big Bopper' Richardson.

The hipper, more discerning elements of society were becoming increasingly leery about America, anyway: too big, too brash, too crass, too rich, too capitalist. Continental Europe was looking far more attractive.

In the early fifties, edgy individuals had done their best to subvert British culture by drinking coffee instead of tea: not, mark you, American cultural imperialist coffee served in a cowboy coffee-pot, but Italian *dolce vita* coffee drawn from a hissing Gaggia by a Sophia Loren lookalike and served frothy. The noisy, oily machismo of the motorcycle was giving way – in some circles at least – to the ice-cream putterings of the Vespa and Lambretta, the mounting of which would not split the rider's mohair trousering nor do damage to his winkle-picker shoes, his pastel socks or his cheeky smile. Wars would eventually be fought between the bike faction and the scooter faction, but for now there was still a measure of tolerance.

The new films coming from France and Italy embraced a new morality, a new style, a new freedom with such élan that their UK release was usually restricted to specialist cinemas. As a result of this, a whole generation was conditioned to be strangely aroused by the sight of a subtitle: and the very names of those foreign stars – Jean-Paul Belmondo, Monica Vitti, Marcello Mastroianni, Brigitte Bardot – could work as a form of foreplay.

And here, bang on cue, comes a new face. Adam Faith, the kid with the French haircut, as continental as Cliff Richard was Elvisified, was ready and willing to bring something new to the party.

Adam had been singing semi-professionally and sometimes professionally for a couple of years by then. The handful of records he'd released had been no better than so-so, and though he'd made enough from a regular spot on *Drumbeat*, a TV pop show, to buy himself a second hand Ford Consul, everybody knew he looked better than he sang.

By 1959, he'd started thinking about jacking in the music business altogether to concentrate on acting. His moody sulks and winning grins on *Drumbeat* had scored him a bit part as a tearaway on the long-running cop show *No Hiding Place* and a featured role in *Beat Girl*, a yet-to-be-released movie.

Adam had met some interesting people on *Drumbeat*. He'd worked with the Lana Sisters (featuring Mary O'Brien, soon to change her name to Dusty Springfield), Cliff Richard & The Drifters, The Raindrops, Roy Young and John Barry, the older, wiser leader of the John Barry Seven.

Since finishing his national service, John had been making a name for himself as an arranger and bandleader. His group had released three records. None of them had done impressive business, but they demonstrated enough twang, honk and thump to impress the suits in the record companies. Mr. Barry was building himself a reputation as a guy who could write a legible score with correct enharmonic spelling but still knew what got those tearaway teenage feet a-tipping and a-tapping.

He and Adam had worked together a lot. They'd even made a record for the Top Rank label: a single – 'Ah, Poor, Little, Baby' coupled with 'Runk Bunk' – which, for good reason, has never been given a spot in the rock'n'roll hall of fame. Mr Barry had also written the score for *Beat Girl* – the first of many movie scores, five of which would eventually have him making acceptance speeches at the Oscars.

To the 19-year-old Adam, he was a fount of wisdom and sophistication, slightly older, better educated, classier, in control and making the connections that would put him at the hub of the sixties smart set.

A few years later, Mr Barry would share a flat with Michael Caine. Terry and Julie would pop round for drinks. Or maybe David and Jean. And in 1965, he would marry Jane Birkin, for God's sake.

Adam watched and learned.

Yani Panakos Paraskeva Skoradalides was another *Drumbeat* contact. Under the more manageable name of Johnny Worth he was a singer with The Raindrops, a four-piece vocal group.

"Adam had an amazing face," Johnny said, "a most endearing face, and something within me said, 'This kid is going to be a star. It doesn't matter that he doesn't sing very well.'"[1]

Johnny was a budding songwriter who had enlisted the help of John Barry's piano player, Les Reed, to make a demo of his latest effort. He played it to Adam. He played it to John Barry. Both could see its potential.

The tune was conventionally structured, elegant pop: an eight bar verse of three lines building to a climactic fourth line and a middle-eight to which a moment of drama is added by slipping in an unexpected chord change – an A flat major in the key of F.

The lyric is one of unrequited love. The singer offers money, gold, ermine and pearls, all the time hoping his inamorata will realise that their value is as nothing compared to that of his heartfelt affection and wishing "you wanted my love, baby". The inamorata, however, unmoved by either material inducement or protestations of sincerity, turns him down and plays it cool, leaving him feeling a clown and a fool respectively.

Mr Barry and Adam shared the same management company. A deal was fixed with EMI's Parlophone label. This meant that Johnny Worth, in order to avoid conflict with his own contract with Oriole records, had to resort to a pseudonym. He chose Les Vandyke, allegedly stealing the 'Les' from Les Reed and the 'Vandyke' from his own telephone exchange. It was the name he continued to use for the many Adam Faith hits he wrote.

A session was booked: Abbey Road, Studio 2, September 26, 1959.

Pizzicato is a musical term used to indicate that the strings of a violin, viola, cello or double bass should be plucked instead of bowed. It has been used as a special effect in orchestral music since at least the 16th century. It is the jaunty, excited sound of a cartoon cat sneaking up on a mouse.

In the forties and fifties, Leroy Anderson's 'Jazz Pizzicato' and 'Plink, Plank, Plunk' and David Rose's 'Holiday For Strings' were all minor hits, frequently aired on the radio. Their sprightliness seemed exactly to match the mood of post-war optimism. Had Prime Minister Harold Macmillan been more musically inclined he might well have ended his 1957 "you've never had it so good" speech with "and here to prove it is a string section, not bowed with sombre sonority, but jauntily plucked".

A few months before he died, Buddy Holly had recorded four songs at the Decca studios in New York: 'True Love Ways', 'Moondreams', 'Raining In My Heart' and 'It Doesn't Matter Anymore'. The Dick Jacobs Orchestra had also been booked for the session. For the first time in his career, Buddy was to be backed by strings.

'It Doesn't Matter Anymore', written by Paul Anka (who had a massive hit with 'Diana' when he was just 16 and later wrote the lyrics of 'My Way' for Mr Sinatra), was a late addition to the schedule. Anka didn't deliver the finished version until a couple of hours before the studio booking. Dick Jacobs jotted down a quick string arrangement.

"I had no time to harmonise the violins or write intricate parts," Dick Jacobs later said, "so we wrote the violins all pizzicato. That was the most unplanned thing I have ever written in my life."[2]

Mr Jacobs is being modest. The strings are not in fact 'all pizzicato' and by modern minimalist standards the score is delightfully intricate.

The record, released in Britain the following February, just a couple of weeks after Holly's death, stayed three weeks at number one.

There is some debate about who came up with the idea of using pizzicato on Adam's record. Johnny Worth thought that he might have suggested it. Bob Kingston, a music publisher, remembered asking Mr Barry to do a pizzicato arrangement for 'Be Mine', a Lance Fortune record, and Mr Barry asking whether it would be OK if he nicked the idea for Adam's session. Most likely, the idea occurred to several people simultaneously, the way ideas that chime exactly with the times often do.

Adam practised the song incessantly.

One of his other friends from *Drumbeat* was a crazy boogie-woogie rock'n'roll pianist called Roy Young, who used to cover the Little Richard and Jerry Lee Lewis material on the show with utter, passionate conviction. The weekend before the session, Roy found himself sharing a car to Oxford with Adam.

They fell to chatting about Adam's forthcoming Parlophone session. Adam sang him the song. Roy sneered. He was appalled that Adam could sing anything with such lack of style and still call himself a pop singer. He told him he needed to inject a bit of pizzazz into it, a bit of individuality, a gimmick: something to make the punters sit up and take notice.

Roy coached him, shaping the vowels so that "want" became "wowan't", "gold" became "gawld" and "baby", the song's killer hook, became an almost whispered "bay" followed by a barely vocalised "be" – with a short 'e'.

Most British pop singers aped their idols by singing in American accents. Adam, under Roy's tutelage, bucked the trend by inventing an accent all of his own that owed nothing to country or region.

The approach to both vowel and consonant, particularly that 'bay–be', caught the public imagination as no mere gimmick could. It was widely imitated, satirised, discussed and debated. It was a stupid noise – and everybody likes stupid noises (a few years earlier Spike Milligan's 'The

Ying Tong Song', the lyrics of which went, "*Ying Tong Ying Tong Ying Tong Ying Tong Ying Tong Iddle-I-Po*" had gone to number three) – but more than that it was a catchphrase, which, like "Loadsamoney", "Does My Bum Look Big In This" and "I Don't Believe It", nailed a thought, a feeling, a trend that was knocking about in the zeitgeist. There was a sly sexuality in that "bay-be", a whisper of defiance, a hint of revolution even, a classless, nationless murmur. The new decade, the sixties, was mere weeks away – bay-be.

The string fixer – the man who supplied the fiddle-players for the session – was a friend of Les Reed's uncle called Sid Margo.

Sid made a few phone calls and on the big day, he, Bernard Monshin, Alec Firm and Charlie Katz assembled, with their fiddles at Abbey Road Studio 2. There is a photograph of them, looking more Capone than Paganini, suggesting that there may have been a moment's apprehension when they showed up at the studio – did those cases contain violins or Tommy guns? They sit, in the photograph, with fiddles under their chins and untipped Capstan Full Strengths burning in the corners of their mouths. If you're looking for *tremolando,* you've come to the right place.

It was a tough job, working for Mr Barry. "Plucking away pizzicato at that E-string got incredibly tense and sharp on your fingers," said Sid Margo, talking about *Hit And Miss,* a later, instrumental track that was used as the sig tune for the TV show *Juke Box Jury.* "After 32 takes on *Hit And Miss,* getting it absolutely the way John wanted it, our fingers weren't just sore, there was blood gushing from them."

"It sounds better when it gets to the bone,"[3] said Mr Barry.

Norman Newell, the presiding genius at EMI, was supposed to produce but he'd just returned from America, where he'd seen Elvis perform live and come to the conclusion that he was rather out of touch with this newfangled rock'n'roll, so retired to a darkened room leaving his young assistant John Burgess and sound engineer Malcolm Addey in charge of the session.

There was a run-through. Burgess heard Adam, he heard the arrangement and he knew just what was needed. "Adam's voice could never soar or compete with bass, drums and twang," he said. "Everything had to be feathery light."[4]

He placed the fiddles in a circle around a single mic and messed with reverb and EQ (or echo chambers and tone controls as they were back then) to give them a hard electronic sound. "That way, the whole thing was relatively polite, the punch just coming from the way I did those strings."

The song was audaciously short: intro, verse, verse, middle-eight, verse, middle-eight, key change and playout verse still only added up to one minute 38 seconds. Record-buyers were used to getting more for their money. Would they feel short-changed?

"If they want to hear more," Adam said, "they can always put it on again."

When Norman Newell heard the acetate he was horrified. He hated the arrangement; he hated Adam's enunciation. He hated the fact that it was nothing like anything else in the charts.

Adam's manager, Eve Taylor, was unimpressed, too. After hearing it, she rushed out a press release stressing that her client would in future be concentrating on his acting career.

'What Do You Want?', released on October 24, 1959, was a slow starter.

Eventually it made its way onto the playlist at BBC TV's record review show, *Juke Box Jury*. One of the panellists said, "This record should do well in China. They'll be the only people who'll understand it." Nevertheless they voted it a hit.

Brian Matthew played in on the Light Programme's *Saturday Club*. Adam gave it an airing on ITV's *Boy Meets Girl*. Jack Good, *Boy Meets Girl*'s producer, moonlighting as a record critic for *Disc* magazine, gave it the thumbs up. But as the days and weeks rolled by, it looked ever more likely that Adam's future career, if he was to have a career at all, would be as an actor.

Then came "The Day I Had My First Hit" – Adam's favourite story, repeated for the rest of his life to anybody who'd listen.

Every Friday, chart day, he'd hang around Eve Taylor's office on Hay Hill in Mayfair, flirting with Eve's secretary, Jan, and hoping the phone would ring with some good news. Four weeks went by. On Friday,

November 20, when no call had come by six, he and Eve left the office and began to trudge despondently down the hill.

They were stopped by a scream behind them. It was Jan.

The *New Musical Express* had rung. They were in. 'What Do You Want?' was sharing the number 18 position with The Coasters' 'Poison Ivy' and was one position higher than the Beverley Sisters' 'Little Donkey'.

"It was," Adam said, "the most exciting moment of my career".

A week later, the record was at number eight. The week after that it had leapfrogged Cliff Richard, Marty Wilde, Neil Sedaka, The Everly Brothers, and even the Avon's 'Seven Little Girls Sitting In The Back Seat' to the number one spot.

Adam Faith was top of the pops.

Thirty years later, Adam took the actor and dramatist Gawn Grainger for lunch at the Savoy to discuss a possible TV series. Adam had, for a while, been a director of the Savoy. He sat among the fine people, the fine décor and the fine dining. The staff treated him like a king. In return, he called everybody, the *maitre d'*, the wine waiter, the manager "cock".

"The Grill Room was full, of course," says Gawn. "And at the end of lunch he said, 'Well, what do you think, Gawn?' And I said, 'About what?' And he said, 'About all this.' And I said, 'It's all right. It's very nice.' And he gets up – and remember the place is full – and he says, 'Do you know what it all comes from?' And I said, 'No' and he goes, 'It comes from... *What do you want if you don't want money* ...'' And he's up and singing in the middle of the Grill Room. He was heaven."

Chapter Two

"The lowest and vilest alleys of London do not present a more dreadful record of sin than does the smiling and beautiful countryside."

Arthur Conan Doyle

M ost war babies claim to have been born in the middle of an air raid. You can't blame them. It adds drama and poignancy to their entry into the world. Everybody wants a fanfare.

Searchlights rake the night-time sky. Satanic mayhem stalks the streets. The earth shakes. Thunder rips through doors and smashes windows. To the agonised screams of the wounded is added another sound: the mewling shriek of a newborn infant. In the midst of death and destruction, new life emerges and with it hope for a better future. That sort of thing.

"I was born on the 9th of October 1940," John Lennon wrote, "when, I believe, the Nasties were still bombing us led by Madalf Heatlump (Who had only one)." The statement in itself is incontrovertible, but the notion that bombs were actually raining on Liverpool Maternity Hospital at the moment Lennon first howled has been subjected to exhaustive anorak research. The verdict is still inconclusive.

"I was born Terence Nelhams," says Adam in his autobiography *Acts*

Of Faith, "in the middle of an air raid on 23rd June 1940. It was the one time my mum's blitz routine broke down. Instead of running for the park, where the shelter was, she got down under the kitchen table and gave birth to me."

In fact, little Terry arrived at 4 Churchfield Road, Acton, West London, a couple of months earlier than the Luftwaffe. If the confinement took place under the kitchen table, then his mother must have had some personal preference for the spot. There were no bombs to hide from.

Anyway, Adam's mum, Nell, was not the hiding kind. She was a formidable woman who came from formidable stock. Grandma, Annie May Hall, was a hard drinker known to all – not at all affectionately – as 'The Old Cow'. She married granddad, Henry Laurence Burridge, on Christmas Day 1907. Nell, Ellen May, was born two years later, the first of three children. Granddad never came back from the Great War.

Left on her own with three kids to support it seems that Annie turned to prostitution to make ends meet, although Adam's Aunt Doll was always outraged by the suggestion. There was a violent streak in her. In drink, and sometimes sober, she'd lay about the kids with a coal shovel, at which time Nell would protectively usher her little brother and sister into the cupboard under the stairs. It was a good place to hide when the gentlemen callers came, too.

Aunt Doll reckoned Nell saved her life several times over.

Nell learned independence, she learned how to stick up for herself, she learned how to survive. But according to Adam, she never learned much about giving or receiving affection, as a result of which, "I've grown up wanting to be loved by the wide world, and all the people in it. Especially the women."

This, of course, is the standard excuse of the womaniser, in much the same way as "we were very poor when I was a child" can be trotted out by either the spendthrift or the miser and "I was bullied" by the brute. And there could be a grain of truth in any of them: maybe even more than a grain.

"She [Nell] was quite an aggressive woman," says Keith Altham, Adam's friend from the early sixties until the end. "She fought her corner and Adam's corner too. She stood up for her children. Typical mum of that period – had lots of energy that, in all probability, if she'd had more opportunities, she could have used to achieve a lot."

Adam's dad, Alf, was a lorry driver who spent long hours and sometimes days away from home. "He was quite passive," says Keith Altham. "A very laid-back man. He was often offered promotion in his job but he would always turn it down. Adam reckoned that he either thought he wasn't capable of doing it or maybe he was just happy doing the simple job that he already got. His dad used to get a lot of flak from Nell over it."

Adam inherited his mother's high cheekbones and sharp jawline – they looked even better on him than they did on a woman – as well as her drive, her ambition, her self–possession and most definitely her survival skills, but he struggled to find any genetic link at all with his father.

"He told me a story that his father might not have been his father," says Keith. "Part of the mystery was that he never understood why the name on his birth certificate was Terence Nelhams Wright. He couldn't understand where the 'Wright' bit came from. When he asked his mother about it, she had a very sketchy explanation. She said that when they were registering the birth, someone in the office had said, 'What do you want the boy to be called?' And his dad said 'Terry' and his mother said 'Right' so they put down 'Terry Nelhams Wright' by mistake.

"But he always had the suspicion that there was a man called William Wright involved – because his mother often called him 'Bill'. William Wright was this shadowy figure that Adam always believed might have been his real father. He thought he was a Canadian GI. There was something strange about it."

The truth of the matter is less glamorous but more complicated. In 1928, Nell, 18 and unmarried, gave birth to a son, Ronald, who, to add to the confusion, was always called Dennis. Five years later, she met and married a gentleman by the name of Cecil G. Wright and took his name. But Mr Wright, as one wag put it, turned out not to be Mr Right after all. So, Nell left him and moved in with Alfred Nelhams, a much nicer chap. Nell and Alf's first child, Pamela, was born just before the outbreak of war in 1939.

In the thirties, divorce could be a costly business. People from Acton had better things to spend their money on. Accordingly, all four of Nell and Alf's children – Pamela, Terry and the twins, Roger and Christine, who came later – were born out of wedlock. Indeed, Adam was 13 before his mum and dad decided to get married – presumably because Nell had at last managed to divorce Cecil G. Wright or because poor Cecil had turned up his toes.

So, Adam's birth certificate is a mess. The baby is Terence Nelhams Wright. Dad, Alfred Nelhams, is recorded as Alfred Richard Wright. Mum is down as Ellen May Wright, formerly Nelhams. It's impossible to say whether this name-fudging was sleight of hand on mum and dad's part to conceal the child's illegitimacy or whether it was merely Mr Elsworthy the registrar's attempt to make sense of it all. Or maybe he was just a bit deaf.

There's nothing on the birth certificate to explain why Nell would go on to call Adam/Terry 'Bill'. If there's any truth at all in Adam's theory that his biological father wasn't Alf, then the 'William' in question was almost certainly not a Canadian soldier, the first of whom didn't arrive in the UK until three or four months after the outbreak of war, which would have been a good two months after Adam's conception.

A diverting afternoon can be spent thinking of alternative Williams of an appropriate age who could be the father of Adam Faith. Billy the Kid was dead, Bill Clinton not yet born, so they're off the hook. Drug-addled literary collagist William Burroughs, however, waspish novelist W. Somerset Maugham and (young but nonetheless post-pubescent) Bill 'Rock Around The Clock' Haley are all possibilities.

When the Luftwaffe finally found its way to Acton, it did its job diligently. There was no shortage of targets: Napier's made aircraft engines on its six-and-a-half acre site in Acton Vale; Evershed and Vignoles on Acton Lane made aircraft instruments; Wilkinson Sword on Southfield Road made flak jackets and commando knives as well as razor blades and swords; on Warple Road, the Sunbeam car factory made military vehicles and CAV/Lucas fuel-injection equipment.

None of these targets was much more than a 10-minute walk from

Nell and Alf's house on Churchfield Road. Luckily the neighbourhood air raid shelter, in Acton Park, was handy too. When the sirens went, mum had everything ready in a pram in the hallway. Grab the pram, summon Alf and the kids, run for it.

The shelter was, by all accounts, a depressing place, nothing like the 'Britain Can Take It' image of the jolly working classes smiling through, swigging tea and laughing in the face of high explosive. Steel bunks, three deep, lined the walls and it had a musty smell, a combination of earth, shit and fear.

In January 1941, a bomb landed on the Nelhams' doorstep. They moved round the corner to 18 Goldsmith Road. If anything, this put them in even more danger. The railway that serviced Napier's ran at the back of the house. Troop trains in and out of London used the line, too. One of Adam's earliest memories was of sitting on the wall at the bottom of the garden with his sister Pamela and the kids from next door, waving at the soldiers as they came past.

The bombing eased off after May 1941, and the raids that came afterwards were never as intense as that first blitz, but still bad enough to have the pram primed and ready in the hall.

Eventually another near miss, in which Nell was showered in broken glass, prompted another move. For a time they stayed in the basement of Uncle Sid's place on the Uxbridge Road, but rats were competing for the space, so they moved on.

Uncle Ernie had found them a place in the country, so the family, including gran and various aunts, uncles and cousins, piled into the back of Ernie's lorry (don't ask where he got the petrol rations from) and drove up the A1 to Bathley, a little village just north of Newark-on-Trent in Nottinghamshire.

Trevor Frecknall describes the place on his "Our Nottinghamshire" website.

"The cottage in which the family stayed is called Sunny View and is situated beside The Green at Bathley. The orchard in which he [Adam] enjoyed a swing was across the Green where bungalows now stand. The first cows he ever saw were in the field behind Sunny View. There were pigs, too. Vegetables came from the Sunny View garden (which was formerly the village's animal pound). Fresh milk and eggs came from the Fryer family Manor Farm at the North end of the village."[5]

Young Terry played on the swing. He took his jug to the dairy to have it filled with unpasteurised milk. He ate eggs and butter and all the other goodies that were so strictly rationed in places with pavements. He lived the life of the Larkin family. Perfick.

It didn't last long. Maybe the owners came back from wherever they'd been. One story suggests that the family's visit to Bathley was occasioned by a pregnancy. While there, Nell gave birth to another child, a girl who failed to thrive.

After heaven came hell. Mum went back to London. Terry and Pam were 'evacuated' for the duration. Most Acton evacuees were shipped off to the West Country or Wales. Some were treated as slave labour by surly farmers and put on starvation diets: others enjoyed the same delights as Terry had known at Bathley.

Terry, still too young for proper school, and sister Pamela, not much older, got sent to Bradford in West Yorkshire. All Adam could remember was that he hated it. At the nursery, he ate handfuls of chalk. Nobody took any notice.

The family was reunited back in London for the last few months of the war. Mum fell pregnant again and Roger and Christine, the very non-identical twins, were born.

After the war, the Nelhams family were among the first tenants to take up residence on a newly built council estate in Ruislip, Middlesex, where their house had an inside lavatory, a proper bathroom and a garden. The estate nudged up against the countryside, so Adam could roam fields and meadows, paddle in a stream, grow vegetables and recreate a little bit of the heaven that had been Bathley.

They stayed a few years, but Nell could never settle. Like most townies, fresh air and grass disconcerted her. She missed Acton, so they swapped the dream home for a top floor three-bedroom flat in Maple Avenue, just off Acton Vale. It was a tight fit: Gran, Pam and Christine in one room; Roger, Dennis and Adam in another; Alf and Nell in the third. There were usually a few cousins and friends around the house, too.

Adam described it as less of a family, more of a "loosely connected gang" who never sat down for family meals but were expected to stick together if there was trouble.

Schooling never took. Young Terry was a smart lad: his intelligence was never in doubt, and all his life he was a fast learner with an almost obsessive curiosity, but school failed to fire his imagination.

He failed his 11-plus – the exam that decided whether 11 year-olds would go to grammar school and maybe on to college or university, or to a secondary modern school which would end, if they were lucky, in an apprenticeship – and went to John Perryn Secondary Modern (which changed its name to Bromyard just before Adam left). He was bright enough, did well in English by all accounts, but he was never a dedicated scholar.

Part of the problem was his stroppy mum. Teachers are often reluctant to impose proper discipline on kids whose mums are a clear and present danger. Nell was up at the school all the time, shouting the odds, sticking up for her boy. It was a habit she never got out of even when he was a teenager.

"One day he went to school wearing a pair of tight jeans," says Keith Altham. "The headmaster hauled him up on the school stage in assembly and told the whole school: 'Take good note of how Mr Nelhams is dressed this morning. This is exactly what I don't want any of you to wear in School. Now go home, Nelhams, get dressed properly and come back.'"

His mum was up at the school, arguing the toss with the headmaster before the bell had rung for morning break.

Most celebrity biographies contain some childhood presentiment of fame and glory. At six years old, the singer-to-be would, perhaps, be stood on a chair and made to sing either 'Soave Sia Il Vento' or 'Daddy Wouldn't Buy Me A Bow-Bow' to a delighted gathering of churchwardens. Or word of mouth would bring top drama critics hotfoot from Fleet Street to witness the actor-to-be's insightful interpretation of Second Angel in a nursery school Nativity Play. Adam had no time or energy for any of that. He was too busy making money.

He was up before the sun most mornings. He worked evenings and weekends. He had paper rounds – more than he could handle, so he subcontracted. He did cleaning jobs, he mowed lawns, he sold papers outside North Acton tube. On Saturdays he did a bread round. School was for sleeping.

Work brought him money and money bought him stuff. He liked stuff. He became an early adopter of the 'live now, pay later' consumer ethos, buying his bike, his record player and all his other stuff on credit, getting mum or dad to sign the Hire Purchase agreements and then diligently keeping up the payments from his pay packets.

He was bang on trend. Before the war, debt had been a matter of shame. 'Buying on tick' had the stink of the pawnshop about it. Post-war optimism, however, brought faith in the future. People had had a crap time in the war and they'd had a crap time dealing with post-war austerity and rationing, and now it was time to party. Today's stuff could be bought with tomorrow's wages because everybody was confident that there would be wages tomorrow. The only thing that could interrupt the cheerful march of progress and plenty was the H-Bomb, and there was nothing in the small print to suggest that HP debts would still have to be honoured after the entire human race had been obliterated.

The same optimism brought an even bolder ambition. If you were young and feisty and lived in Acton, Aston, Anfield, Armley or anywhere else that was grey and grimy and stuck in the cracks between *Sons And Lovers* and *The Road To Wigan Pier*, even though your parents and grandparents and great-grandparents had lived there, this looked like a time when you might, at last, be able to break out.

In 1959, Lionel Bart wrote a song called 'Big Time' for the hit musical *Fings Ain't Wot They Used T'Be*. Adam recorded it the following year.

> *"When the big times come,*
> *I'm gonna have me some*
> *I'm gonna do the things*
> *My daddy never done.........*

I won't be double-crossed
I know the things I want
I know the price they cost
I'm gonna get my share
While I've got my hair
I'm on the upward climb
Big Time."

Nell and Alf were old school. Nell knew about graft, she knew about drive and she knew about squirrelling the coppers away. When Adam was born, she was a part time cleaner in a factory. By the time he was a star, she was running a sizeable contract office cleaning company.

But Alf was happy just driving. After the war, he moved on to charabancs and took coach parties to Margate and Southend. Sometimes Adam tagged along for the ride. Alf thought the way he could make the Big Time was winning on the horses or the pools. He read the racing papers. He studied form. He worked out complicated accumulators. He never won.

Adam's generation knew that gambling and graft were for squares. And the 'professions' – doctoring, lawyering and so on – were only open to kids who'd passed their 11-plus. This basically left three routes open to the Big Time: crime, sport and show business.

Though little brother Roger tried his hand at crime later on in life, Adam could never see the point. His dad was no good at it either. During the dark days of rationing and austerity, black marketeers made big money dealing in stuff that 'fell off the back of a lorry'. Alf, a lorry driver, could not have been better placed, but apart from one incident when he came home carrying a huge slab of butter on an old door, his conscience was too active for the spiv's life.

Adam, too, had tried his hand at crime. When he was little, he and his sister had nicked a couple of pocket diaries from Woolworths. Alf and Nell found out and made them take them back. He learned his lesson. Crime had its downside. You got caught.

Later in life, Adam excelled at martial arts and became a fiercely competitive golfer, but back then, at school, he was a little runt who never got picked for teams. He wasn't quite what they called 'a delicate child' but he suffered migraines and never had the most robust of constitutions so sport seemed a non-starter, too.

Which left show business.

The main source of entertainment for everybody back then was still the pictures. Telly, unless you had a particular penchant for watching *Billy Bean And His Funny Machine* or *The Appleyards* (a soap opera that made drying paint look like *Star Wars*) on a nine-inch screen, was a waste of time.

No, the pictures was best.

Adam was spoiled for choice: he could go to the Dominion on the Uxbridge Road, the Globe, just off Churchfield Road, or the Odeon on King Street. The Crown in Mill Hill Place was a dreadful flea-pit, but did have the attraction of double seats in the back row for people who preferred snogging to Margaret Rutherford.

In 1956, just before his 16th birthday, Adam went to the pictures with his friend Ray Tibbles and saw the picture that changed his life.

Chapter Three

"Here is a figure worthy of the status of hero – a new youth in a new world. His own country can offer him little – a dream, exploitation, the culture of the older generation. His world awaits a new culture, a new art in the age of the common man."

Ray Gosling, *New Left Review*, May–June 1960.

Rebel Without A Cause, directed by Nicholas Ray and starring James Dean, Natalie Wood and Sal Mineo, didn't invent teenage angst any more than Bill Haley invented rock'n'roll or Alfred Kinsey invented sex, but it didn't half get it talked about. It sets out to explore 'what makes the modern teenager so alienated, so antsy, so uppity' but it couldn't really be called a 'teen movie'. It has all the thematic resonances of Dostoevsky, Sartre and Camus but with better hair and pointier bras.

The snottier critics disapproved. "It is not necessary to be a bigoted reactionary out of all sympathy with the emotional problems and difficulties of youth," said the *Times*, "to hold that Mr Ray's specimens deserve not commiseration but a visit to the headmaster's study – although the school they attend seems not to have such an animal and discipline is not one of the subjects on the curriculum."

If you were under 25, though, the film was like cocaine, sex and God all in the same noseful.

James Dean's performance as Jim Stark remains, two generations later, a benchmark for cool. He is cool when he is drunk. He is cool when he plays stupid games with Natalie Wood. He is cool when he giggles. As his loopy geek friend Plato says of him, "He doesn't say much, but when he does, you know he means it."

On a school trip to the planetarium he is told, "Life will be destroyed in a burst of gas and fire" and "mankind is an episode of little consequence". Judy, the Natalie Wood character, wants "a man who can be gentle and sweet like you are, but a man who doesn't run away".

What's more, Jim Stark is bothered by his passive father and his utterly dominant mother. He has cheekbones and a square jaw. He prefers not to fight but, if pushed, can give as good as he gets. When he takes Judy up to the deserted mansion he says, "You can trust me Judy," and because of the straightforward way he holds her gaze, because of the way he moves his shoulders, because of his sincerity, because he drives a 1956 Ford Coupe with whitewall tyres, a bench front seat and column change, and because of his hair (a long crew-cut, combed back, but with the odd clump allowed to escape anarchically, razored definition around the ears and a tapered rather than Boston back), she does.

Rebel Without A Cause was a sort of style guide for war babies, particularly those who preferred sensitive angst to macho strutting, teaching them how to dress, behave, think and woo.

Best of all, James Dean's cool would never be tainted. He would never grow old, get fat, go bald, change his shopping habits, change his mind, have regrets. His perfection would be preserved, just as it was, for all eternity, because he died just a few months before *Rebel Without A Cause* was released. At the age of 24, he crashed his brand new Porsche 550 Spyder smack into a black and white Ford Tudor coupe. He was travelling at 85 mph.

Terry left the cinema knowing what he wanted to be. He wanted to be James Dean in every respect except for the dead part. He obsessively read everything he could find about his idol in newspapers and movie magazines.

He read that when Dean, the new boy, was co-starring with Elizabeth Taylor, Queen of Hollywood, in the film *Giant*, the way in which he overcame his nerves on the first take – a scene shot in the desert – was to ask everybody to hang on for a moment, walk a few steps away from the cast, crew and the crowds of excited fans gathered to watch the shoot, whip out his Johnson and have a piss.

The story had a profound effect on young Terry. "It became my motto for life," Adam wrote in his 1996 autobiography. "Always attack the thing you most fear. Don't just sit there, in your armchair, letting life frighten you – go out and piss on your fear."

The original James Dean was dead. They weren't interviewing for a replacement: and even if they had been, Paul Newman, Steve McQueen and Clint Eastwood were all better qualified for the job than a 16-year-old twerp from Acton. Terry Nelhams had the jaw line and the cheekbones, did his best with the hair and the attitude, got the jeans and eventually even tracked down something like the red blouson jacket Dean had worn in *Rebel*, but the Ford Coupe way out of his price range and though there were a couple of girls around who looked a bit like Natalie Wood in the back row of the Crown picture house, if you told them things like "mankind is an episode of little consequence" they tended to say they were going to the kiosk for some Payne's Poppets and never came back.

Terry couldn't be James Dean. He couldn't even be an actor like James Dean. He didn't think he could anyway. In 1955, actors still needed a monkey suit and round vowels.

He consulted his big brother Dennis, who was wise to the ways of the world. Dennis suggested that rather than being a film star, he should do something behind the camera. He should be a film director.

Acton was well placed for film studios. Ealing, where the Ealing comedies were made, was just up the road. Shepperton, Pinewood, Teddington, Twickenham and Elstree were all within a 15-mile radius. Terry had the bike he'd bought on Hire Purchase. He made the rounds and got the same response everywhere: "Bugger off."

Eventually, Nell got him sorted out. Her contract cleaning business was on the up and up. She 'did' the Mayfair offices of J. Arthur Rank, a company Terry would have known not only for its man-with-a-gong logo on the front of the films they distributed but also as popular rhyming slang.

Nell had a word with the personnel manager and fixed her son up with a job as a messenger boy.

He was on the bottom rung of the ladder.

Rank was a huge enterprise, involved in film production, distribution, and advertising. It had its own processing labs and would later get into the record and photocopying businesses. The 'Rank Charm School' was where Donald Sinden, Joan Collins, Dirk Bogarde, Diana Dors and Christopher Lee were groomed for stardom.

Messenger boys working at Rank knew that they were in with a chance of the big time – or at least the ever so slightly larger time. The custom was that they would work their way up the pecking order and, if they kept their noses clean, would be transferred from Mayfair to Pinewood and a job in the studios as clapper boy or something equally menial. At Pinewood you could see actual films being made. You could rub shoulders with Dirk Bogarde, Diana Dors, Kenneth More and Shirley Eaton.

But Terry didn't want to be a clapper boy. At the age of 16, straight out of school, he was focused. He had a goal from which even Diana Dors and Shirley Eaton could not detract him. He was going to direct.

He had been advised that the way to learn the director's art was not on the studio floor, but as an editor in the cutting room. Rank's Mayfair offices had a cutting room in the basement where adverts were spliced together: an airless, windowless space that smelt of tobacco, cellulose and latex from the rubber-numbering machine next door. Other messenger boys came, kept their noses clean and rose up the pecking order until the great day came when they were sent away to work the clapperboard and meet the stars, but Terry stayed put, refusing all offers of betterment and promotion until something came up in a cutting room.

Again, the break he was looking for came from his mum, bless her. Another of her cleaning contracts was with a company called Television Advertising – TVA – based in Wardour Street in Soho. As the name suggests, it put together ads for the then relatively new Independent Television and was looking for a trainee assistant editor/tea boy/ dogsbody – what today would probably be called a runner.

Terry was in like Flynn.

He crossed Regent Street from Mayfair to Soho, a walk of a few hundred yards that nonetheless was – and still is to some extent – like crossing the border from Mundania into Excitementville. Soho of the fifties was a dangerous and delectable haunt of prostitutes, gangsters, razor boys, French, Spanish and Italian restaurateurs, punters of every race and creed on earth, artists, musicians, actors, film people and, above all, drunks. If those few acres south of Oxford Street, between Regent Street and Charing Cross Road, did not boast the highest concentration of alcoholics in the UK and possibly the world, they certainly boasted the poshest alcoholics. It has been estimated that, on an average day, the blood-alcohol found in the habitués of the Colony Room and the French Pub combined could have powered a small industrial estate.

The prostitutes held a particular fascination for Terry. On the other side of Regent Street, Mayfair prostitutes were called 'call girls' and did everything discreetly behind closed doors. In Soho they were on the streets. Terry got to know the Wardour Street regulars by their assumed first names and they got to know him. He was a fresh-faced kid, wet behind the ears. He was short, too. Having reached five-five and a bit, he stayed there for the rest of his life. The sex workers teased him mercilessly. He liked that.

Since the late forties, Soho had also become the UK's centre of coffee bar culture. A radical and almost treasonous alternative to the endless cups of tea that had sustained us through the war, coffee – Italian coffee made in a hissing machine and served in see-through Pyrex cups – had become a fetish not just among young, left-wing, bohemian, intellectual jazz fans with a deep understanding of abstract expressionism, unmilitary facial hair (men), too much eye make-up (women), a duffel coat and a Vitamin D deficiency, but also among people who wanted to be seen as young, left-wing, bohemian, intellectual jazz fans with a deep understanding of abstract expressionism, unmilitary facial hair (men), too much eye make-up (women), a duffel coat and a Vitamin D deficiency even though they were actually 37-year-old insurance actuaries.

Coffee bars quickly became 'pubs for young people' – places where they could read, meet friends, listen to music and, if business was slack and the proprietor indulgent, hang about for hours. They stayed open longer than pubs, too. Some of them all night.

On July 5, 1954, Elvis Presley, a white-skinned truck driver, on his third visit to Memphis Recording Services, having tried many songs in many styles, began to mess around with an old Arthur "Big Boy" Crudup number, 'That's All Right'. Sam Phillips, the owner of Memphis Recording Services and of Sun Records, liked what he heard.

Eight days after that, on July 13, 1954, Chris Barber and his band assembled at the Decca Studios in Broadhurst Gardens, West Hampstead, London. They recorded a few jazz standards like 'Chimes Blues' and 'Stevedore Stomp'. While the rest of the band took a tea break, Chris Barber on double bass, the singer Beryl Bryden on washboard, and the band's banjo player, Lonnie Donegan, on guitar and vocals, ran through a couple of numbers that had been going down well in their live shows. One of them, 'Rock Island Line', was a train blues that John Lomax, the American folk-song collector, had recorded at the Arkansas State Prison. It tells the not very stirring tale of a goods train driver who evades a toll by misrepresenting his cargo. Donegan sang it with laser-beam passion. Sixty years later it still has the power to excite.

The track mouldered in Decca's vaults and wasn't released as a single until January, 1956, a full 18 months after the session, by which time, on the basis of live performances and album tracks, a grassroots enthusiasm for 'skiffle' – the name given to Donegan's style of music – had already seized the country.

Like the punk revolution 20 years later, skiffle was essentially "this is a chord, this is another, this is a third, now form a band" music, with the added advantage that it was much cheaper: no amps, no drum kit, just an acoustic guitar or banjo, a washboard (still a fairly common household appliance, at least at your gran's), a broomstick-and-string 'bass', and a check shirt. Bigger than the Davy Crockett hat or the hula-hoop, skiffle blew like a hurricane and before long there was an uncountable number – sometimes it must have felt like trillions – of skiffle groups up and down the country singing a repertoire of slave plaints, railroad shuffles, murder ballads, prison moans, spirituals, songs of rambling and gambling; songs with sentiments as comprehensible to the average16-year-old in Acton, Erdington, Ipswich or Taunton as the Latin Bible or logical positivism. And even though, in the cack hands of amateurs, Donegan's white-hot passion was usually replaced by a generalised boy-scout bonhomie, the music had drive. It had energy. Above all, skiffle, even in its most cheerless form, was a release from the stifling, Lord's Day Observance Society, sports jacket and grey flannels, Perry Como and Eddie Calvert, meat and two veg, post-war pusillanimity of the fifties. It was, in its delightfully suburban way, a rebellion. Indeed, in comparison with the monkey-suited granddads with clarinets and wire brushes who customarily provided foxtrots for weddings, socials and do's, even the most inept skiffle came across like a jungle howl of teen revolution.

Skiffle was where the stars of tomorrow learned their trade. Tommy Steele and Lionel Bart were in The Cavemen. Mick Jagger was in the Bucktown Skiffle Group. Cliff Richard was in the Dick Teague Skiffle Group. John Lennon and Paul McCartney were in the Quarrymen. Roger Daltrey was in the Sulgrave Rebels. The James Page Skiffle Group appeared on the kids TV show *All Your Own*.

"What do you want to do when you leave school? Take up skiffle?" asks the show's presenter Huw Weldon, with a patronising smile.

"No," says the freshly scrubbed 13-year-old Jimmy Page, "I want to take up biological research" – as good a euphemism as any for Led Zeppelin's subsequent career.

Just before he left Rank, Terry got his school mate Roger Van Engel, known as Hurgy, a job there. Hurgy and Terry used to meet after work at the recreation ground in North Acton, sit on the wall and sing. Sometimes Hurgy would play air washboard. Kind friends told Terry he sounded a bit like Lonnie Donegan.

After they'd sat on the wall for a while, sometimes they'd go on to 'record hops' (the 'discothèque' was still, like food and sex, something you could only experience in France) at the YWCA youth club, where, to break up the monotony of scratchy vinyl through duff speakers, a local skiffle group would now and then do a turn. The general ineptitude of the local groups convinced Terry that he and Hurgy, rather than just being crap on a wall in the recreation ground, could be crap on stage, wearing check shirts and everything. Girls would look at them: and though only the most deluded of teenage boys can ever have nurtured a belief in the pulling power of a washboard, a stage is nevertheless a fine vantage point from which to see every girl in the room, possibly make eye contact and, with head gestures alone, suggest a liaison outside as soon as Tom Dooley's been safely hanged.

Hurgy had a washboard. Terry got a Framus acoustic guitar for £12 and 10 shillings (contemporary commentators have suggested that he was done). Another of the Rank messengers, a boy called Pete Darby, also had a guitar and a dad who played the banjo in the Salvation Army and who could show them how to hold their guitars (strings *away* from the body) and approximately where to put their fingers to make the three chords required to play the skiffle repertoire (usually G, C and D7, but Jimmy Page on *All Your Own* seems to have favoured E, A and B7 – the A and the B7 in the hard-to-master barre positions which, in skiffle circles, made him a virtuoso).

Cheap guitars in the fifties were invariably strung with hawsers from an ocean liner. Their actions were set such that those hawsers would have to be pressed anything up to half an inch down to the fret and then held there for several bars before the relief of a chord change came and the fingers could be moved to an equally painful but at least different position. The agonised expressions you see on the faces of those old guitar players are rarely the result of passionate identification with the music. Their fingers really hurt.

Terry, Hurgy and Pete would rehearse with bleeding stumps either at Pete's house in Putney or in their lunch hours in the screening room at the Rank offices. They were called something like The City Ramblers – although hazy memories might have confused them with another, more famous City Ramblers. Their first gig was a free concert for the staff at Rank, where the general consensus was the boys were well-suited to being messengers.

Their first paying gig, recalled by Adam in his autobiography, was at Wandsworth Boys Club. Terry wrote out all the chords and lyrics of the set and balanced them on a music stand. The curtains opened. The music stand went flying, scattering Terry's crib sheets hither and thither. The curtains were hurriedly closed again. Terry scrabbled and retrieved his prompts. The curtains opened again. Again the music stand went flying. The curtains closed again. This time Terry came up with the brilliant plan of moving the music stand six inches backwards. The curtains opened again. They were off.

Despite the two false starts, Terry, Hurgy and Pete went home ten bob (50p) richer. Each.

Terry, networking around Soho, got them more gigs in jazz clubs and – skiffle's natural home – coffee bars. They played The Cat's Whisker where the hand-jive was allegedly invented, the Mars Club on Berwick Street and the Skiffle Cellar on Greek Street.

By this time they had a new name. One of the skiffle standards was 'Worried Man Blues":

"It takes a worried man
To sing a worried song
It takes a worried man to sing a worried song
To sing a worried song
It takes a worried man to sing a worried song
I'm worried now
But I won't be worried long."

Terry, Hurgy and Peter were not yet fully grown men and they had precious little to worry about. Nevertheless the name combined the skiffle ethos with a splash of the James Dean pre-apocalyptic angst that Terry was so keen on. They became the Worried Men and set their sights on the hallowed Formica of the 2i's Coffee Bar in Soho's Old Compton Street – skiffle Mecca and gateway to The Big Time.

Chapter Four

"I always felt rock'n'roll was very, very wholesome music."

Aretha Franklin

The 2i's took its name from its one-time owners, Sammy and Freddie Irani. They sold it to two wrestlers, Paul 'Dr Death' Lincoln and 'Rebel' Ray Hunter, who lacked the funds for a new sign so kept the name. It was a wrestler's caff, not much favoured by the Soho bohemian set who tended to prefer the more Gothick surroundings of the Heaven and Hell just up the road, where the door to the basement ('Hell') was a Devil's Mouth and the walls were painted with flames.

The fortunes of the 2i's changed on July 14, Bastille Day, 1956. That year the Soho Bastille Day Parade, started by Soho's French community, featured the Vipers Skiffle Group playing on a flatbed truck. It rained. The Vipers abandoned the truck and made for the shelter of the 2i's. They ordered coffee and started to play. A crowd gathered. The management asked them to come back some time and play some more.

The Vipers started regular skiffle sessions in the basement of the 2i's. They were good. Within a month or so, they were packing the place out every night.

Lionel Bart (then co-proprietor of a down-at-heel silk-screen printing firm, soon to become the country's top songwriter and author of *Oliver!*, the best British musical of all time) and his friend Mike Pratt (who later starred in the TV series *Randall And Hopkirk (Deceased)*) were hired to decorate the basement. They chose black for the walls with an Egyptian-style eye motif over the tiny stage. They were paid in beer. The black paint came off on people's jumpers.

When a merchant seaman called Tommy Hicks played the 2i's and sang 'Rock With The Caveman', a song that he, Lionel and Mike had written for a laugh, he was "discovered" by John Kennedy, a news photographer and ace publicist who, with help from a rag trade contact called Larry Parnes, changed Tommy's name to Tommy Steele and got him column inches and a record deal with Decca. Tommy's record of that spoof song, 'Rock With The Caveman', went Top 10 and entered the history books as (give or take Tony Crombie & His Rockets' 'Teach You To Rock') the first British born and bred rock'n'roll record.

Overnight, the 2i's gained a reputation as a place where stars were made. Harry Webb who became Cliff Richard, the Drifters who became the Shadows, Vince Eager, Terry Dene, Wee Willie Harris, Joe Brown, Eden Kane, Screaming Lord Sutch, Tony Sheridan, Lance Fortune, Ritchie Blackmore and Paul Gadd (later known as Gary Glitter and later still as 'Aaargh!') were all either 'discovered' at or at least played the 2i's. Some of them went on to earn enough money to buy cars and driving lessons and still have change for proper insurance. They walked around in two guinea shirts and 10 guinea suits that girls tried to tear off their backs.

Terry wanted some of that.

The Worried Men's first appearance at the 2i's was probably around May 1957. They'd grown to a six piece: Terry, now calling himself Terry Denver, on acoustic guitar and vocals, Hurgy on washboard, Pete Darby on bass, Terry's cousin Dennis on another acoustic guitar, Freddy Lloyd, a neighbour from Acton, poached from a rival group called The Sinners, on a third guitar and vocals, and Chas Beaumont on electric guitar.

Freddy had transport – a 1932 London taxi painted yellow, covered with graffiti and big enough to carry a tea-chest bass.

For his definitive work on the period, *The Restless Generation*, Pete Frame interviewed Freddy. "At that time, he [Terry] really looked like James Dean, no question about it... hair brushed up in an exact copy, white T-shirt and blue jeans, leaning up against the wall looking exceedingly cool – as only Terry the poseur could! He was certainly very image conscious, even then. He was always convinced he would become a star – always big time!"[6]

Terry, "exceedingly cool", was still not quite 17.

The resident group at the 2i's, Les Hobeaux, were on the up and up. When, a couple of months after the Worried Men's first gig, Les Hobeaux landed a spot in a movie, a record contract and a tour, Terry's group took over as the 2i's house band.

They played seven to 11 every night to an audience of two or three hundred. The pay was 30 bob a week each – £1.50p. Dreams of a car were still a long way off. Thirty bob was about enough to buy half a tank of petrol.

For a time there was some doubt as to whether Terry was the main attraction in the group or Chas Beaumont, the new guitar player who could play fast and fancy on a proper America Epiphone guitar with a De Armond pick-up. The cheekbones usually won.

By the autumn of 1957, the Worried Men had genuine cause to worry. Tommy Steele only had to play a handful of gigs at the 2i's before being 'discovered'. Terry had been strumming his Framus night after night for three months – a lifetime in skiffle – and was no nearer the Big Time than he had been when he'd been sitting on the wall at the recreation ground with Hurgy. Nobody thought the skiffle craze would last forever. Maybe the bubble had already burst. Rock'n'roll was proving a more robust contender. Rumour had it that Calypso was the next big thing. Maybe they should team up with some West Indians so as to be ready to jump on the new bandwagon when it came along.

Then one night, Jack Good walked in.

Jack Good, 26 years old, had been President of OUDS (the Oxford University Dramatic Society) and had appeared on the West End stage before signing up with the BBC.

His stewardship of BBC TV's first proper go at teen music – *Six-Five Special* (so named because it came on after the six o'clock news) – had made him one of the most influential men in British rock'n'roll.

Six-Five Special was a hideous mishmash of pop, light entertainment, youth club worthiness and misplaced jollity – a cross between *Top Of The Pops*, *Blue Peter* and Alan Partridge. But it was all there was and consequently regularly notched up ratings of 12 or 13 million.

The show seemed to be informed by a conspiracy not to take this teenage business too seriously and to do everything possible to play down any suggestiveness or sexuality.

On the Ed Sullivan show, Elvis had been shot from the waist up lest his gyrations caused unwanted pregnancies. No such precautions were needed on *Six-Five Special*. BBC employees, both staff and freelancers, were contractually obliged to hand in their pelvic flexibility at reception. As Lonnie Donegan once said, "It's a wonder show business ever survived the BBC at all."

"Welcome aboard the *Six-Five Special*," said Pete Murray the DJ/ geeky older brother/trendy vicar who hosted the show. In patrician tones he announced, "We've got almost a hundred cats jumping here, some real cool characters to give us a gas, so just get on with it and have a ball." Never has the disjuncture between script and delivery been more marked.

Vouchers for long playing records were offered as prizes to the couple who 'cut the coolest capers'. A pair of Hungarian wrestlers was featured in the 'Sports Section'. "If you're going to rock'n'roll properly," said Pete, "you're going to have to have your muscles in pretty good shape." In response to which most spirited 13 year-olds decided to smoke more.

Mike & Bernie Winters provided light comic moments. Tony Hancock had passed on the opportunity.

"I remember Jack Good coming down to the 2i's to see us," said Freddy Lloyd. "He wore an American baseball jacket and looked down through his glasses, with his head raked back. I think he was hard pushed to find enough talent to fill his programmes. We were the next act along and he came to see if we were any good."

Jack was always on the lookout for ways to make his shows livelier, more spontaneous, more *now*. For the *Six-Five Special's* first anniversary, he came up with the idea of a live outside broadcast from the cellar of the 2i's.

On November 16, 1957, the huge BBC Mobile Control Unit was parked in Old Compton Street, miles of cable were laid and the Marconi Mk III cameras, weighing 12 stone each, were lugged down the rickety stairs. The show featured a roster of cool cats including Terry Dene, the King Brothers, Jim Dale, the Chas McDevitt Skiffle Group and comic funsters Mike & Bernie Winters. Gilbert Harding, a 50-year-old curmudgeon who'd found fame on the TV panel game *What's My Line?,* was also on hand to look on disapprovingly. Wee Willie Harris, the pink-haired rock god who was one of Ian Dury's 'Reasons To Be Cheerful', called him "Daddy-O". The press thought that was pretty much as wild as wild could get.

The Worried Men, the resident band, opened and closed the show. The viewing millions were exposed to the cheekbones, the blue eyes and the matchless charm.

Six-Five Special, Live From The 2i's cemented the coffee bar's status as the epicentre of the teenage earthquake. Decca signed Wee Willie and released, as his first single, 'Rockin' At The 2i's, a composition of his own which didn't make hit parade history but gave him enough encouragement to give up his job at the biscuit factory. The song also gave its name to and was featured as Track 1 Side 1 of a 10-inch LP – an album which also carried two tracks by the Worried Men, '900 Miles From Home' and 'This Little Light'. The former provided a showcase for Chas Beaumont's fancy picking and Hurgy's rock-steady washboard: the latter made a decent stab at whipping up a bit of excitement, but neither track is distinguished by its vocal performance and neither do they display any more talent or promise than you could have heard on Skiffle Night at St Jude's Church Hall, Mansfield or the Washwood Heath Trades & Labour Club.

They were Adam's first record releases, yet he chose to make no mention of them in either of his autobiographies. Another Decca track, 'Fräulein', released on a later Decca compilation *Stars Of The Six-Five Special,* is airbrushed out of the story, too. Terry Denver made those records not Adam Faith.

In the week that *Six-Five Special, Live From The 2i's* was aired, there were just two skiffle songs – Lonnie Donegan's 'My Dixie Darling' and Johnny Duncan's 'Last Train To San Fernando' – in the Top 30. Harry Belafonte's 'Mary's Boy Child' was at number three and his 'Island In The Sun' at number 23 but, other than that, the much vaunted calypso boom didn't seem to be happening, either.

Rock'n'roll had beaten off the competition and was king of the heap with no less than 10 fine examples gracing the charts. They included the satanic sex of Jerry Lee Lewis' 'Whole Lotta Shakin' Goin' On', Buddy Holly's 'That'll Be The Day' and Jackie "Mr Excitement" Wilson's 'Reet Petite (The Sweetest Girl In Town)'. Elvis Presley was at numbers two, 16, 18, 19 and 22 with killers like 'Lawdy Miss Clawdy' and '(Let Me Be Your) Teddy Bear'. These were among the finest rock'n'roll records ever made. Spoiled for choice, punters stood at the juke box, thru'penny bit in hand, quivering with indecision.

Why would anybody want to sing 'Mamma Don't Allow No Guitar Played In Here' or 'This Little Light Of Mine I'm Gonna Let It Shine' when they could be singing 'Lawdy Miss Clawdy' or 'Whole Lotta Shakin' Goin' On'? It was the equivalent of Making A Stir At Debating Society vs Storming The Winter Palace, or Cheese'n'Wine At Your Auntie's vs Bacchanalian Orgy With Unimagined Variations.

Things started to go sour for the Worried Men. The crowds at the 2i's dwindled. The TV appearance and album tracks had not led to offers from Hollywood. Terry's chance of dying in a new Porsche or even of owning a second hand Vauxhall 10 seemed to be getting slimmer.

The strain of working the seven to 11 shifts at the 2i's on top of his job at TVA was beginning to tell, too. He was knackered and uncharacteristically aimless. He left the Worried Men. The rest of the group soon followed. Freddy Lloyd defected to the Vipers who by now had a record deal, and regular tours and TV shots.

By the beginning of 1958, Chas Beaumont looked around and noticed that he was the only original member of the Worried Men left. He kept the group going. Tony Meehan played drums with them before going off to join the Shadows. He was replaced by Brian Bennett, who went on to replace Tony in the Shadows. Chas himself later played with the Jets in Hamburg, just up the road from where the Beatles were rolling drunks and thinking about haircuts and just round the corner from where Chris Andrews, who would later write many of Adam's hits, was playing. As they say on Disneyland's most disheartening ride, 'It's A Small World'.

Chapter Five

"The working class kid was born in a working class home at the time of our Finest Hour, bought up in a council house, taught in a secondary modern school, thrown out into a causeless world of affluence and opportunity (for other people) and left to look for his own dream by himself. He drifted about the eddies of pop music until he found his man and became a Dream Boy. Tommy Hicks, the merchant seaman from Bermondsey, found John Kennedy and Larry Parnes and became Tommy Steele, Terry Williams, the record packer from Newington, found Hymie Zahl, and became Terry Dene. Reg Smith, the timber hunker from Greenwich, found Larry Parnes and became Marty Wilde. Ron Wycherley, the deck hand from Birkenhead, found Larry Parnes and became Billy Fury. Terry Nelhams, the film boy from Acton, found John Barry and Evelyn Taylor and became Adam Faith ...”[7]

Nicholas Walters

Very little of Adam Faith's life was down to chance or luck. Some accounts of what happened next, including his own in his 1961 autobiography, *Poor Me,* have him 'bumping into' Jack Good on Wardour Street. Others suggest that Jack Good rang him. It is almost impossible to imagine that Terry Nelhams, having been on telly and made records, would have shrugged his shoulders and walked away when the Big Time had been close enough for him to taste. If Jack rang him, then it's a tanner to a quid that he was responding to a growing pile of messages left on his desk.

Anyway, Jack remembered how good those cheekbones looked on telly. He invited Terry round to his flat on the Goldhawk Road one Sunday afternoon for a chat. He wondered whether Terry would be interested in a solo career away from the Worried Men. Terry said he would. Jack wondered whether anybody had ever told Terry he looked a bit like James Dean. Terry said, "Now you come to mention it ..."

Words like 'mean', 'moody' and 'magnificent' were bandied.

Jack pointed out that Terry's name was rubbish. There is nothing mean, moody or magnificent about "Terry Nelhams" or even "Terry Denver": "Terry Denver" is a scaffolder's name – maybe a scaffolder who also sang skiffle but a scaffolder nonetheless.

The naming of rock stars had already been brought to a fine art by the uber-manager Larry Parnes. Under his tutelage, Reginald Smith had become "Marty Wilde", Ronald Wycherley "Billy Fury", Roy Taylor "Vince Eager" and Clive Powell "Georgie Fame". Joe Brown, who had threatened to punch Larry up the bracket at the first sign of nonsense, remained plain Joe Brown.

A pattern had developed. The first name should be something reassuringly boy-next-door (Billy, Georgie, Vince). The second name should evoke the abstract quality of which the star was the personification. These rock boys were gods. Like Mars was war and Venus love, Billy was Fury, Vince was Eager and Georgie Fame.

Jack and his wife, Margit, had just had a baby. A book of baby names was handy. Jack and Terry browsed it for inspiration. Rejecting Aaron, Abel, Absalom and Abraham, they came to Adam. Then they turned to the girl's section and found Faith.

Another version of the story has it that Jack Good took the names of two of his friends, Adam Fremantle and journalist Nicholas Faith, and made the smart choice. Nicholas Fremantle wouldn't have stood a chance on *Six-Five Special*.

George Melly, in his book *Revolt Into Style,* saw great significance in

Adam's name. 'Wild', 'Eager', 'Fury' were all sex names, but here, "in place of sexual promise − a religious amalgam: the first man fallen but convinced of his redemption."[8]

Nell wasn't so impressed. When Terry told her about his new name "she screamed with laughter and said, 'Don't you dare mention that name round here. I'll be laughed out of the flats'."

"But I much preferred Adam to the name Terry," Adam said. "There were too many Terrys around at the time and I think it's the worst namby-pamby, nonentity, nothing sort of name."[9]

Name sorted, Jack introduced him to an agent, Teddy Summerfield, who got him a contract with HMV. If you had Jack Good and the full weight of *Six-Five Special* on your side, record execs fawned.

The James Dean image was worked on. A black leather jacket, casual shirt and proper Levis, shrunk to fit, were acquired. Most important of all, Adam made his visit to Eddie Jones and got the haircut.

Terry Denver, who had been Terry Nelhams, had become Adam Faith.

Jack tried hard to make him a star. He gave Adam a spot on *Six-Five Special*, singing covers of American hits. But keys were badly chosen. Adam didn't make the high notes. Instead of moody, he looked petrified. The world was not set on fire.

He released an HMV single, '(Got A) Heartsick Feeling' with "The Rita Williams Singers and Geoff Love & His Orchestra": a dreary track with a 12/8 'Blueberry Hill' feel that refuses to swing or establish any momentum.

The B-side, 'Brother Heartache And Sister Tears', is marginally better but you wouldn't cross the street to listen to it.

Jack gave Adam a second shot on *Six-Five Special* to publicise the record, tactfully suggesting that he should mime to it rather than sing live like most of the other acts.

The record tanked.

Adam was, as they say, in a bad place, under the weather and suffering from stomach pains. A doctor told him he probably had an ulcer.

Mean, moody, magnificent, mixed-up kids did not have stomach ulcers. Overpaid executives had stomach ulcers. Mixed-up kids had neuroses. Adam went to see a psychiatrist. Just the once.

The psychiatrist came up with an eminently sensible diagnosis. Adam was working too hard.

Something had to give. Certain that the big time was just around the corner, Adam gave up his day job.

Jack Good was in flux, too. Around the time of the *Live From The 2i's* show, the BBC had brought a new co-producer to *Six-Five Special*.

This was Dennis Main Wilson, an older man and a broadcasting legend who had nurtured two of BBC Radio's most successful comedy shows – *The Goon Show* and *Hancock's Half Hour* – and went on to make everything from *The Marty Feldman Show* to *A Little Bit of Fry And Laurie*. But he was, and remained, essentially a comedy producer. And he was also, according to many, quite boring.

"I think of him as the kind of man," said Barry Took, "who, if you asked him the time, would say, 'Ah, it's interesting you should ask me that because I've just been talking to the man whose grandfather built Big Ben', and would then proceed to describe in detail the man, the clock, the history of parliamentary democracy, and in the process would forget what you'd asked him in the first place."

Dennis Main Wilson liked Mozart. He wasn't very rock'n'roll.

Jack Good liked Little Richard. He was ever so rock'n'roll.

Jack had been rubbing the BBC up the wrong way for some time. It wanted to entertain, educate and inform. He wanted to put Satan into the teenation's jeans. The crunch came with disagreements about Jack's plans to take *Six-Five Special* on the road as a stage show. Memos flew. It was clear that Good, for all his Oxbridge pedigree, was turning out to be an upstart.

On January 9, 1958, the corporation announced that it would not be renewing Mr Good's contract. It was no great loss for Jack. In return for his inventing – or at least doing his best to invent in the face of BBC recalcitrance – proper rock'n'roll TV, they had paid him £18 a week, about the same as a junior clerical officer in the Civil Service. There would always be a better paid home for this upstart in upstart commercial TV.

Remarkably, the stage show did actually happen, albeit truncated to a four-date mini-tour. It starred *Six-Five*'s presenters, Pete Murray and Josephine Douglas, along with English/Dutch/Ghanaian bandleader Cab Kaye, The Five Dallas Boys, Kerry Martin, the Vernons Girls, the John Barry Seven (billed as 'John Barry and his Seven') and, at the bottom of the bill, Adam Faith. The audiences clapped. They cheered. But when the show was over they did not refuse to leave the theatre until Adam had treated them to six encores. Only in his dreams.

It wasn't happening. Desperate for some progress, Adam contacted Hymie Zahl of Fosters Agency, who kindly subbed the lad a fiver a week until he got on his feet again.

Despite Jack Good's best attempts with *Six-Five Special,* British rock'n'roll had never got off the launch pad. Rock'n'roll was, it seemed, an exclusively American product: so while Jerry Lee, Little Richard, Chuck Berry and Elvis – particularly Elvis – did terrific business, the British presence in the Hit Parade consisted for the most part of old-style big-band singers – Michael Holliday, Frankie Vaughan, Alma Cogan, Petula Clark – singing songs that could have been written 10 years earlier.

Tommy Steele – once the great grinning hope of British rock'n'roll – seemed to have veered off course and into the middle of the road. His latest hits, the arguably racist 'Nairobi' and the frankly senseless 'Happy Guitar', put him resolutely in the bracket of tomorrow's all-round family entertainer. Marty Wilde's 'Honeycomb' had made no impact. Cliff Richard & the Drifters were gigging, but didn't make their first record until the end of the year. Adam couldn't even get a gig.

He had a one-nighter at the upmarket Astor Club and a couple more ho-hum tellies, but other than that he depended on Hymie's fivers. He got a job in a print works for a bit, then blagged his way into a cutting room at Bushey Studios, 20 miles north of Acton, up near Watford.

Luckily Jack Good still hadn't given up on "Britain's Singing James Dean". He got Norman Newell, EMI's A&R man without portfolio, otherwise known as the "Queen of Denmark Street", to give Adam another chance on the HMV label.

The result must represent some sort of low point for the British record industry. The A side was a cover of Jerry Lee Lewis' magnificent 'High

School Confidential'. The Jerry Lee Lewis version makes you want to break something: a cinema or a classroom, a teetotal pledge, or maybe a heart. Adam's didn't even make you want to break wind.

Part of the problem, it must be said, was Adam's diction. Like many Londoners, Adam swallowed his consonants and had particular trouble with the letter 'r'. Jonathan Ross has the same problem. Under most circumstances it doesn't matter. It can even be charming. But it makes mush of rock'n'roll. Jerry Lee liked lyrics you could spit: fast, hard consonants that came out like syncopated machine gun bullets. The opening of 'High School Confidential', done right, is a full St Valentine's Day Massacre. In Adam's mouth, "Listen to me sugar, all the cats are in the High School rockin'" turns into a wobbly "Listen to me shog a wall the cat a winner High Schoo wockin". It fails to nail.

The backing musicians sound, like they usually did on British rock'n'roll records of the period, as if their previous gig was in the pit orchestra for *The Desert Song* and they're still in thrall to the righteous rhythms of Sigmund Romberg. The guitar is too loud and too clangy, the drums are so quiet it was hardly worth the trouble of setting them up in the first place and the backing singers are possibly in Swindon. Two or three times, Adam peters out as if realising he's flogging a dead horse.

The B-side, 'Country Music Holiday' was, implausible though it may sound, written by Burt Bacharach and Hal David and is as far away from 'The Look Of Love' or 'Do You Know The Way To San Jose' as an acute understanding of cosmology is from an antelope. Like a lot of terrible songs, it was written for a film: this was called *Country Music Holiday* and starred country stars Ferlin Husky, Faron Young and June Carter Cash together with Hungarian temptress Zsa Zsa Gabor and middleweight champ Rocky Graziano. The tune never quite gets off the ground. The lyric celebrates a day when "everybody's going to rock around the fire pump" and "all the ice-cream sodas will be free": and if it had added "the sun will become as black as scorched sackcloth" and "the scorpions of the earth will have great power" it could not have been presented more joylessly. It also repeats the phrase "it's a country music holiday" so often that the temptation, just once, to leave off the last six syllables must have been near overwhelming.

Apart from a pointless stress laid on the occasional 'p' or 't', Adam sings in the manner of somebody who just remembered a suit he forgot to pick up from the dry cleaners.

Adam Faith's 'High School Confidential' never came close enough to the charts to glimpse the foothills much less the upper reaches.

Jack Good, loyal to a fault, had one last shot at doing good by rock'n'roll and by Adam Faith. He had a new show, on ITV, called *Oh Boy!*. Broadcast live from the Hackney Empire, *Oh Boy!* was everything that *Six-Five Special* should have been: fast, slick, dark, dirty and all music. Jack gave his stars – Cliff Richard, Marty Wilde, Billy Fury, Tony Sheridan – detailed direction to maximise their theatrical impact: legs apart, toes in, look down on this line, up on this line, head back as it goes into the middle-eight, now sneer.

But whatever its glories, *Oh Boy!* could never fully escape the pall of fifties British Light Entertainment. The house band, for instance, Lord Rockingham's XI, looked tough (Benny Green, one of the sax players, wore dark glasses so that people wouldn't recognise him as the jazz critic who railed against rock'n'roll in the *Observer*) but sang novelty songs as cute as Max Bygraves' 'You're A Pink Toothbrush' and did so in a Scottish accent. "Hoots Mon, There's A Moose Loose Aboot This Hoose" the band would chant and everybody would hope Marty Wilde would come back on soon.

Cherry Wainer, another regular, smiled a lot, dressed like Barbara Cartland and played an organ that had been quilted like a World of Leather headboard.

It must have been while infected by this evil Djinn of Light Ent. that Jack contacted his James Dean lookalike, reunited him with Freddy Lloyd of the Worried Men and got the pair of them to learn the old folk song 'Go Tell Aunt Rhody (The Old Grey Goose Is Dead)' with synchronised dance steps.

Cliff Richard & the Drifters' 'Move It', a proper rock'n'roll record fit to stand beside the American product, and Marty Wilde's 'Endless Sleep', a death song about a drowned girlfriend summoning her living lover to suicide, had both gone Top 10. And Adam Faith was singing 'Go Tell

Aunt Rhody (The Old Grey Goose Is Dead)' with synchronised dance steps. It was worse than embarrassing, it was humiliating.

Adam abandoned all hope and became Terry Nelhams again. He got a job at the Danziger Studios, on Watford Road in Elstree, and spent the freezing winter of 1958/59 splicing sound effects tape together in a hut in the car park. After a couple of months, he landed himself a better billet as an assistant editor a couple of miles away at the National Studios in Clarendon Road which had recently been acquired by Lew Grade's ATV. Here, he found himself working on two of Lew's hits: *The Invisible Man* and *William Tell*.

Maybe he should have stayed there. Maybe Terry Nelhams would have become one of the most respected film editors of the 20th century. Maybe he would have gone on to direct a couple of Bond films or something Oscar winning with Julie Christie and Albert Finney. But it wasn't to be.

One day in March 1959, John Barry phoned the cutting room and asked to speak to Adam Faith.

"Who?" they said.

It was a while before the mystery was solved and Terry came to the phone.

Chapter Six

"Adam, Billy Fury and Cliff Richard were the triumvirate that dominated pop around 1960. Of the three, Fury was the most exciting, Faith the most intelligent, Richard the most competent. What they had in common was that they ended up smooth. They had tidy smiles and noncommittal accents and nice manners. They tended not to make fools of themselves in public. Between them, they made pop singers almost respectable.

"The best of the bunch was Adam Faith, who was at least an original. He had a marvellous face, classic bone structure, but he was also very short and had to wear monstrous high-heeled boots if he wasn't to be dwarfed by his infant fans. He didn't have much of a voice either. He was all nose and tonsil, a poor man's Buddy Holly. What he did have, though, was good management, good song writing, good plugging and most important, a certain persistent oddity, a real individuality."[10]

Nik Cohn, *Awopbopaloobop Alopbamboom.*

Phase One Training for a military bandsman includes skill at arms, field craft, lots of PE and, these days, CBRN – chemical, biological, radioactive and nuclear defence training. Phase Two includes instrumental performance and technique, music theory, orchestration and aural perception. A bandsman ends up with most of the skills he would have acquired at, say, the Royal College of Music, together with an ability to walk up and down in impressively choreographed directions, kill an opponent in several different ways and protect himself and his comrades in the event of biological attack.

John Barry did his National Service playing trumpet with the Green Howards. He served in Egypt and Cyprus. He could strip and reassemble an EM-2 bullpup rifle with one hand while servicing the spit-valve on a Boosey & Hawkes Sovereign with the other. He knew what he was up to all right.

He was a half-Irish Catholic Yorkshireman born John Barry Prendergast. His dad, the exotically named Jack Xavier Prendergast, known as 'JX', owned a chain of cinemas in the North of England. The boy's earliest memories were all of Mickey Mouse and the great, sweeping scores of Erich Korngold, Max Steiner and Alfred Newman. His mum, Doris, was a talented pianist who played Rachmaninoff and Beethoven while little John scampered about with his Dinky toys.

He went to school at St Peter's, York, a public school founded in AD 627, where he had some piano lessons, then took up the trumpet, discovered jazz and joined a local band, the Modernaires. He signed up for a correspondence course – the 'Music By Maths' Schillinger System of Musical Composition by Ukrainian mastermind Joseph Schillinger.

The army, apart from giving him discipline, self-respect, a trade for life and all the other things the recruiting ads tell you about, provided him with a pool of highly skilled musical comrades on tap, often with time on their hands. He started coming up with compositions and arrangements for him and his mates to play.

When he was demobbed, John started trying to flog his arrangements to the big bands of the day, Johnny Dankworth, Ted Heath, Jack Parnell. It was the mid-fifties. The glory days of the big bands had come and gone. The market for arrangements – especially those scored, like Ted Heath's were, for four saxes, four trumpets, four trombones and rhythm section – was all but non-existent. The economics of keeping a 16-piece band on the road didn't make sense any more.

Jack Parnell advised John that the best way of getting a showcase for his work was to start a band of his own. He also told him that you have to take your audience with you. Start out pandering to their tastes and gradually bring them round to the more challenging stuff.

It was good advice. John got in touch with some old army pals, poached around the local bands and started rehearsing on Sunday mornings at the Rialto on Fishergate in York. Sometimes JX, who owned the Rialto, would come along and listen. He was impressed and lent John £5,000 to get the band established.

The John Barry Seven made their professional debut at the Rialto on March 17, 1957, a couple of months before the Worried Men played their first gig at the 2i's. Taking Jack Parnell's advice to 'take the audience with you' they were mostly playing the British species of rock'n'roll with a few calypsos chucked in for good measure. But they played tight, with army discipline, and they looked good, too, in matching grey suits.

The promoter Harold Fielding signed them for a summer season in Blackpool with Tommy Steele – then the biggest star in the British rock'n'roll heavens. This led to a prestige booking in the Top 20 Hit Parade All-Star Show, featuring Lonnie Donegan, at the Royal Albert Hall. Inevitably, Jack Good, ear, as always, close to the ground, heard tell of these newcomers from Yorkshire and hired them for *Six-Five Special* towards the end of September, again a couple of months ahead of Adam's first appearance on the show.

In a world where every agent and record company wanted some of this new rock'n'roll thing but were alarmed to discover that most of its purveyors actually were juvenile delinquents, John Barry was a great source of comfort. Admittedly he was from the North, but he was clearly a middle-class lad who knew which fork to use and he'd served in a very respectable regiment.

Allegedly, Philips, Decca and EMI fought to get his signature on a contract. EMI won and put him on its Parlophone label.

Later, John Barry had the good grace to apologise for having the nerve to take the vocal on the band's first single, 'Zip Zip', although actually the vocal is by no means the worst thing about the record. The worst thing about the record is that it suffers from the misconception, common to most examples of British rock'n'roll of the period, that the key elements to the new music were nonsense lyrics, an inanely honking sax and a generally Neanderthal approach: as if rock'n'roll was a bit like proper music except much, much cruder. There is, of course, every species of xenophobia, class warfare and racism inherent in this assumption but that was unremarkable in the fifties. Nobody, except maybe for one or two of the more enlightened Communists and, of course, a whole underclass of juvenile delinquents, knew any different.

The record-buying public were not fooled and continued to buy the American product.

'Zip Zip' was followed by another, even worse, single, with an inept attempt at an Elvis impersonation. After this Mr Barry abandoned vocals and stuck to instrumentals. These didn't sell much, either.

As a live act, though, the band were doing well. They backed Paul Anka on his British tour. They were regulars on *Six-Five Special* and on *Oh Boy!*. And they appeared, along with Lonnie Donegan, Petula Clark, Jim Dale and a host of others in *Six-Five Special* – the movie. (Imagine *Apocalypse Now* without the distractions of helicopters and bloodshed but with the added attraction of no less than 25 songs sung by top recording artistes of the day and you'll have some idea of the treat that *Six-Five Special* offered to cinemagoers. At 85 minutes, it's also more than an hour shorter than *Apocalypse Now*. Watch and learn Francis Ford Coppola.)

By the end of 1958, it was clear that in comparison with ITV's *Oh Boy!*, *Six-Five Special* was slow and stuffy. But if the BBC programmers had been tempted to try and coax Jack Good back into the fold to come and save them from their own joylessness, ingrained frugality would have stood in their way. ITV was paying Jack £100 a week – nearly six times more than he'd been getting at the BBC.

Nevertheless, in January, 1959, the BBC launched a new, Jack Good-style faster-paced contender, *Dig This!*, promising that it would provide "good clean fun with no hysteria" and wouldn't "clutter up the studio and screen with juvenile delinquents", which was most likely why it didn't last more than one series.

Once again it was back to the drawing board.

A 29-year-old producer, Stewart Morris, was given the job of coming up with something new. He produced a show so fast paced that the occasional lapse into hysteria and even hints at juvenile delinquency were barely noticed, and he called it *Drumbeat*.

The John Barry Seven were among the first to be hired. Just like *Oh Boy!* had featured Cliff Richard and Marty Wilde as regulars – in fact the show pretty much made their careers happen – Stewart Morris wanted *Drumbeat* to develop its own star.

Which is why John phoned Adam at the Elstree cutting rooms inviting him to audition. Adam did some quick calculations. Working at Elstree, with overtime on Saturday and Sunday, he could earn £25 a week, about twice the national average wage. He had prospects. He had security. He'd already given show business his best shot and ended up back where he started.

So he decided to play safe. He took a day off work to audition for *Drumbeat* and when he got the thumbs up he wangled Thursday afternoons and Fridays off from work to rehearse and do the show in return for working on Sundays.

Stewart signed him for three shows, with more to come if they worked out, at £60 a week.

The first *Drumbeat* aired on April 4, 1959 at 6.30, thereby conceding the 6.00 slot to ITV's *Oh Boy!*. This provided any teen viewer prepared to get off their arse and change channel with an hour of TV heaven – unless there was a younger child in the house, a cowboy fan, perhaps, who wanted to watch *Wells Fargo* on BBC at 6 and who was always favoured in sibling rows: in which case the teen viewer would probably have no option but to buy a flick knife, kill a policeman and get hanged. This is how juvenile delinquency happened back then.

Most of the shows were transmitted live from the Riverside Studios in Hammersmith and they were, if anything, even faster paced than *Oh Boy!*, usually cramming 18 songs into half an hour. *Drumbeat* was glitzier, too. A lot of *Oh Boy!* was black screen punctured by a follow-spot picking out Marty or Cliff. *Drumbeat* was big studio set-ups with fancy lighting changes and ambitious camera moves.

The John Barry Seven were duded out in matching pink suits; Bob

Miller and the Millermen in blue. On black and white telly – the only kind there was – it all came out as a uniform grey, but the thought was there.

The formula worked. Soon Stewart was claiming more viewers than *Oh Boy!*.

The show was mostly powered by the regulars: Vince Eager, Sylvia Sands (who later married Stewart Morris), the Raindrops, the Lana Sisters (with Dusty Springfield), the Kingpins, Roy Young, Bob Miller & the Millermen, Dennis Lotis and Adam Faith. Guest stars came and went: Billy Fury, Petula Clark, Ronnie Carroll, Anthony Newley, Cliff Richard & the Drifters.

Adam, with his Elstree money and his *Drumbeat* money, was coining it. The first £80 went as down payment on his first car, a Ford Consul: top speed 80 mph and 0-60 in the time it takes to soft-boil an egg, but it had a lot of shiny chrome and styling features borrowed from the American Ford Fairlane so you could at least look impressive while you waited for the engine to work.

"When I bought my first car," Adam later said, "I just didn't want to go to bed. It was only an old Ford but I couldn't leave it alone. It was a fantastic feeling."

A lifelong car-buying habit was born.

Every Thursday, Terry the assistant film editor would hurry down to the Riverside Studios and become Adam Faith the TV singing sensation. It was never an easy gig. The studios had no air-conditioning and Stewart Morris was a perfectionist, prone to outbursts.

By the time Stewart Morris died in 2009, his CV included series and specials starring everybody from Les Dawson to Sammy Davis Jnr. and encompassed the *Eurovision Song Contest* and *The Royal Variety Performance*. He had also earned himself a peerless reputation as a man who "didn't suffer fools gladly", although less diplomatic associates use terms like "arrogant, bullying bastard" and catalogue the obscenities he liked to scream into his talkback microphone.

When old TV technicians sit around, eventually they will start telling Stewart Morris anecdotes. A favourite concerns his direction of the Opening Ceremony of the 1986 Commonwealth Games, an all-stops-out affair at the climax of which sky divers were supposed to descend on the arena.

"Cue the parachutists!" Stewart commanded as the moment approached. "Cue them. Now. Cue them." Nothing happened. "Just get them to fucking jump. Tell them to fucking jump." Stewart upped the volume. His veins threatened to burst. "Get them to jump. Jump. JUMP. Fucking JUMP."

And a plaintive voice replied from the plane. "We're five miles from the stadium. Do you still want us to jump?"

Adam had trouble with him, too.

"Stewart Morris liked to present him [Adam] with a stern, rocker, motorbike image," said Johnny Worth/Yani Panakos Paraskeva Skoradalides/Les Vandyke whom we met in Chapter 1. "And I told Adam to smile at the camera, gently, and the world would light up when he did. Stewart Morris was furious when he was stuck with a smiling Adam Faith singing 'Love Is Strange'. He tore him off a colossal strip and told him never to do it again, but I knew he was wrong. When he smiled that wistful smile, he went zonk! into the hearts of millions."

Adam was doing a seven day week – four at Elstree, three in the pressure cooker at Riverside. It couldn't last.

The end came not with the whimper of nervous collapse but the bang of being nabbed sagging off work. The studio manager at Elstree, Aida Young, was a kind, if formidable, presence. She would wander around from time to time saying, "Has anyone seen Terry?" and his workmates would loyally reply, "Well, he was here at lunch time…"

Then, one day, Aida's teenage daughter mentioned that she'd seen Terry on the telly. He was grassed up.

Aida summoned him and told him a choice had to be made: Elstree or pop.

Elstree offered security, a career in the film industry which could – who knows – end up with his becoming an established film director, his long-held ambition. *Drumbeat* offered more than twice the money, the slim chance of ending up earning as much as Lonnie Donegan, Tommy Steele or... dare one dream such dreams... Elvis, and the chance further to develop the Adam Faith brand, a business in which he had taken a close personal interest. On the other hand he could be out on his ear in a week.

He phoned Stewart Morris and managed to secure a six-month contract on *Drumbeat* – all the security an 18 year old needs. He gave in his notice at Elstree.

It was time to put the Adam Faith project on a proper business footing. John Barry steered him towards his own manager, a woman – and thus a rarity in showbiz management even today – called Eve Taylor.

Chapter Seven

"Eve Taylor was managing Adam Faith, trying to turn him into Grace Kelly. There'd never been any class in the music business before Brian Epstein."[11]

Chris Hutchins

In some circles, the mention of the name 'Eve Taylor' is enough to send people running out of the room screaming. Others merely hide under the table.

"The Queen Bee of Show Business" had a loud voice, was remorselessly protective of her clients and sometimes grew, in the words of Sandie Shaw, "emotionally violent". She was, without doubt, redoubtable.

"Yes, I'm tough," she told Pamela Coleman in a *Times* profile. "Very, very tough. I'm the most hated woman in show business – but I am also the most respected."[12]

Her pedigree was faultlessly showbiz. Mum was a singer and dad an impresario and agent. He had the Brummie comedian and lifelong alcoholic Sid Field on his books and young Eve, sometimes under the name "Sue Brett" (geddit) became one of Sid's comic 'feeds'. Under his guidance, young Eve acquired the lore and language of showbiz. He would cue each of her lines with a little squeeze of her hand and thus she learned the art of comic timing.

After eight years with Sid Field, she went solo as a comedy dancer. Bob Henrit, drummer in the sixties with Adam's backing group, the Roulettes, described her act: "She wore a long skirt and under her skirt attached to her knees were a pair of cymbals. At the end of her act she would hoist her skirts and bash her cymbals together with her knees. That was it."

Eve gave up the stage at the age of 35, when her mother died. "I was doing comedy when I lost my mum. I didn't feel very comical any more, so I went into management."

With her husband, Maurice, and his business partner Colin Berlin, she set up the Starcast Agency and thus moved on from being Eve Taylor, soubrette, to reinvent herself as the Redoubtable Eve Taylor.

Her first client was Des Lane, who played the penny whistle. He did steady business for years. She then went on to discover Mike & Bernie Winters and manage Jackie Dennis, a Scottish rock'n'roller who wore a kilt onstage. She got Jackie a £650 gig in the USA on the primetime *Perry Como Show*. That didn't happen much to British acts before the Beatles, but the Redoubtable Eve Taylor made it happen for Jackie. Some people began to suspect she practised the Dark Arts. She put it down to graft and resilience.

"I thrive on the aggravation of this business," she said, "although it makes me ill. It's a lonely job as well as being hectic. I thought success would bring me much more happiness than it has done."

Having signed Adam, Eve decided that he needed another change of image.

"I'll never forget the first time I saw him," said Eve, lifting her eyes to the ceiling. "He looked like a dying duck in a thunderstorm. He was wearing a powder blue pullover and blue jeans worn white at the knees. His hair was all over the place."[13]

Eve subbed him £50 and they went shopping for stage clothes. The James Dean tearaway look was replaced by a new, softer, rebel-without-his-claws Adam Faith. He wore suits. He wore sport jackets. The shaggy Roman Emperor fringe was neatly parted and combed with water.

While she never quite stood on stage and squeezed his hand to teach him timing, all the same, before every performance, Eve would give Adam notes on how to walk, how to stand, when to move, when to smile and how to bow, passing on the stagecraft she'd learned from Sid Field.

Adam listened. He did as he was told. He respected Eve. "We trust one another completely... " he said in his 1961 autobiography, *Poor Me*. "She's my friend, my watchdog, my producer, my banker and my big sister, all rolled into one. I'm nuts about her. We really need each other as much as the original Adam needed Eve."[14]

"So many butchers boys came up in the skiffle era being managed by butchers," he said, "or someone who knew nothing about show business. Eve knows the business."

He signed with her for 10 years.

Eventually the relationship soured. Then it went from rancid to poisonous.

"This woman made Cruella de Vil look like Snow White," he said in his later 1996 autobiography, *Acts Of Faith*. "She'd use every trick in the book to get what she wanted. Emotional blackmail, tantrums, threats and, if all else failed, she wasn't backwards in coming forwards with the old water works. [...] She was the commandant from hell. A dreadful woman."[15]

A month after *Drumbeat* started, Fontana released a six-track EP called *Drumbeat* that featured tracks by the show's regulars including the Lana Sisters, Bob Miller & the Millermen and Sylvia Sands. It was, according to the sleeve notes, a "feast of powerful beat music" and "a knockout for the teenager".

Adam's contribution was a cover of 'I Vibrate', a Conway Twitty song that was itself a shameless rip-off of Jerry Lee Lewis' 'Great Balls Of Fire'. Recorded live (by the sound of it) in the TV studio and backed by John Barry, it was Adam's best record to date. It had punch. It had energy. It had commitment. It presented Adam for the first time as a credible contender. He'd got the hang of it. He could do rock'n'roll.

His contract with HMV had expired. The Fontana EP was a one-off, but Eve was busy sorting him out a new contract, this time with Top Rank – the music wing, as the name suggests, of Adam's former employer, the Rank Organisation.

It was a new label, managed by Dick Rowe (the man who, a few years later when he was working for Decca, turned down the Beatles with the words, "Guitar groups are on their way out, Mr Epstein") and Tony Hatch (who later wrote, with Jackie Trent, 'Downtown' for Petula Clark as well the themes from *Crossroads, Emmerdale* and most other pieces of music in existence).

The label had so far released no more than a handful of mostly lacklustre singles including a honky-tonk version of 'If You Knew Suzie' by Knuckles O'Toole. Indeed, he only feather in its cap was its release of 'Guitar Boogie Shuffle' by 'Play-In-A-Day' Bert Weedon, which had just about sneaked into the Top 10.

Adam's contribution to the catalogue – with backing from the John Barry Seven – did little to brighten the label's lustre. 'Ah, Poor Little Baby' was a cover of a Presleyish rocker that hadn't done too well when Billy "Crash" Craddock had released it in America. Most six-year-old girls and one or two of the larger breeds of domestic cat can do a better Elvis impersonation than Adam ever managed.

The B-side, 'Runk Bunk', might have created something of a stir in Sweden – where 'runk' means 'wank' – had any Swedes been made aware of the record's existence, but it was released amid a resounding hush of publicity caused by a printing strike. For the burgeoning careers of both Adam Faith and John Barry, this was undoubtedly a boon.

Drumbeat came to an end after 22 weeks. It had provided excellent publicity for the Adam Faith brand while it lasted, but, without it, the brand barely existed. To sustain the momentum, Adam badly needed a hit and the Swedish wanking song was clearly not hitting the spot.

As she so often did when things looked like they were going tits up, Eve Taylor advised Adam to announce that he was planning to concentrate on his acting career. This time he even mentioned the possibility of elocution and stagecraft lessons.

To back up the claim, he landed a part in the long-running TV cop show *No Hiding Place*. In an episode thrillingly entitled *Wheels Of Fury,* he plays Vince Kinley, a tearaway biker. It was aired on September 30, 1959.

"Isn't that the bloke off *Drumbeat?*" viewers asked, sleepily.

"Who?"

"No, he's gone now."
Bigger things followed.

George Willoughby, a film producer, had acquired a script by Dail Ambler, a writer who had had success with a couple of *Armchair Theatre* TV plays. It was set in the seamy, seedy world of Soho coffee bars and drenched in beatniks, vice and frothed-up milk.

George's daughter, a *Drumbeat* viewer, suggested that Adam might have the right sort of look. George got in touch with Eve Taylor and Eve, never one to miss an opportunity once she'd got a foot in the door, recommended another client, John Barry, to compose and arrange the music.

It was Mr Barry's first film score. Later, he would win Oscars for *Born Free, The Lion In Winter, Out Of Africa* and *Dances With Wolves*. He would score the Bond films, *Midnight Cowboy, The Cotton Club, Zulu, Walkabout, The Deep, Body Heat,* 80 equally illustrious titles and *Howard The Duck*. But this one was important because it was his first.

Beat Girl (released in the USA as *Wild For Kicks*) had little in the way of an intelligent plot but was full of energy and spark. The screenplay took a prurient *Daily Mail* look at themes like juvenile delinquency, teenage angst, the shadow of The Bomb, amorality and the unreliability of French women and concluded, reassuringly, that Young People were, just as you'd imagined, going to hell in a handcart. And it gave the viewer the opportunity to enjoy a peep into strip clubs and Soho vice joints with the safety of a very moral conclusion tagged on.

It had a European flavour. Jennifer, the Beat Girl of the title, was played by 15-year-old Gillian Hills, who was truly cosmopolitan: born in Cairo, childhood in Switzerland, England and Germany, most recently living in Nice. While she was still at convent school she had written a letter, with accompanying photograph, to Roger Vadim, the film director who had discovered, directed, married and divorced Brigitte Bardot. Gillian bore a startling resemblance to Bardot. What was a Frenchman to do? Vadim gave her a small part in his 1959 version of *Les Liaisons Dangereuses*. *Beat Girl*'s director, Edmond T. Gréville, was French, and often directed the cast in his native tongue.

The cast found this bloody useful. "*Parlez-vous anglais?*" they would ask.

The story is as follows. Jennifer's father (David Farrar) has remarried a French woman who is only eight years older than Jennifer. As a result, Jennifer has 'gone off the rails'. She hangs around dodgy coffee bars with her friends, Dave (Adam), Dodo (Shirley Anne Field), Tony (Peter McEnery) and 'Plaid Shirt' (Oliver Reed). Then Jennifer finds out that her new stepmother has a questionable past, possibly as a stripper, maybe even as a prostitute – with predictably dramatic consequences. Along the way there's a certain degree of filth. At one point Gillian Hills almost does a striptease: at another, a genuine exotic dancer, known only as 'Pascaline', does a bit more of a striptease. Oliver Reed probably wanted to do a striptease as well, but was discouraged.

Adam was Jennifer's bit of rough: a leather-jacketed moody troubadour – although not as moody as Oliver Reed who manages to combine frantic dancing with massive sulking. Dave's a boy who's grown up scraping a living on bomb sites and playing truant. The other characters are similarly alienated: Tony spends most of the film swigging gin from a cough mixture bottle because his father is emotionally distant; Plaid Shirt dances and sulks; Dodo is a teasy boho siren who spends a lot of time on Tony's lap. There is no attempt at a psychological explanation for Dodo's behaviour, but it, like most other things in the film, can probably be justified by Jennifer's key line: "Next week – boom! – the world goes up in smoke. And what's the score? Zero!"

Adam has some deep and meaningful lines, too. "If you wanna fight," he says, "go and join the Army, that's the place for squares!" Also: "Drink's for squares, man."

"Why can't you sit up properly?" Jennifer's dad asks.

"I like floors," says Jennifer with cool, defiant and, in a sense, defining aplomb, because that's what these modern kids want. They want floors. Chairs are for squares.

There's a good deal of jiving in cellars to John Barry's jazzy score: there's a chicken drag race, just like the one in *Rebel Without A Cause*, and there's a lot of sleazy chicks.

Adam had three songs in the film, all written by John Barry with lyrics by Trevor Peacock, the actor/presenter/singer/songwriter who'd been one of the presenters on *Drumbeat*.

'The Beat Girl Song' is a one riff number with a talking bit in the middle that achieves a level of literacy uncommon in rock songs until the advent of prog more than ten years later: "That's the Beat Girl, feeding coins into the jukebox," Adam raps. "Long black stockings and no make-up. She makes like she's not over-concerned about this extravagant adventure."

'I Did What You Told Me' is a distant relative of 'Heartbreak Hotel', but without the heartbreak or, obviously, the hotel: a 12-bar blues, with stops, and a mooching shuffle beat.

'Made You' is a medium tempo rocker with a riff stolen from Eddie Cochran's 'Somethin' Else'. It was later re-recorded for a B-side.

Adam didn't much enjoy the movie-making experience. He found Gillian Hills a pain to work with and complained that she had tantrums on set — although to be fair 15 year olds are often given to that sort of behaviour.

The antipathy was not entirely reciprocated. "What impressed me about Adam was that he often talked about the business side of things," said Gillian. "He seemed unusually adult. When he came close, I was aware of him, but I didn't show it and he didn't notice. He was 18 and I was 15. 'Jail bait,' he said to me later."[16]

Adam didn't like the director much, either: *sans doute parce qu'il parlait français tout le bloody temps.*

He did, however, take to the gorgeous flame-haired actress from Bolton, who played Dodo. Shirley Anne Field was almost exactly two years older than Adam. She was brought up in children's homes, trained as a model, then did some pinup work for *Reveille* and *Titbits*. She made her first film in 1955. Given that she'd just worked with Michael Powell on the deeply disturbing but critically acclaimed *Peeping Tom,* and Laurence Olivier, Tony Richardson and John Osborne on *The Entertainer,* she was doing *Beat Girl* a favour. Slumming it.

Adam used to give her lifts in his Ford Consul to Chingford, a suburb in North West London, just beyond Walthamstow, not generally associated with the bohemian lifestyle.

Cramped housing. At home with Nell and Alf in Acton, 1959. PERKINS/ASSOCIATED NEWSPAPER/REX FEATURES

"And when the Big Times come, I'm gonna have me some …" GEORGE ELAM/ASSOCIATED NEWSPAERS/REX FEATURES

Good clean fun with no hysteria. *Drumbeat*, 1959. ASSOCIATED NEWSPAPERS/REX FEATURES

Adam Faith Gets With It. GAB ARCHIVE/GETTY IMAGES

studying the master. John Barry, 1960. POPPERFOTO/GETTY IMAGES

We were divided into two camps: Cliff fans and Adam fans." HARRY HAMMOND/V&A IMAGES/GETTY IMAGES

Counting the house. The Palladium, 1960. PAUL NAYLOR/REDFERNS/GETTY IMAGES

Dealing with one of Eve Taylor's outbursts of 'emotional violence'. BEVERLEY LEBARROW/GETTY IMAGES

Never Let Go, 1960. ITV/REX FEATURES

Mix Me A Person, 1962. REX FEATURES

Steeling himself to sing 'Lonely Pup". Panto, Wimbledon, 1960. RAY BELLISARIO/POPPERFOTO/GETTY IMAGES

It had been a very good year. GAB ARCHIVE/GETTY IMAGES

The Roulettes: John 'Mod' Rogan, Russ Ballard, Peter Thorp, Bob Henrit. RUSS BALLARD, PRIVATE COLLECTION

Adam with Russ and sister Pam. RUSS BALLARD, PRIVATE COLLECTION

"Better than working in my dad's shop" – Russ and Adam, 1963. RUSS BALLARD, PRIVATE COLLECTION

'Faith Castle'. ASSOCIATED NEWSPAPERS/REX FEATURES

"I thought it was shot on the streets of Soho?" said Mark Lawson in a 2009 interview with Shirley Anne.

"No, we shot a lot of scenes in some caves in Chingford."

"This was a gritty little picture in itself," says Lawson, "reflected in the character names such as Green Pants, Duffle Coat and Plaid Shirt. A harder version with even more explicit scenes was filmed for European cinemas. Were you aware of that?"

"Yes, I remember that, come to think about it. They had extras waiting when we finished. I wonder who did my body?"[17]

At the studio, Gillian Hills had the dressing room next door to Adam's. Whenever she heard Shirley Ann slip in there, "my materfamilias bustled loudly in my dressing room," says Gillian, "to cover any eventual sound coming from theirs."

Shirley met Nell and Alf, Adam's mum and dad. She got on well with Nell, who harboured hopes of something serious developing. But Shirley and Adam were busy people on the up and up. "Marriage and all that jazz," as Dave in *Beat Girl* might have said, "that's for squares." And anyway, "Next week – boom! – the world goes up in smoke. And what's the score? Zero!"

"The days were fun because of the people I was working with," said Shirley. "Adam Faith was beginning to be a teen idol at that time. With his striking face, which reminded me of how I thought Hamlet should look, I could see why. He could always make me laugh, and was a dreadful flirt."

But Adam had at least two rivals.

"John Barry wrote [...] a song for me to sing called 'I'll Never Be Bad No More' that was released on the soundtrack," said Shirley. "He had an intensity about him that was very attractive. John and Adam were great friends, but I felt there was a competitiveness between them. John often did sweet unexpected things like arriving on the set with a flower for me."[18]

Everybody fancied Shirley. One day a photographer from the *Daily Sketch* came to the studio to do some publicity stills. This was the young Terry O'Neill.

Over 50 years, Terry has produced many of the images of rock stars, film stars, royalty and assorted rogues that are burned into everybody's brain: the windswept Bardot with the fag in her mouth; Bowie's *Diamond Dogs* cover; the one of Faye Dunaway by her pool the morning after she won the Oscar; loads of the Beatles and the Rolling Stones; Mr Sinatra with several associates in Miami Beach; and Adam Faith at every stage in his career.

"I first met him when I was a photographer on the *Sketch* and I went down to Pinewood – when he was making *Beat Girl*," says Terry. "I fancied the girl in the film – Shirley Anne – that's one I pulled off him. He was an incredible bloke, but he was a rascal, an absolute rascal. Birds – I mean women – used to love him. He was just a little scruff of a kid – but he had the greatest face. We just became friends."

By the time the movie was made, Eve had negotiated a new record contract for Adam, this time with Parlophone. Johnny Worth wrote a song. Roy Young taught him how to sing it. John Barry wrote a pizzicato arrangement, and the rest … is Chapter One.

Chapter Eight

"If your dreams are black and white, try this: walk around a Galaxie by Ford. This is a daydream of a car… steel made beautiful by the power of design. Here, in Ford, you find distinctive automotive luxury at its finest… the first fashion of the sixties in America's best-selling car – the car with the silver curve of success."

Ford Galaxie advertisement

Eras of history don't switch from one to the next like channels on a TV. When at midnight on December 31, 1959, the allegedly black-and-white fifties became the allegedly Technicolor sixties, there was no announcement on the radio: "Ladies and gentlemen it is now the nineteen-sixties. Please remove your trilby hats and foundation garments and dance a wild watusi."

But there is, perhaps, a significance in the similarity between the title of Adam Faith's 'What Do You Want?' which slipped from the number one position the week before Christmas, and that of the song which replaced it, 'What Do You Want To Make Those Eyes At Me For?' by Emil Ford & The Checkmates.

Would it be too extravagant to suggest that not just Adam, but the zeitgeist itself was asking not only 'What Do You Want?' – to which the reply would have been "acrylic paint, a contraceptive pill, decriminalisation of homosexuality, cassette players, Letraset, Astroturf, Teflon, legal abortion, soft contact lenses, an end to theatre censorship, better record production, colour supplements, *Lady Chatterley* and Habitat" – but also 'What Do You Want To Make Those Eyes At Me For?' – to which the reply would have been "because I haven't got the soft contact lenses yet"? Yes, of course it bloody would.

'What Do You Want?' entered the chart at number 18. A week later it had jumped 10 places. The week after that it had gone to number one and Adam Faith was Big Time.

Journalists queued for interviews, but could seldom get a word in edgeways. Adam would sit in one corner of the room, smoking, and the journalist would sit at the other end of the room, scribbling, while Eve Taylor sat between them, talking.

Jeremy Banks from the *Daily Express* was pinned to the wall: "'What do you want to know about my boy?' she [Eve] asked, pausing for about a hundredth of a second for a reply. 'I can tell you here and now that I have sleepless nights about my Adam. Oh, dear, I have fostered him ever since he was a nobody. But I never dreamed he would one day be up there beating all the records. Now I am so excited I have to take sleeping pills, isn't it all fabulous? His sudden success? He has such a sexy face, you see? He has classic lines and he is a good actor. Already he has made a film and he's earning £600 a week. Soon he'll be in the £1,000-a-week class."

Eve pauses for another hundredth of a second, maybe to draw breath, maybe to let the magnificence of that "£1,000-a-week" sink in.

Adam, sitting in the corner, smoking, with an open matchbox on his knee to serve as an ashtray, takes Eve's pause as his cue to speak and says, apropos of nothing: "I've always like classical music. Dabbled in poetry a bit, but I don't get much time for that sort of thing now."

"It was just unreal," Adam said, years later. "Pop was so different in those days. If you made the charts you were a star. I think I regarded myself as a film cutter playing about in showbusiness. It went to number one. Incredible. The record company rang me and said one Friday it sold 49,500 copies. Crazy. What about the money? I hadn't a clue how much I was earning.

"I didn't even realise I'd arrived until one night at Edmonton. When I looked out of the dressing room window there were fans all down the High Road. Thousands of them. Mobbing and adulation was something new then. Now everyone has grown used to it – artists and fans. But then it was outrageous"[19]

Eager to capitalise on the record's success, Eve sent Adam on a string of one-nighters: Sheffield, York, Worksop, Doncaster, Halifax, Leeds, Bradford, Hull, Harrogate, and on and on, involving long drives, mostly on pre-motorway A-roads in unreliable vehicles; grim provincial hotels and B&Bs with damp sheets; nowhere to eat – not even a chippie – after 10 o'clock. Adam had spent time in Bradford as an evacuee and hated it. Now he was finding out about Burnley and Scunthorpe, Park Drive and parkin, coin-in-the-slot gas fires and "hot water available only between the hours of 7 and 8 am". In 1960, this was the rock'n'roll lifestyle.

Adam's brother Dennis often went on the road with him, acting as his tour manager.

"Here's the routine," Adam told fans. "My brother Dennis and I get to the house before the show. Dennis does everything for me. Books my hotels, plans my day, sees my stage clothes are all there, gets them cleaned and so on."[20]

But the 'Adam Faith' phenomenon soon grew beyond anything a bloke and his brother could handle. The "bay-be" had unleashed a tidal wave of animal sexuality that came crashing over the stage every night.

At the 2i's, sexuality had all been sublimated into frantic jiving, sultry looks across the Pyrex and the occasional heart-stopping touch of ribbed sweater sleeve against ribbed sweater sleeve. On *Six-Five Special* and *Drumbeat* the 'hysteria' had been regulated to what was permissible on early evening television. Any fan found in possession of an orgasm was summarily ejected.

At the Regal, Worksop and the Rialto, York, on the other hand, often only a thin blue line of elderly gents drawn from the ranks of the Corps of Commissionaires stood between seemliness and saturnalia. And those Commissionaires were powerless against the tide of stirrings and awakenings, of churnings and concupiscence.

For many, the experience of being at one of those concerts, of thrilling to the sight of Cliff or Adam and the sound of your screeching neighbours in the audience, and emerging dazed, dreamy and spent, made actual intercourse pale into insignificance.

"There was something blokish about him," says his friend, Keith Altham. "There was always something a little bit feminine about Elvis – or Cliff and Billy, who were both doing Elvis imitations. Adam wasn't doing that – he was doing something more butch and you felt, as a boy, that you could relate more to him than the other pop stars of the period."

Everybody who met him bears witness to his extraordinary charm and his charisma. An enquiry as to its source – "How did he do it?" – will be met with furrowed brows and half-finished sentences. Some talk of the smile, of the self-confidence, of the focus. He himself put it all down to his facial anatomy: "It's the cheekbones, mate. You can't buy cheekbones like that." One commentator has suggested that the driving force was another, disproportionately large, anatomical feature. "He could have ruled the world with a thing like that." The authors, however, have been unable to validate this bold assertion because they're too shy to ask.

The rest of him was tiny. Even in heels he was dwarfed by those around him.

It is tempting to make something of this; to play the 'Hitler and Napoleon were both quite short' card. On the other hand, it must be remembered that many of below average height have perfectly affable personalities, devoid of any trace of chippiness, twitchiness or megalomania. And many, many dictators, bullies and serial killers are of average height or above. Pinochet was huge.

Perhaps the real key to Adam's charm was his bottle. As he put it, "Go out and piss on your fear."

When he approached the most intimidating person in the room, the moody model, the brooding bishop, and gave them the benefit of his smile, made them laugh, they thought he was charming; he thought he was pissing on his fear.

And now the Nureyev cheekbones, the charisma, the blokishness, the smile, the self-confidence were unleashed night after night on a packed house of adoring fans.

"It was the most fantastic sight I'd ever seen," Adam said, looking back in his 1996 autobiography. "It was obvious what you were supposed to do – smash all that sexual energy back to them. So that's what I did. It was as basic as that, and as simple as that, and it was no act: I meant it – I was living every young man's dream."[21]

And, as he freely admitted, he did his best to "smash all that sexual energy back at them" individually as well as collectively. While on stage he would pick out the liveliest contenders and communicate their seat numbers to Bert, who sometimes came out with Dennis. Bert would then approach the chosen one at the end of the show and say something like, "Mr Faith would like to say hello to you in his dressing room." And Adam would either get lucky or not. Any similarity between this and pimping is entirely coincidental.

"It was the most wonderful introduction to promiscuity a 19-year-old ever had," he told the *Daily Mail*. "I was at the centre of 2,000 screaming girls every night. But when I looked at myself as a singer I thought, 'Jesus, I'm not dedicated to this. I'm no good at it.'"[22]

He was hooked on 'carnal mileage' as he called it, but managed to avoid other destructive influences. Jazzers did drugs but rock'n'rollers at the time, apart from a bit of Benzedrine or a handful of "diet pills", usually stayed clean.

Adam was never a drinker either. "I never touch beer or spirits – no matter who asks me," he reassured his fans in a 1960 fanzine. "The only time I relax this rule is when a toast is proposed. Then I take a glass of wine."[23] This might sound like anodyne tosh to allay any suspicion that he was a bad influence on the younger generation but, by all accounts, it was actually true. He was certainly never coy about smoking.

"'Relax'," he says at the beginning of the fanzine, "and I'll tell you all about it." This is the caption to a picture of him offering an untipped cigarette to the readers and thus turning 50% of pubescent girls (the other 50% being non-smoking Cliff fans) on to the joys of pulmonary and cardiovascular diseases.

If you didn't have much of it when you were growing up, money can never be taken for granted. Adam was spellbound by its wizardry; its magical powers to make wishes come true and to give an ordinary bloke from Acton like him extraordinary powers to transform the mundane into the special. Fame was good, too, but that was less measurable. Money was the magic stuff: bits of paper that, in the right circumstances, could reproduce. Money was the stuff he made standing on stage and singing.

Sometimes he didn't have to do a thing. While he was sitting still at home, customers would go into shops and buy copies of his record and that would put more money in his pockets. It's an alchemy that shopkeepers and captains of industry get used to after a while, but for Adam the novelty never wore off until the day he died.

Lionel Bart, the songwriter, once said that if you've got enough money, you can walk into the finest hotel in the world and piss on the furniture and nobody complains. Adam pissed on fear, Lionel pissed on *chaises longues,* it's horses for courses, but they amount to pretty much the same thing.

In later years Adam took immense pleasure in getting out of his Roller in ripped jeans, trainers and T-shirt, walking into a fancy restaurant, calling the *Maitre d'* "cock" and asking the chef to make him some proper trifle the way he liked it.

When the gift of money's magic has been granted, its potential still has to be learned. The lore of spending and the language of flash are arcane arts: a mentor was needed.

John Barry, a man of rapidly developing sophistication, had picked up a tip or two and happily passed them on. It was he, for instance, who told Adam the difference between a car that would impress the lads down the pub and a car that would impress God. Adam had already traded up his Consul for a yellow Zodiac, with its own built-in 'radio phone'. "It's one of those handy luxuries that make you say 'This is living'," he explained.

But, one day, Mr Barry showed up in a Chevrolet next to which Adam's Zodiac, of which a moment before he had been so proud, looked like a clockwork invalid carriage. Mr Barry had but to mention the name of the dealership at which he had bought the Chevvy and Adam was down there handing over £2,800 for a Ford Galaxie – 17 feet long, nearly six foot six inches wide with white-wall tyres and twin aerials sticking out of fins the size of albatross wings. The transaction took 20 minutes. In 20 minutes he'd abracadabraed a car the size of a council flat. That was the magic of money. And with the car he could make more magic happen wherever he went.

"He gave me a lift home once," Terry O'Neill, the photographer, says. "He lived in this really poor street in Acton. But he had this bloody huge American car – it took up the whole road. When he dropped me off at home, my mum couldn't believe her eyes."

Adam bought clothes, too. His tailor, Bernie of Kingly Street, Soho – bang next to Carnaby Street which a few years later would pioneer the mod revolution – made him suits of "the best mohair that money can buy". A two-piece cost 38 guineas (£39.90).

Even when Adam's talking to the fan-mags, money is a constant presence.

"I had a white suit made, with white boots to match," he says, "the bill clicked up to £80."

Austin's in Shaftesbury Avenue was another favourite spend-venue. "It sells gear that's really up to date." It imported American Ivy League clothes – coloured shirts with button-down collars, penny loafers and neat little jackets with narrow lapels. He bought zip-up chisel-toe cowboy-style boots, with Cuban heels to give him a bit of height, four pairs at a time. And he loved his big sheepskin-lined car coat.

Having lived for most of his life on egg and chips, he also began to acquire a taste for rarer delicacies. "I dislike cheese, spicy foods, Chinese food and coffee. I like lobster, chicken, sole, turbot, steak, milk, tea, coke – and egg and chips." Turbot, Galaxie, classical music, poetry and chisel-toed boots four pairs at a time. He was learning good.

Eve knew from her experience with her one-and-a-half hit Jock Rock Superstar Jackie "The Kilt" Dennis that you have to cash in quick in the rock'n'roll business. Even cheekbones can go out of fashion. Accordingly on January 15, 1960, while 'What Do You Want?"' was still riding high in the chart, Adam's second Parlophone single hit the stores.

The record did what all follow-ups should do: closely copy the recipe of the first hit while adding one or two subtle new ingredients. 'Poor Me' was another Johnny Worth song recorded at Abbey Road and produced by John Burgess.

Mr Barry's arrangement begins by nailing its colours to the mast with three strident pizzicato notes, then relaxes into a lilting chromatic figure mostly sustained by the backing vocals' "Aaaahs". It's vaguely reminiscent of Buddy Holly's 'Raining In My Heart' but, more exciting perhaps for John Barry anoraks, it anticipates the chromatic figure that underpins the 'James Bond Theme'. John himself pointed to this similarity when authorship of the 'Theme' was brought before the courts in 1997.

The tortured vowels from 'What Do You Want?' are here, too, and the Buddy Holly hiccups, and, in the first bar of the middle-eight, a "bay-be" exaggerated almost to the point of self-parody.

The lyric refined the little-boy-lost vulnerability that some heard in 'What Do You Want?' into modest self-pity: nothing histrionic, nothing Johnny Ray, just a bloke taking a moment to mutter in the corner of the pub before pulling himself together and rejoining the darts game.

A few days after the release, Adam unleashed the song on the viewing millions, appearing on the lovely *Beverley Sisters Show* on BBC. Joy, Teddie and Babs – the Bevs – in capris and snow-flake jumpers looking like tipsy maiden aunts – all joined Adam singing 'What Do You Want?' and then he sang his new number. It hung around in the Top 10 for a while, then, on March 5, knocked Anthony Newley's 'Why?' off the number one spot.

'What Do You Want?' had wormed its way into the national consciousness by this time. Milkmen whistled it. Teachers had heard of it. "Bay-be", usually mutilated into "boi-bay", had become a catchphrase. 'Poor Me' went one further, achieving the accolade of a playground parody:

"Poor Me, sitting on the lavatory," the 10 year olds of Accrington, Aldershot and Axminster sang, "Poor Me, sitting on the lavatory, someone came and pulled the chain, now I'm falling down the drain."

It's worth mentioning that, as far as academic research has been able to establish, no such honour was bestowed on Cliff Richard until the reprehensibly homophobic version of his 'Summer Holiday' did the rounds in 1963.

Chapter Nine

"At school we were divided into two camps – Cliff fans and Adam fans. It was mad really but we were very competitive. I remember buying six copies of a comic that was having a 'vote for your favourite singer' and sending them off to people I knew who might vote for Adam!"

Sylvia Ashton, fan.

By an odd movie industry quirk, the 'flash of nipple cut' of *Beat Girl* was released in Finland and West Germany before the 'cleaned up version' came out in the UK.

This gave Adam time to make and release another film while waiting for his first to hit the cinemas.

Never Let Go was a gangster flick, seeped in the seaminess of the Krays' 'Firm' and the Richardsons' 'Torture Gang'. It was topical. Reggie Kray had just been put away for 18 months for his involvement in a protection racket.

Peter Sellers plays, in uncharacteristically understated manner, an ultr-violent criminal called Leonard Matthews who locks horns with an Honest John cosmetic salesman played by Richard Todd. Adam was cast, inevitably, as a tearaway on a motorbike, Tommy Towers, who steals cars to order – including Richard Todd's 1959 Ford Anglia.

The 17-year-old Carol White – later to find fame and acres of credibility in the TV plays *Cathy Come Home* and *Poor Cow* – played Peter Sellers' girlfriend. She was blonde: Adam was blond. She had the pout: Adam had a square jaw. In one scene, while Adam wore his sheepskin-lined car-coat, Carol wore black underwear. One thing led to another in what was beginning to seem like a pleasantly repeatable pattern of Adam romancing his leading ladies.

The film also gave John Barry his first proper shot at scoring a dramatic movie. Despite its not being a musical, Adam had one song – a reworking of the 1863 American Civil War song 'When Johnny Comes Marching Home' with an updated lyric by Lionel Bart – which was used as the film's title theme.

On June 7, 1960, *Never Let Go* premiered at the Odeon, Leicester Square. Generally the film and Adam's performance were well received. But though the *Times* critic thought it was "well made" and commended the way in which John Barry's "music is turned to imaginatively sinister use", he deplored the "graphic depiction of sadistic violence" (Peter Sellers shuts Adam's hand in the lid of a record player, beats up Carol White and treads on some goldfish), and concluded, "Now that this so unnecessary film has been made will Mr. Sellers please go and do something precisely the opposite."

Mr Sellers took the advice. His next film was *The Millionairess*, a mound of delightful froth he spun with Sophia Loren.

Back in March, the *Bristol Evening Post* had been pleased to announce, "Filming on Adam Faith's current picture is ahead of schedule, enabling him to accept an extra variety date. He will star at the Bristol Hippodrome for a week from March 28."

He was joined by Italian rocker Little Tony, The Honeys (three sisters from Portsmouth, formerly known as the Liddell Triplets, although the 'triplets' was a lie), comic Larry Grayson (later known as the 'shut that door' host of TV's *The Generation Game*), Don Aroll (another comedian who briefly hosted *Sunday Night At The London Palladium)*, Joan & Paul Sharratt (puppeteers) and, of course, the John Barry Seven. You got your money's worth at a pop concert in those days.

The carnival moved on from Bristol to Slough, Birmingham, Norwich, Grantham, Manchester, Glasgow, Liverpool and a couple of dozen other venues, not to mention a trip back to London on April 12 for a huge star-studded concert at the Royal Albert Hall.

As Buddy Holly had proved, touring was never the safest of enterprises. A lot of the theatres were death traps. The shoddy electrics turned microphones and amplifiers into lethal weapons. The ABC Theatre, Blackpool, for instance, was, one night, filled with the smell of roasting meat which, investigations established, emanated from the house electrician, dead and slowly frying in the wings.

The dressing rooms, when there were dressing rooms, would have been condemned as unsuitable for farm animals. Vibrations from bass guitars and loud saxes brought stucco crumbling from ceilings and any number of things tumbling from the flies. Once, the John Barry Seven and the Lana Sisters suffered a near-death experience when a safety curtain came adrift from its moorings and crashed to the stage in the middle of 'My Mother's Eyes'. In theatrical circles the safety curtain is known, not without good reason, as 'the iron'.

In Pontefract, Dennis King of the King Brothers fell into a hole in the stage that stage hands had thoughtfully covered with rubber mats.

For one tour (they all merge) a fancy set had been built. The Seven opened the act with an instrumental number, standing on a rostrum – or rather two rostra which, at a key moment, would be pulled apart in a single fluid movement opening a space through which Adam would make his entrance. More often than not the stage-hands responsible for handling the ropes that achieved this miracle would pull in spasmodic jerks, or the rostra would snag. Either way it resulted in musicians struggling to keep their balance. Vic Flick, the guitar player, eventually learned to dismount while the move was in progress, then get back on again when all was calm and still. Doug Wright, the drummer, didn't have that option. The odd tumble, and the risk of decapitation from a skidding cymbal, was an accepted occupational hazard.

And if the theatre didn't kill you, the drive home would. When the next night's gig wasn't in an adjacent town and home was less than four or five hours away, driving home was always preferable to, and cheaper than, shelling out for theatrical digs or a B&B. The M1 had opened by then, at least the London-Rugby stretch. There were no speed limits on motorways until 1965. Anybody who couldn't do Crick to Hendon in under an hour was a wuss.

John Barry and Adam would regularly race home from a gig in their huge American cars. "She can really move," Adam said. "I've had the needle off the clock... and the clock stops at 120mph. Why do I do it? Why do I go so fast? I don't know, I suppose it's the risk of death that's the kick. But that sounds too corny, don't it? This is one of the biggest problems in my life, to try to analyse why and what I do things for."[24]

The Blue Boar Services at Watford Gap, just south of Rugby, had become the assembly point where musicians, on the way back from Birmingham, Derby and all point north to London, could meet in the middle of the night, get something to eat and exchange horror stories. Every one of them had a catalogue of near misses – the night the car turned over or smacked into a tree or the tour bus hit a train. Eventually Adam would lose a bass player to the road and, in the early seventies, come close to death himself.

On April 16, Eddie Cochran, Gene Vincent, the songwriter Sharon Sheeley, who was also Eddie's fiancée, and Pat Thompkins, their tour manager, were being driven in a Ford Consul taxi back to London after a gig at the Bristol Hippodrome – the last date on their UK tour. On Rowden Hill, just outside Chippenham, the car hit a lamp-post. Pat and the driver, George Martin, walked away. Eddie, Gene and Sharon were taken to St Martin's hospital in Bath. Eddie died the following afternoon.

Everybody knows this story, but just in case: one of the first coppers to arrive on the scene of the accident was a young cadet called Dave Harman. Eddie's Gretsch guitar was taken into custody and languished at the police station long enough for Dave to pick it up from time to time and teach himself a few rudimentary chords. Later he changed his name to Dave Dee and formed a band that was first called Dave Dee & the Bostons, then Dave Dee, Dozy, Beaky, Mick & Tich whose 1968 hit 'The Legend Of Xanadu' was a number one million-seller.

It's an ill-wind.

Adam's tour was interrupted on April 17 – coincidentally the day that Eddie died – by a booking on TV's top-rated *Sunday Night At The London Palladium*. He was topping the bill which, in the showbiz world of 1960, was the equivalent of winning a Nobel Prize.

He was not yet 20, but Sinatra could not have been more relaxed on stage, more self-assured, more skilled at wrapping the audience of 2,000 in the theatre and several million at home into a package small enough to hold in the palm of his hand.

Dressed in a strange PVC overshirt and what can only be described as "slacks", he takes complete control of the stage and, staring straight into the camera, proceeds to flirt outrageously with the mostly middle-aged audience. There is nothing overt about his performance, no hip swivelling, posing, vogueing, twerking, snarling or brooding. But nobody ever worked boyish charm more successfully.

He's inclusive. Sometimes a line is addressed to the balcony with a finger pointing to you up there – and you – and you. And you. Sometimes he throws a kiss to the stalls. There's nothing condescending about it. He's just – the hardest thing to represent on stage – an ordinary bloke singing a couple of songs, so casual he seems almost distracted …

… and, as you watch, you wonder – could it be? – no surely not.

He's counting the house, that's what he's doing. He's thinking, all the people over there have paid 10 and six a seat and there's say, two hundred seats in that block ….

Other singers inhabit the song. They emote or at least go through the motions of emoting. They mug. Sometimes they even cry. Adam derived a sizeable proportion of his charm, on stage at least, from his detachment, his focus on what really mattered. He knew exactly what he was doing up there. He was making money, that's what he was doing. Magic, innit?

He had just released his third Parlophone single, 'Someone Else's Baby', another Johnny Worth number coupled with 'Big Time'. On the Palladium, he sang both sides of his new record and the big hit, 'What Do You Want?'. There is no doubt that the pronunciation of "baby" in 'Someone Else's Baby' is deliberate self-parody.

The host of the show, Bruce Forsyth, these days Sir Bruce Forsyth – in the *Guinness Book of Records* for having the longest career in show business – joins Adam on stage. Brucie's dressed identically to Adam. He wears a flaky blond wig. He and Adam chat. Adam can do this. Like the Beatles later, he could 'gag it up'. He looks as relaxed with the comedy material as he was with the songs.

"I'm a fan, you know," Brucie says. "I know all your numbers. What shall we sing?"

Adam thinks for a moment, "What about 'Poor Me'?"

Brucie's always had catchphrases. "Nice to see you, to see you nice" has done him well for 40 years and he's got considerable mileage out of "Didn't he do well?"

In 1960, his front-runners were "I'm in charge" and the one he deployed now: "That's my *fa-a*-vourite". The audience laughs. The orchestra strikes up the intro to 'Poor Me'.

Adam sings the verses. Bruce sings the middle-eight, laying great stress on the "bay-bee". Adam laughs like nobody's ever mentioned his idiosyncratic pronunciation before. He's a terrific sport.

At the end, as the audience applauds, Adam asks "Was that all right?" and Brucie replies, "They love it."

Then the Jack Parnell Orchestra strikes up the sig. Adam and Bruce jump on the revolve with the other acts, the Apache dancers, the Tiller Girls, Beryl Reid, Risë Stevens and the John Barry Seven – and they all wave.

Adam's made. He's established. He's sung a song with Bruce. He's nailed it.

A month later Adam became Adam Faith, Mangler Of Vowels By Appointment to H.M. Queen Elizabeth II.

The Royal Variety Performance, 1960, ran for two and a half hours and was broadcast live on ATV. It featured a cast of thousands including Liberace, Nat "King" Cole, Vera Lynn, Hughie Green, Bruce Forsyth, Sammy Davis Jnr., Max Bygraves and Pearl Carr & Teddy Johnson.

It was crowded backstage. Liberace was the only star to have his own dressing room. Adam shared with Cliff Richard, Ronnie Carroll, Dennis Lotis, Paul Carpenter, Jackie Rae, Ivor Emmanuel and Lonnie Donegan. The John Barry Seven were in an upstairs room at a pub across the street.

Along with various jugglers, acrobats and dancers, they had to cross the street in full make-up and costume. People stared. They felt like dicks.

Adam wore white – not the white suit that had cost him £80, but an even showier outfit – white shirt, white trousers, white leather jacket, and white kid leather Western boots. He was heard complaining that he'd had to spring for the gear out of his own pocket, which meant he was £100 down before the evening had started.

At the traditional line-up afterwards where the showbiz royalty got to shake hands with the other sort, Prince Philip, the Duke of Edinburgh, noticed the outfit. "This isn't your usual garb is it?" he quipped. Nobody knows why, but it is one of the few comments he's ever been recorded as making that contains no hint whatsoever of racism. Then, however, he moved on to Sammy Davies Jnr.

In June, as the tour was winding up, Herbert Kretzmer of the *Sunday Dispatch* went to interview Adam in his dressing room. They talked mostly about girls. Adam told him that he had more luck with women when he was working at the film studios.

"'Can't take girls anywhere, you see,' he explained. 'I get mobbed. Still, I go out with as many as I can.'"

Had he thought of marriage?

"'The kids like me to be erratic, to move around, to be alive. If I married and settled down they'd look for something new. Look at this.'

"He picks up a handful of trinkets – bracelets, crucifixes, beads. 'You wonder how many weeks they saved up for this stuff. They throw it on the stage for me. They do. Without those kids I'm nothing. Nowhere. I like it when I have a lot of girls in the front rows going bleedin' mad.'"[25]

The fans spent a fortune on the widely advertised 'Adam Faith Locket'. It cost 2s 11p (nearly 15p). Adam responded to their generosity by ensuring that at all times he was erratic, moving around and alive.

On June 17, Parlophone released 'When Johnny Comes Marching Home', the track used in *Never Let Go*, with a re-recording of 'Made You', one of the songs from *Beat Girl*, on the B-side. This version is spiced up by some tricky guitar fills from Joe Brown.

Shortly after the record's release, the pipe-smoking arbiters of taste at the BBC (having presumably been alerted to the potential problem by advisers who were *au fait* with the current hep-cat jive-talk) took the precaution of listening to the lyric ...

"Every time I make a play
Baby you just run away
I never make first base
You're a gasser that's a fact
And I never can relax
Until I've made you"

.... came to the conclusion that it was 'lewd and salacious' and banned it from the airwaves.

In spite – or perhaps because – of this, it sailed to number five.

Summer was relatively quiet with Adam and the Seven, along with Emil Ford, the Lana Sisters and the Honeys booked for a 12-week twice-nightly season at the Blackpool Hippodrome. Adam rented a house in genteel Lytham St Annes and invited the family up to stay. But he and John knew there was unfinished business to attend to. They had to make an LP.

In 1960, LPs, long playing records, were icing on the cake for a pop star. Grown-ups might buy Frank Sinatra's *Songs For Swinging Lovers* or the soundtrack from *South Pacific*, but at 30s (£1.50, the equivalent today of maybe £30) the purchase of an LP was not an enterprise to be undertaken lightly. Kids bought singles.

All the same, it was generally felt that an artiste who had arrived should have one LP in the shops. Cliff Richard had released two. Marty Wilde had just released his third, *The Versatile Mr Wilde*, which showed him off, no doubt reluctantly, singing standards like 'Autumn Leaves' and 'Try A Little Tenderness'.

On August 14, well into the Blackpool run, John and Adam, straight after the Saturday night second house, drove through the night down to London for a six-hour Sunday session at Abbey Road. They did the same thing the following Sunday and eventually knocked out an album's worth of songs and a new single, 'How About That?'.

Johnny Worth had written 'How About That?' as a joke, based on one of Eve Taylor's pet sayings. John announced that he intended to "keep the pizzicato down to a minimum" and in so doing produced one of his most sophisticated arrangements to date, with cascading strings and sparse percussive pizz. Adam's in good voice, too. It's his best crack at the Buddy Holly hiccup.

In the *New Musical Express* poll, 'How About That?' was voted third best disc of the year, behind the Shadows' 'Apache' and Cliff's 'Please Don't Tease'. Adam also came in as Britain's second most popular Male Singer.

Second. Bloody Cliff Richard again.

All this success delighted George Willoughby, producer of *Beat Girl*. Even though Adam's role in the film was relatively minor, by the time it premiered on October 28, he got second billing on the poster and his image was bigger than Gillian Hills'. It opened to mixed reviews, although nobody had a bad word to say about Adam or the music. It was, however, banned in Italy, South Africa, Turkey, Malaya and Singapore and when you watch the exotic dancer Pascaline run through her '101 things you can do with a yard or two of flimsy chiffon' routine, it's not hard to see why.

The LP, called simply *Adam*, was released on November 4 and was, like *The Versatile Mr Wilde*, a chance for Adam to show off his range. There are rockers on there like Doc Pomus and Mort Schuman's 'I'm A Man', there are novelty songs like 'Greenfinger' (about a man who buys his girl a gold ring from a dodgy jeweller and suffers the consequences when the ring gives his girl a ... you can guess the rest), and selections from the Great American Songbook like 'Singin' In The Rain' and 'Summertime' – clearly an attempt to show that Adam can handle mum and dad music and well as the uptempo numbers that get the kids' feet a-tappin'. Unfortunately the attempt failed.

When mums and dads who listened said, "I can sing better than that," they were usually right.

John Barry comes out of it well, though. His arrangement of Gershwin's 'Summertime' – all low register woodwind, shimmering strings and a tinkling celeste – could be an object lesson in orchestral texture, which is why it's such a damn shame Adam has to come in and ruin it. And when he hits the high note at the end it's easy to believe that your dad actually could have done a better job.

There was, however, worse to come.

Chapter Ten

"Cinderella's got a brand new frock
And, goodness, i'n't it a gaudy un'
So we'll… hang on, what's behind this clock?
It's Mouse! And his piano accordion!"
                    from *Cinderella*, Gravelly Hill Little Theatre, 1961.

In theory it should have worked a treat. Christmas pantos made money. Rock'n'roll made money. Combine the two and buy a bank. What could possibly go wrong?

The basic formula had been there for at least 10 years before rock'n'roll was invented. Hit Paraders like David Whitfield, Ronnie Hilton and the Beverley Sisters had been swapping cows for beans, buying lamps, marrying princes and trading pussy jokes at Empires, Alhambras and Hippodromes all over the country since the end of the war.

When the Chiswick Empire booked Lonnie Donegan to play Wishee-Washee in its 1957 *Aladdin*, it felt it was on safe ground. It knew that Donegan, the undisputed King in that year of skiffle, would sell tickets. It also knew that as well as singing death ballads and prison blues with a passion none has ever rivalled, Donegan could and did wrap his tonsils and banjo around 'My Old Man's A Dustman' and 'Does Your Chewing

Gum Lose Its Flavour On The Bedpost Over Night' without wetting himself. Such versatility could take the pie in the face and the bouncing ball in its stride.

Similarly, a year later, when Tommy Steele was cast as Buttons in the Coliseum's *Cinderella*, nobody was risking the farm. The benefits were mutual. The theatre would sell tickets, Tommy would make big strides on his charted course from Flash In The Pan Rock'n'Roller to Futureproof All-Round Family Entertainer.

Sticking Marty Wilde in *Robin Hood* at the Hippodrome, Stockton-On-Tees was more worrying. Marty was a real rock'n'roller who made no secret of his disdain for the pap he'd often been required to perform. His acting skills were yet to be proven. Accordingly, neither he nor his co-stars, the Chas McDevitt Skiffle Group, were given actual parts in the show. Instead they were wheeled out now and then at diplomatic moments to appease the teenage ticket-buyers, who stank up the back stalls with their Brylcreem and hormones and looked dead set on bottling the next Merry Man who made a tree joke.

By 1960, no panto was complete without at least one teen idol on the poster. Lonnie did *Robinson Crusoe* at the Finsbury Park Empire, Cliff did *Babes In The Wood* at the Stockton Hippodrome (and went on to be a panto regular, the highlight of his career being a 1966 *Aladdin* when he shared top billing with an elephant), Vince Eager played *Aladdin* at the Swansea Grand, Frank Ifield was a yodelling Jack in *Jack And The Beanstalk* at the Birmingham Hippodrome and Mark Wynter was being Mother Goosed twice nightly by Frankie Howerd at the Palladium.

Panto brings out the best and worst in people, mostly the worst. The nightmare of nine shows a week, every week, from bleak December to cruel and seasonally inappropriate February, by which time the tinsel has rusted and tempers are as frayed as the costumes, takes its toll. The tales of tears, of outbursts, of unwise couplings in the props room, of drunkenness and dereliction, of injury ("Oh, shit, Jimmy Clitheroe's fallen out of the beanstalk again") and death are endless. And not one of those rock'n'roll stars ever divided the audience into two teams for a singing competition without thinking, "The career, the credibility, the ideals, the dreams – it's behiiiiiind you."

The pop industry of 1960, had not, however, yet worked out that credibility could be woven into a saleable asset. It only knew showbiz. It was where pop come from. It was the tradition it was steeped in. Eve Taylor was a former dancer and comic feed. Tito Burns, Cliff Richard's manager, had for years been better known as leader of the Tito Burns Septet, an accordion combo. Most of their pals, the theatre managers and TV execs, had once trodden the boards, too: Lew Grade was a former charleston champion; his brother, Bernard Delfont, had been a professional dancer for 14 years before taking a desk and phone job as an impresario.

If the young rock'n'rollers wanted a lasting career in the business, they had to round themselves out. They had to master a few dance steps, learn how to tell jokes and tie a bow tie. Most of all they had to accept that drainpipe trousers and moody sneers might get you to the top but to stay there you needed a smile on your face, a crease in your trousers, a shine on your shoes, a twinkle in your eye and a chuckle in your voice. These were the basic requirements for any performer. No questions. Stop grizzling.

Adam was booked to play the Bosun in *Dick Whittington* at the Wimbledon theatre. He was also given a new song to sing.

It was written by a Scottish bandleader called Archie Alexander, who'd previously enjoyed some success with 'Ev'rybody Loves A Soldier' and 'Did Santa Have A Daddy Just Like Mine?' – the kind of song that keeps the Samaritans so busy at Christmas time.

As far as Eve could see, Archie's latest composition, 'Lonely Pup (In A Christmas Shop)', had Adam's name all over it. Adam disagreed. John Barry was horrified. But the Redoubtable Eve Taylor was insistent.

Eve had also come up with a brilliant idea to promote the song. At the climax of his act in *Dick Whittington*, Adam would sing 'Lonely Pup' and then ... you'll like this ... *give a child in the audience a real little puppy to take home and keep.*

Fortunately good sense prevailed before any animals were harmed. Even before the RSPCA and anybody else with a shred of decency could raise objections, the theatre vetoed the idea. Live puppies notwithstanding, 'Lonely Pup' was released on October 30.

The record came up for appraisal on *Juke Box Jury*. Actor David McCallum (soon to become heartthrob Ilya Kuryakin in *The Man From U.N.C.L.E.*) in a pompous mini-rant, lambasts the record for trivialising the true meaning of Christmas while viewers shouted "Lighten up, Dave, it's just a song" – or its 1960 slang equivalent – at their 21" Fergusons.

Two of the other panellists, Nina & Frederik, the Danish singing duo, also voted it a 'Miss'. The remaining panellist, actress Jill Ireland, at that time Mrs. David McCallum, merely looked alarmed.

Despite which the record slimed its way up to number four and earned Adam another Silver Disc.

Eve, determined to prove the validity of her original idea, made him sing it on the *Alma Cogan Show* and, as a surprise encore, give Alma a Cocker Spaniel puppy. After the show, Alma discreetly disposed of the beast – gave to friends not gassed it, this is Alma Cogan we're talking about.

Dick Whittington opened on Christmas Eve and lasted three and a half hours.

"He excites frenzied partisanship in the audience," the *Times* said. "They scream every time he comes on and, 'No, Adam, *look out!*' they shriek whenever some typical pantomime trap is set for him, as though his life depended on their assistance."

Towards the end of the evening, the Sultan of Morocco would cry, "Now that we're rid of the rats, let the celebration commence." Adam would come in powder blue trimmed with gold and do a 25-minute set, at the climax of which he'd sing 'Lonely Pup'. Children from the audience were invited to join him on stage. No live puppies were thrown. Adam took to it all like a duck to water.

"He joins good-naturedly in the nonsense, has water squirted in his face with the best of them and generally plays his part in what remains, for the most part, a good old-fashioned traditional panto."

Panto aside, 1960 had been a good year for Adam. He'd had six singles, an EP and an LP in their respective Top 5s. Two of the singles had gone to number one. He'd been in two film releases. He'd met the Queen,

Prince Philip and Bruce Forsyth. He'd been screamed at. He'd sung with Alma Cogan and the Beverley Sisters. He'd had more sex than any 20-year-old has a right to expect, some of it with film stars. He'd bought a huge American car and suits of clothes that had set him back £100. He'd been to places that his contemporaries had only read about in geography books: places like Manchester (cotton), Birmingham (canals), Glasgow (shipbuilding) and Hull (fish). He'd eaten turbot and lobster.

It had been a very good year.

Chapter Eleven

"For those with eyes to see it, something important and heartening is happening here. The young are rejecting some of the sloppy standards of their elders... They have discerned dimly that in a world of automation, declining craftsmanship and increased leisure, something of this kind is essential to restore the human instinct to excel at something and the human faculty of discrimination."

William Deedes,
Speech to Young Conservatives.

Face To Face was a TV interview show in which John Freeman MBE, an ex-MP and distinguished journalist, interviewed a celebrity. Though commonplace today, the idea of interviewing somebody not about a specific issue but about *them* was new at the time and, in some circles, regarded with revulsion.

"It produces a pervasive triviality," said one critic, "a constant descent into the lowest human common denominator, at which poet, philosopher, politician, comedian and athlete will be asked indiscriminately what is their favourite weather, do they always travel with a hot water bottle, what is their favourite colour, is there a type of person they particularly dislike, and what (in not more than 30 words) have they learned from life – the general aim being, it seems, to assure us that the famous and talented are just like anyone under the skin."[26]

Interviewees had included Bertrand Russell the philosopher, Dame Edith Sitwell the poet, John Huston the film director, Carl Gustav Jung the psychiatrist, Tony Hancock the comedian, Evelyn Waugh the novelist and King Hussein of Jordan the king.

Freeman kept his back to the camera (Kingsley Martin, the Editor of the *New Statesman*, said, "John is the only man who has made himself celebrated by turning his arse on the public"). The subject was shot in unforgiving close-up. A lot of nervous smoking went on. By today's standards, the questions seem anodyne, but then they were seen as searching, challenging, impertinent. Gilbert Harding, the curmudgeon whom Wee Willie Harris on *Six-Five Special* had called "Daddy-O", cried when he was on the show. Real tears.

When the idea of doing a pop star struck the producers, their first thought was of Cliff. Then, John Freeman had the good sense to ask his teenage daughter, Liz, for advice. She said, "Cliff never, Adam forever," or words to that effect, and appropriate enquiries were set in motion.

Eve Taylor didn't want her boy to do it. "She didn't tell him about it for a couple of weeks," says Adam's friend Keith Altham. "She just didn't see much money for herself. But one day, she let it slip in conversation and Adam exploded, 'Bloody hell, Eve, I'd give my life to be on that show.'"

"I think really they decided to invite this pop star on for a bit of fun," says writer and broadcaster Robert Elms. "I think they were doing it to slightly take the mickey out of him. They thought, he's a working class boy so he's going to be stupid."

Most people agreed. Adam was cruising for a bruising.

The interview took place at the Lime Grove Studios on December 11, 1960. Journalists swarmed on the Goldhawk Road outside the studio. They warned Adam that he was in for a mauling, but they were wrong. The working class boy more than held his own. The camera homed in on his chiselled beauty and Adam gave thoughtful and truthful answers to John Freeman's questions.

Freeman seemed almost as fascinated by money as Adam was.

FREEMAN: It's said about you quite often that you earn about a thousand pounds a week and, as you don't deny that, I suppose that it's perhaps about true.

FAITH: Yes it's true to a certain extent. It is difficult to average out what one [*one!*] earns in a week because with records you get a royalty on them and you get that in a lump sum, so it's very difficult.

FREEMAN: Quite. But if you divided a year's earnings by 52, I dare say that we would come to something like a thousand a week.

FAITH: I should think so – yes.

FREEMAN: Good. Well now, do you have professional advice as to what to do with that?

FAITH: Well, I have. I've been in the business now for just over a year and I've taken advice from my manager and her business associates and their advice is to keep it. So I've been saving now for a year and I intend to do so for another six or eight months.

FREEMAN: Does that mean – when you are saving – I don't want to be impertinent about this – does that mean you're not investing it, you're just literally saving it in the bank, or does it mean you are putting it out into investments?

FAITH: Well, at the moment I'm not investing because come the time next summer – that'll be the time I start to invest. Then I shall buy the best brains possible.

And thus it continues. No flick-knives. No jive-talk. No crazy mixed-up kid. No secondary modern gaffes. Straightforward, sensible – possibly even dull – answers. To forestall the possibility that they'd end up talking about the inadvisability of buying gilts in a bear market, Freeman changes to a different tack.

FREEMAN: Do you read a lot?

FAITH: Fair amount. As much as I can.

FREEMAN: Again – any particular tastes?

FAITH: Well, I'm varied again. I like – I've read some of Huxley's books.

FREEMAN: Aldous Huxley. Yes?

FAITH: And – have you ever read any of Salinger's?

[Note the way Adam's making literary recommendations to Freeman]

FREEMAN: Yes – *The Catcher In The Rye*.

FAITH: Yes, that's my favourite book. *The Catcher In The Rye* by Salinger, and I'm going to start on Hemingway and Steinbeck now.

FREEMAN: Do you read ever because you think you ought to read something or do you always read just because you enjoy it?

FAITH: Well, I started to read because I enjoyed it, but then I found I got so much benefit in reading and got so much from it that I determined myself to read as much as possible. And as variable as possible.

Freeman tries him on music.

FREEMAN: The newspaper cuttings say you like classical music. Now is that just a story, or is that true?

FAITH: Well you see I always take interviews myself and I never put out any press releases, so most of it, what you read in the newspapers, is true, if slightly exaggerated. But I do enjoy classical music.

FREEMAN: What particular composer?

[See the trap he's setting there?]

FAITH [without a moment's hesitation]: Sibelius and Dvořák I enjoy very much. Tchaikovsky I like.

[Radio 3 announcers have been known to mispronounce Dvořák. Adam's pronunciation is irreproachable.]

FREEMAN: Do you ever have time to go to a classical concert?

FAITH: I haven't been to a classical concert for about nine months, the last one I went to see was at the Royal Festival Hall – Toscanini.

The nine months was clearly 'misremembered'. Arturo Toscanini died in 1957. The last time he played the Royal Festival Hall was 1952. If Freeman was aware of this, he kindly lets it pass.

Finally, Adam speaks up for teenagers everywhere.

FREEMAN: Probably millions of teenagers would copy you whatever you did. If you shaved off all your hair like Yul Brynner, a million other young men would do this tomorrow morning. Now, do you think that makes sense – that a young man of 20 should be the idol of so many millions?

FAITH: Sense? I don't know. You see I don't feel they would shave their heads if I had a Yul Brynner haircut. I don't think that if I put my head in a gas oven – they wouldn't do it. I don't think they would.

FREEMAN: You think they are more independent than we give them credit for?

FAITH: I think so, you see, because I meet teenagers all the time. When I'm working, I always meet them in the dressing room and I've found them completely independent. This is another thing that the press have taken. Because in the world with many, many millions of people and millions of teenagers, a few teenagers do things that get into the press and immediately every teenager in the country is put into that category.

FREEMAN: Let me ask you as a last question. What's quite certain is that, whether they copy you or not, you're very much admired by millions of teenagers. Now if you could say it for yourself, what are the qualities that you would like to be admired for most?

FAITH: Sincerely, being an individual. I think all teenagers should try to be individuals and – let me see – I don't know – there are so many different things that I'd like people to like me for. But I think being an individual, being sincere and being frank with other people are the most important things.

"He holds his own under this really quite extreme grilling by this man with a very posh voice who looks down on him and talks down to him," says Robert Elms. "Adam is brilliant. This kid who should really be driving a bus like his dad does – holds his own."

"I reckoned I gained an extension, a sort of lasting level of stardom by appearing with John Freeman on *Face To Face*," Adam said a couple of years later. "Suddenly I was accepted as a social voice, although that wasn't the original idea. I just came over as myself. If I was a berk, I would have emerged as a berk. Whatever else I was, I wasn't a berk."

The programme was transmitted at 10.25 on a Sunday night. Ratings weren't great. About four-and-a-half million people watched Adam on BBC, while 20 million watched James Garner in *Maverick* on ITV. There were only two channels of course.

The BBC's postbag was full, though. Some of the letters were in green ink along the lines of "get this adenoidal little pleb off my TV screen" or words to that effect, but most were guardedly favourable.

"I admit to some prejudice at first," said "A Housewife". "But this evaporated as the programme continued."

A "Retired Businessman" confessed: "In my ignorance I switched on this programme with a feeling of anticipated distaste. It taught me a lesson not to pre-judge a generation with which I am not in personal contact."

After the *Face To Face* interview, Jocelyn Ferguson, a BBC mandarin, sent a memo to Lorna Moore, Talks Organiser, saying, "His television personality was enchanting, but I doubt whether it is worth a repeat on sound [radio]. Although he is more intelligent, what he has to say has much in common with the Cliff Richard *Frankly Speaking* and perhaps we've had enough of teenage pop singers for the present. He speaks rather slowly, too."

Slow speech or not, it was Adam, not Cliff, who became the "the spokesman for British Youth". When the British Medical Association set up a committee to look at "young people and morals", Adam was invited along. And when the Archbishop of York appeared on the BBC to talk about youth, Adam appeared with him. He was the mystery guest on the TV panel game *What's My Line?* and did *Desert Island Discs* in April.

Desert Island Discs was, and still is, a long running radio series in which guests are invited to choose the eight "gramophone records" they'd most like to keep them company if they were cast away on a desert island.

Holding true to the classical tastes he'd expressed on *Face To Face*, Adam chooses Sibelius ('Symphony No. 2 in D'), Dvořák ('Slavonic

Dance No. 2') and Tchaikovsky ('Capriccio Italien') along with Sammy Davis Jnr's 'Because Of You', Lonnie Donegan's 'Lost John', Ray Charles' 'What'd I Say?', Johnny Mathis' 'What'll I Do?' and his own 'What Do You Want?'.

"You know how quickly crazes spring up and die nowadays in popular music," Roy Plomley, the presenter, asks, "do you think you'll be able to ride those waves and change your style as required?"

"Well, I don't know," says Adam. "I'll have to wait and see."

"What's your big ambition?"

"To direct films."

"Films?"

"Yeah."

"You'd rather direct than act."

"No, I'd just like to do both. Direct a film and maybe act in another one."

According to the rules of the game, as well as the eight gramophone records to keep him entertained on the desert island, he's given the Complete Works of William Shakespeare and a Bible, and is allowed to choose one other book and one "luxury item". This "luxury item" may not be anything 'practical' that could, for instance, be used to escape.

The book once again concurs with his *Face To Face* answers – Aldous Huxley's *Brave New World*.

"One luxury... well, I would like to take a deterrent against colds because as you realise I've got a cold now so that my voice sounds a little peculiar. I must apologise, but as we can't take anything practical ..."

"Well, you can take a cold cure. Put that in your pocket. Choose something else."

"How about a pack of cards?"

"You can put that in your other pocket. Choose something a bit bigger."

"Well, I'm planning to write a novel soon and if I get shipwrecked it seems I'll have plenty of time, so I'd take some notepaper and a pen."

"Yes, yes a big supply of both."

"Yes."

"Have you got a theme for the novel already?"

"Well it keeps coming and going."

No novel ever emerged, but Eve Taylor secured Adam a publishing deal for an autobiography. The ghosted result, at 95 pages, is a slim volume, but still seems a stretch for a twenty year old who claims selective amnesia.

"I'm not going to tell you much about my childhood for the best reason of all," he writes. "I can't remember. My memory is a bit of a joke in the family."

While hazy about names, dates and historical events, however, his recall of fees and prices is unfaltering. He earned 7s 6d for his first weekly newspaper round, 10s for his first gig, he was now earning £1,000 a week, he was buying a house for £6,000... and so on. Even the title, *Poor Me*, has pecuniary ambiguities.

Much of the book – pandering shamelessly to the fans – is written in the breathless photo-comic style of *Valentine*, *Mirabelle* or *Roxy*. Accordingly, Adam makes it clear that he has known love and heartbreak. He is vulnerable. He talks at length about the anguish caused by a girlfriend called Jane who toyed with his affections and drove him wild with jealousy when she revealed a 'pen pal' in Germany: and then he tried to break it off with her but couldn't... (*to be continued next week*).

He talks of his career plans. Eve's been preparing him for a summer season in Stockton, we're told, working to create bits of comic 'business' to perform "to stop people thinking of me purely as a singer".

The book is "profusely illustrated" with photos of Adam playing golf, badminton, riding a horse, sporting a Pringle sweater and shaking hands with the Queen Mother. Knitting pattern models have looked more rock'n'roll.

The end papers are filled with a reader competition. The first prize is a chance to meet Adam in person, a portable record player and five long-playing records. Second and third prizes are just the five long-playing records and a signed photograph. All you have to do is write, on a postcard, please, in 50 words, what you like about the singer and his recordings, attach the coupon to your postcard and send it to The

Secretary, International Adam Faith Club, 60 Great Russell Street, London WC1. Before you get your hopes up, reader, be warned that the closing date was August 1, 1961.

The appearance on *Desert Island Discs* and the publication of the autobiography were both, along with buying a house for your mum and dad, on the standard checklist of things that were required of pop stars.

The house he bought for Nell and Alf was in Sunbury-On-Thames. It was the right location. In the fifties and most of the sixties, stars of stage, screen and television were almost obliged to make their homes in that area of the Thames Valley. Eve Taylor already lived in Sunbury-On-Thames. So did Eddie Calvert ("The Man With The Golden Trumpet") and crooner Dickie Valentine. Charlie Drake and, later, John Lennon, Ringo Starr and Michael Aspel lived in nearby Weybridge. George Harrison would live up the road in Esher.

Nell and Alf's new home was not exactly the sort of thing one might gawp at on a 'Homes of The Stars' coach trip. It was a newly built four-bedroom detached, with garage and front-drive parking for two cars, up a cul-de-sac of lookalike properties. As soon as it was finished, Adam moved the whole family in. He lived there himself for a while, too, while he was looking for his own dream home. His bedroom was modest in size but desirable for having its own telly and – a sophisticated continental luxury in 1961 – a duvet.

Nell was sympathetic when she found women lurking underneath that duvet – sometimes bringing them a cup of tea in the morning and perching on the bed to have a chat.

"Show business is a lonely business," Adam said. "I've got maybe five friends – like my manager and my arranger and my songwriter and some that I've known from school. But you don't make friends in show business. Why? I can't sort of put my finger on it, but you don't. I don't call girlfriends friends. I mean they're – like – girls and you don't want to get involved, do you?"[27]

At the *NME* poll winners' concert in March, Cliff got "British Male Singer" but Adam got "British Vocal Personality of the Year". The awards were presented by the winner of "World Female Singer" Connie Francis, with whom Adam, according to the British press, was romantically involved – a rumour that was almost certainly true if only on the grounds that she was a woman, he was Adam Faith and they were in a room together for at least 15 minutes.

Chapter Twelve

"Show me what life could have been, up and down, happy and sad; a life with a spontaneity and a movement and a generosity, and a living pitch and a depth of feeling, show me this. Show me life through coloured spectacles because that is how I wanted it, how I still want it."

Ray Gosling, *Sum Total.*

The Adam Faith brand had been able to report a tidy profit for 1960–61, but experience had shown that keeping the balance sheet healthy in the foreseeable future would take some fancy footwork. Pop stars had a tendency to be nine-day wonders. The evidence was everywhere to be seen: remember the Three Chuckles, the DeJohn Sisters, The Ferko String Band, Gerry Granahan or Gary Stites?

Even if you were Adam Faith, the £1,000 a week did not come from sitting on your arse. It was standard procedure for managers, when their clients were at the top of their game, to work them like prisoners in a gulag. Eve, remember, was the "commandant from hell".

At the beginning of 1961, Adam tried to wipe out the shame of his failure to reach the number one spot with 'Lonely Pup', not to mention the embarrassment of having recorded it in the first place, by releasing a proper Johnny Worth double A- side: 'Who Am I?' and 'This Is It'.

Don Nichols in *Disc* magazine was as relieved as anybody to see that the follow-up wasn't 'Little Puppy Isn't Lonely Any More'. "'Who Am I?'" he wrote, "is a very brisk romancer which lilts along brilliantly to a strings and chorus backing (the Vernons Girls) directed as always by John Barry. I like the wide open noise of this half. Faith's performance is as good, perhaps better than ever. 'This Is It' is also riding a quick pace with strings a-plucking and chorus ah-ahing in the rear. Tune's a simple one, and the lyric matches. Polished arrangement and performance lift it high. With either half – another hit."[28]

This was a good few years before rock criticism became a respected literary genre.

The record went to number five and stayed in the chart for 14 weeks.

On March 18, Adam was back on the road again with the John Barry Seven. "Popular Young Vocalist" Gerry Dorsey, who later changed his name to Englebert Humperdinck, closed the first half. The first gig, at the Gloucester ABC Regal, was sold out in less than an hour.

In April, he was back at Abbey Road recording another new single, a Lionel Bart song called 'Easy Going Me'. The music press wondered whether the songs, and particularly the arrangements, were becoming predictable. The public, too, seemed to have fallen out of love with pizzicato. 'Easy Going Me' was Adam's first Parlophone record not to make the Top 10, hovering just outside at number 12.

At the beginning of May he was at the ATV studios in Aston, Birmingham to appear on ITV's new pop show, *Thank Your Lucky Stars*. Then there were more one-nighters in May, moving from Doncaster and Stockton all the way into Scotland, to Aberdeen and Ayr and Leith. Then June took him around the seaside resorts to Southend, Brighton, Blackpool and Cleethorpes.

The third single of the year, 'Don't You Know It?', is a dark song. "One kiss from your deadly lips and I feel the pain" is about as far away from 'Lonely Pup In A Christmas Shop' as you can get without actually entering Madame Jojo's Whiplash Wonderland.

John's arrangement features a clavioline – a sort of early synthesizer – timpani (the big sound of 1961 as heard on Tony Orlando's 'Bless You' and the Brook Brothers' 'Ain't Gonna Wash For A Week') and some kind of dinner gong, possibly a tam-tam.

Adam and John couldn't win. Having previously criticised them for being too samey, the critics panned 'Don't You Know It?' for being too gimmicky. Again it went to number 12 but never made that push into the Top 10.

In September, Eve tried to up Adam's "mum and dad appeal" by sending him off for two weeks cabaret at the Room At The Top, a club above a department store in Ilford, Essex. It was not the Talk of The Town, it wasn't even the talk of Ilford, but Eve said it would be good for the business, so Adam bore it like a soldier.

The slog continued.

There were 15 consecutive one-nighters in October without a night off, starting in Colchester, working through Wolverhampton, Walthamstow and Worcester, and ending up in Peterborough. His November schedule included an afternoon gig for the inmates of Leicester prison before his evening concert at the De Montfort Hall.

But the money kept pouring in. The fees he could command, even from the parsimonious BBC, had skyrocketed. In January, 1960, his fee for an appearance on *Saturday Club*, BBC radio's Saturday morning pop show hosted by "Your Old Mate" Brian Matthew, was a niggardly 10 gns. By August 1961, the same gig made him 50 gns, which, by BBC standards of the time, was breathtaking.

"What do you spend it on?" Roy Plomley had asked.

"Well, clothes and a car," Adam had replied.

The latest car outclassed even the Ford Galaxie. In the summer of 1961, Jaguar introduced a new model, the E-Type. It was, and remains, one of the most beautiful cars ever designed: a tiny cabin sat behind an unashamedly phallic bonnet housing a six-cylinder engine that had the throaty roar of Leslie Phillips on heat.

Eventually George Best, Steve McQueen, Brigitte Bardot, Caroline Stafford and Tony Curtis all became E-Type owners.

"There was a five-year waiting list or something," says Andrew Tribe, a business associate and friend. "Adam decided that he'd got to have one so he got on the phone to Sir William Lyons who owned Jaguar. Got his phone number and phoned him at home. He said, 'Can I have one of your Jags?' And as it turned out, Sir William Lyons' daughter was a fan, so he said, 'Yes, as long as my daughter can come and meet you." So Adam agreed and got something like the fourth E-Type ever made."

It was silver grey, with a blue hood.

Because it's nice to have a bigger car as well to drive the family around in, he also bought himself a powder blue Rolls Royce from a friend of Eve's – a used car salesman by the name of Bernie Ecclestone.

Adam pushed himself as much as Eve pushed him. The constant one-nighters, the cabaret clubs, the records and the TV and radio appearances, it seemed, weren't enough. Now, and forever, he would always want more.

"Me and my manager," he told the *Evening Standard*, "have got to have a meeting soon to discuss my film career. You can certainly say I am considering this business of being a film star. Definitely. I'd like to be a film star. I'd get a satisfaction out of that, you might say. Like you get a satisfaction out of...."[29] He trailed off suggestively.

Eve obliged by getting him a starring role in a film called *What A Whopper!*. The title tells you pretty much all you need to know. It was not set in beatnik coffee bars where tearaways with names like "Plaid Shirt" could hide from the existential threat of "Boom! – the world goes up in smoke." In fact, for the first time in his acting career, Adam Faith wasn't playing a tearaway at all.

The cast of *What A Whopper!* includes every comedy stalwart of the day: Sid James (playing a Scotsman), Charles Hawtrey, Wilfred Brambell, Clive Dunn, Freddy Frinton, Terry Scott, even Spike Milligan puts in a cameo appearance as a tramp. It was written by Terry Nation, the man who later, when called upon to provide a new adversary for the second series of *Doctor Who*, came up with the Daleks. Adam plays a struggling writer who fakes photographs of the Loch Ness monster blah blah blah.

During filming at Pinewood on June 23, the film's star celebrated his 21st birthday. *Disc* magazine presented him with a special tribute EP containing spoken tributes from John Barry, Johnny Worth, Norman Newell, Jack Good and even Adam's arch-rival Cliff Richard.

Adam's *What A Whopper!* co-star, pouting, blonde Carole Lesley, helped him blow the candles out, posing primly for the photos. This led, of course, to rumours of another romantic liaison.

What A Whopper! was supposed to have had a John Barry score, but Mr Barry, busy with other commitments, dropped out during production. He did, however, arrange Adam's two songs for the film, both written by Johnny Worth.

The film's title song, 'What A Whopper!', is a truly spirit-sucking take on 'Oh Dear What Can The Matter Be?'. "Oh, what a whopper," the chorus goes. "O-wow-wow-what a whopper, one day you're gonna come a cropper, for telling such a low down lie." Luckily the song at least has the decency to be unmemorable.

The other song, 'The Time Has Come', was released as Adam's next single. It's up there with the best. Devoid of pizzicato, clavioline, timpani or other gimmicks, it's a straightforward string arrangement against which Adam lounges, his vowels unmangled, his delivery relaxed and honest. Deservedly, it made number four.

What A Whopper! opened at the Rialto, Coventry Street, London on September 28. Nobody liked it much. It opened a few weeks later in Sweden under the title, *Nu tar vi monstret* (*Now We Take The Monster*). Nobody liked it much there, either.

Chapter Thirteen

"Sexual intercourse began
In nineteen sixty-three
(which was rather late for me) –
Between the end of the Chatterley ban
And the Beatles' first LP."

Philip Larkin, *Annus Mirabilis*

It is impossible to write about pop music in that period between the *Lady Chatterley* ban (August 25, 1959) and the Beatles' first LP (March 22, 1963) without a sense of dramatic irony creeping in. It's like writing about 1B.C., 1913, 1938, or the presidency of J.F. Kennedy. Or seeing the bucket of water balanced over the door just as Teecher is about to enter the room in a Bash Street Kids cartoon. Something big is about to happen and the key people in the story don't know about it, but we do.

All the elements that were to create the sound and shiny fury of the sixties were assembling in the wings waiting for the big show to get going. In those couple of years: the Beatles performed their first gig at the Cavern Club in Liverpool and released their first two singles; Mick Jagger and Keith Richards started a band called Little Boy Blue & the Blue Boys; the Marquee on Oxford Street started something called "Rhythm

& Blues" nights; Bob Dylan released his first album; Mary Quant opened a second branch of her shop, Bazaar; David Bailey was hired by *Vogue* magazine and started taking different kinds of photographs of different kinds of models; *Beyond The Fringe*, the 'satirical' revue, transferred to the Fortune Theatre in the West End; the first edition of *Private Eye* magazine was published; Peter Blake won the John Moores (Junior Section) Prize for his *Self Portrait With Badges*; Andy Warhol produced his *32 Soup Cans*.

Fings Ain't Wot They Used T'Be – the Lionel Bart/Frank Norman musical of seamy Soho running in the West End – was cocking an inappropriately angled snook at the Lord Chamberlain. And, in the already mentioned case of *Regina versus Penguin Books Ltd.* concerning the publication of D.H. Lawrence's *Lady Chatterley's Lover*, the jury found for the defendant, which meant that perfectly ordinary men – yes and their wives and servants – could now go into perfectly ordinary bookshops and buy a book in which both men and women had the nerve to take pleasure in the act of sexual congress without even having the decency to use Latin words when they talked about it.

There were rumblings on the wider stage, too. On July 8, 1961, Stephen Ward introduced John Profumo, Secretary of State for War, to Christine Keeler, model and showgirl – a meeting that, in the fullness of time, would shake the Tory party to its roots and bring down a government. Kennedy became president of the USA; Hugh Gaitskell died and Harold Wilson became leader of the Labour Party.

Yuri Gagarin became the first man in space, orbiting the earth once. Then, Alan Shepherd, an American, went round three times. Work started on the Berlin Wall. There was increasing clamour for the US, already deploying several thousand troops in Vietnam as 'advisors', to engage openly and directly with the North Vietnamese. A CIA-funded counter-revolutionary militia landed at the Bay of Pigs in Cuba with the intention of overthrowing Castro's new government. This led to the Cuban Missile Crisis – probably the nearest the world ever came to "Boom! – the world goes up in smoke. And what's the score? Zero!"

And so on ...

There was a general feeling that the forces of decency and rectitude were bracing themselves against the coming onslaught from communists, sex maniacs, perverts, tearaways, non-Caucasians, tarts, wide boys and working-class oiks who were doing their damnedest to take Western Civilisation to hell in a hand-job. They were edgy times, all right.

And all this uncertainty played havoc with the charts.

When skiffle and rock'n'roll were deemed to have gone the way of all passing crazes, there was an attempt by journalists and record companies to convince the punters that 'trad' – a ninth-hand pastiche of antique New Orleans jazz mostly played by Acker Bilk, Chris Barber and Kenny Ball (all fine musicians) – was the New Big Thing. Nobody except men who were 40 when they were 20 believed it.

Then came the twist. For 18 months or so, the twist – a mostly static dance that involved swivelling the hips and gyrating the arms in an imitation of a bather giving his or her lower back a brisk rubdown with a towel – dominated the world's dance floors, charts and press.

The proto-twist records were Chubby Checker's 'The Twist' and 'Let's Twist Again', but it was an unmissable bandwagon even for old stagers like Frank Sinatra ('Everybody's Twistin''), Frankie Vaughan ('Don't Stop Twist') and Petula Clark ('Ya Ya Twist' – rendered oddly erotic by being in French).

The more extravagant, cavalier scholars of popular culture have claimed that since the dance required independent movement of the hips – an action anatomically unfamiliar to Northern Europeans and WASP Americans – it fuelled the sexual revolution of the sixties and revealed to many the mysteries of the orgasm. Similarly, feminist scholars have claimed it as a catalyst to their cause, if only on the grounds that, unlike conventional ballroom dances, it required no man to 'lead'.

While some clergymen denounced it from the pulpit, others, hoping to ingratiate themselves with the teens, did it in their cassocks. Doctors expressed their concern that 'excessive twisting' could result in slipped discs and spinal deformities. When a teenager was stabbed outside a Twist Club in Acton, a full-fledged moral panic was launched.

The Egyptian government and most of the Arab countries condemned it as filthy. The Soviets banned it as decadent, though poet Yevgeny Yevtushenko, after a visit to the West, described it as 'very OK'. Even at the height of the Cuban missile crisis, the pros and cons of the twist were considered news.

In general, though, the twist was enthusiastically embraced as an egalitarian dance that, it seemed, even the ill-coordinated and arrhythmic could have a shot at. HRH Prince Albert of Belgium did it with Anna Neagle while his pregnant wife, Princess Paola, watched. Garbo did it alone. Princess Margaret did little else for the best part of two years. Olympic bronze medallist Liz Ferris did it underwater. Carlo Ponti and Sophia Loren did it at their wedding. The Kennedys did it at The Peppermint Lounge – New York's Twist Central. Three police display motorcyclists came to grief trying to do it in the saddle.

In the UK, a tabloid without at least three twist-related stories was considered an editorial failure and that's not counting the ads, most of which tried to give their copy for anything from Beechams Powder to ex-Russian Navy binoculars a little twist. Tampax boasted that it gave women 'the freedom to Twist'. Horlicks gave everybody the sound sleep they required to embark on another hard day's twisting.

By the autumn of 1962, except in one or two out-of-the-way social centres in rural Lincolnshire, it was all finished. On the whole people were glad. Chubby Checker's attempts to engender the same enthusiasm for the Fly, the Hucklebuck, the Pop-Pop-Popeye and the La-La-Limbo met with little success.

There was also, over those two years, a terrifying proliferation of 'novelty records' and general pap. When the keen-eared pop-picker listened to the chart rundown on *Pick Of The Pops*, it often seemed that between every Roy Orbison, Ray Charles or Duane Eddy track, you were forced to endure a couple of Charlie Drakes, a Bernard Cribbens, a Russ Conway, an Andy Stewart, or Makadopoulos and his Greek bloody Serenaders doing 'Never On Sunday'. The records were harmless enough, but those who had thrilled to Lonnie's laser-beam whine, who had heard Jerry Lee Lewis invoke the Lord of Darkness with his punishing left hand and Little Richard call the Gadarene Swine with his whooping and his hollering found themselves dismayed. In *Jailhouse Rock* (1957), Elvis had killed a man in a barroom brawl and, shirtless, endured the lash in prison; in *GI Blues* (1960) he sang 'Wooden Heart', the musical equivalent of low-fat Petit-Filous, to a marionette.

Rock'n'roll was cinema-wrecking music. Nobody ever wrecked a cinema while listening to 'Wooden Heart'. Bob Wallis & His Storyville Jazzmen doing 'I'm Shy Mary Ellen, I'm Shy' did not shake nerves and rattle brains. Joe Loss & His Orchestra doing 'Wheels Cha Cha' did not set anybody's sex on fire.

Babes suckled on White Lightnin' were being weaned onto Tizer. It wasn't right.

In the spring of 1962, Adam, exhausted from the previous year's punishing schedule, undertook an 11-day nature cure at a Surrey rest home. He (or possibly Eve) invited a reporter from the *Sunday Express* down to interview him while he languished in his bathrobe.

"I was a physical wreck. I thought all I needed was a little tuning up. But when I went downstairs for my analysis yesterday, they told me about all sort of things that I hadn't even known were wrong with me. They go right back to the beginning, as far as you can remember. If your big toe hurts, they'll find out why. You know what I mean?"[30]

He was accompanied by his older brother, Dennis.

"He works as my assistant," he told the reporter. "My mother, father, sisters and brothers are all directors in one or other of my companies. We all share. I asked my mother and father whether they wanted to retire. They both said no. My mother supervises in a cleaning firm. My dad drives a coach."

The phone rings. Adam answers it. It is a new member of the team – his stockbroker.

Just as he'd indicated to John Freeman nearly 18 months earlier, the time for saving was over. The time for 'investing' had begun.

"Think we ought to buy some?" he says. "Yeah... How long are we staying in Shell?... I think I bought some at 128 and some at 131."

The same theme was picked up in a *New Record Mirror* profile. "I've no time for anything except business at the moment. I see my future much more clearly now with two films a year and the rest of the time devoted to singing tours and television work. I thoroughly enjoy big business and I've so much to learn at the moment that it takes up all my spare time."[31]

As if sensing the change in the air, he was diversifying the brand.

The *Face To Face* interview had made him a regular on serious TV discussion programmes. These didn't pay as much as *Saturday Club* or *The Billy Cotton Band Show*, but they were good exposure and held out the possibility of leading to something that could be genuinely lucrative – like being a politician. Prime Ministers didn't make anything like as much as pop stars, of course, but all the same they pulled decent money and there were a lot of perks. And they were never asked to do two weeks at the Room At The Top, Ilford.

In January 1962, Adam made a splash on *Meeting Point*, a highbrow religious discussion programme, hosted by Ludovic Kennedy, in the Sunday 7 pm God slot. Earlier in the year the Archbishop of York had invoked the name of Adam, saying, "Adam Faith tells youngsters the meaning of life is sex – the propagation of the species. Adam Faith tells us nothing of the life of the hereafter."

The show put Adam in the blue corner and the Archbishop of York in the red corner. At the end of the show, most people concluded that Adam won on points.

The Archbishop of York's first mistake was in speaking to Adam as if he was trying to demonstrate the word 'patronising' in a parlour game. From time to time, when Adam said something pertinent, his Right Reverence turned to Ludovic Kennedy and said, "He's got a point, hasn't he?" Adam bore it all with Christ-like restraint.

Peter Forster, TV critic of the *Spectator*, made great sport out of the discovery that Adam did not speak like the Queen or the Prime Minister: "I wish to say we all fink a lot abaht religion. We also fink a lot abaht bints and pools and the palais; but religion is somefing extra good, specially some of those ballads like 'I Believe'. What we don't fink much of is the Archbishop of York, who we fink is a proper Charlie of York."

He concluded that Adam was no fool but would be better off singing rather than wasting his time hanging around with losers like Archbishops and hoped that "somehow, sometime, soon, the Christian Church, which has been the most accomplished propaganda movement since the world began, will find a formula for presenting its ministers today on television in a persuasive and acceptable manner."

Extraordinarily, news of the confrontation went international and even made the pages of *Time* magazine: "It was as though Elvis Presley at his prime had challenged Cardinal Spellman to a theology debate on NBC," it said. "For in England, mop-haired Adam Faith, 21, is the current king of rock, and last week he argued religion for half an hour on BBC-TV with the Most Rev. Frederick Donald Coggan, 52, Anglican Archbishop of York. Faith proved rather more than the archbishop had bargained for."

'Lonesome', Adam's first single release of 1962, was a country song that could adapt itself to the pub style of singing favoured by drunken uncles at weddings and thus went straight to the hearts of the mums and dads generation. The choice of the B-side – a cover of Bobby Parker's 'Watch Your Step' – was infinitely more interesting and put Adam at least six months ahead of the game.

Bobby Parker was a proper blues musician from Lafayette, Louisiana. The song was later covered by Spencer Davis, Dr Feelgood, Manfred Mann and a thousand others. It is underpinned by one of the great guitar riffs of all time, a riff which all the young guitar players of 1962 with an interest in the blues and some rudimentary plectrum technique would inevitably have learned to play. Many of them are still playing it. Everybody who formed a band around that time – the kind of band that didn't wear bow ties tucked underneath their shirt collars, anyway – would have included 'Watch Your Step' in their set list. John Lennon later admitted to adapting that riff for 'I Feel Fine' and several other Beatles songs. It is the riff that Led Zeppelin were proud to steal for 'Moby Dick'.

In at alternative universe Adam's B-side could have put him at the forefront of the new wave. But it was too late. Already he was, in the eyes of young guitar players flexing their plectrums in 1962, a *Sunday Night At The London Palladium* sell-out has-been. If one of those young guitar players had dared own up to having listened to an Adam Faith record at all, if he (and they nearly always were 'he') had said, "Have you heard the B-side of Adam Faith's new one", he would immediately have been trumped with, "Not a patch on the Bobby Parker version, though, is it?"

In March, a new 14-track LP, *Adam Faith*, was released. It's not to be recommended except as a reference work for those researching John Barry's progress as an arranger. 'Come To Me' for instance, with its minor key, its French horn intro and its bold descent from the ninth in the first line of the melody, is like a rehearsal for the many Bond scores on which Mr Barry was soon to embark

More historical interest comes from the possibility that the album might contain the first ever commercially recorded fragment of a John Lennon song. The story goes as follows.

In May 1960, Larry "Parnes Shillings And Pence" Parnes, the most influential man in pop, travelled to Liverpool to audition bands to back Billy Fury on tour. John, Paul, George and Stu Sutcliffe, calling themselves The Silver Beetles, had a go. They didn't get the gig, but Mr Parnes offered them a seven-show tour of Scotland with another of his stable of stars, John Askew, whom he had rechristened Johnny Gentle.

Ten days later, they opened at Alloa Town Hall, travelled to Inverness, Fraserburgh, Keith, Forres, Nairn, and finished up the Rescue Hall, Peterhead.

One night, in the hotel after the show, Johnny Gentle was working on a song. He was stuck on the middle-eight. Luckily young John Lennon was on hand to help him. John came up with "*We know that we'll get by / Just wait and see / Just like the song tells us / The best things in life are free.*"

Admittedly it's not, "She said I know what it's like to be dead", and the last line could hardly be described as original, but it's a start.

The finished song – 'I've Just Fallen For Someone' – was Track 2 Side 1 on Adam's new LP.

It would be nice to say that the song's comfortless progress is redeemed by John Lennon's alleged middle-eight, but it would be a lie. It doesn't even scan properly.

Another single, 'As You Like It', was released at the beginning of April. The song had originally been earmarked for Jess Conrad but Adam bought it from him for £25. Jess definitely got the better end of the deal. It was not anybody's finest hour.

Despite which, miraculously, the record climbed to number five, becoming Adam's 13th consecutive Top 20 hit, which was, all importantly, one more than Cliff.

Adam was never unerring in his choice of quality material. In the summer of 1962, an aspiring songwriter called Mitch Murray (who later in the year had a minor novelty hit with 'My Brother' for Terry Scott) offered Adam a song he'd written for him. Adam passed on it.

An acetate of the song hung around Abbey Road for a while. Eventually George Martin, a Parlophone staff producer, thought it might be suitable for a new signing he'd made. The new group, the Beatles, made a half-hearted recording of it but preferred the songs they'd written themselves or obscure American covers.

Their manager, Brian Epstein, however, had another band on his books. The song was offered to them. And that is how Gerry and The Pacemakers came to record 'How Do You Do It?', the song that propelled them to number one a full three weeks before the Beatles scored their first number one.

In May, Adam started work on his fourth film.

Mix Me A Person is several cuts above *Beat Girl* and in an entirely different universe to *What A Whopper!*. It's a crime drama – a message picture – about a miscarriage of justice. Adam, back in his 'young tearaway' role, is accused of a murder he did not commit. Will his lawyer's wife, a psychiatrist, be able to save him before he falls victim to the hangman?

The script is by Ian Dalrymple and Jack Trevor Story, a writer with the knack of turning everyday speech into poetry. "I don't need no getting off cos I've done nothing that I need getting off of," says Adam, summarising the plot in words of nearly one syllable.

The film's directed by Leslie Norman – Barry's dad – and co-stars Donald Sinden and Anne Baxter, a genuine Hollywood name whose starring role opposite Bette Davis in *All About Eve* earned her an Oscar nomination. Ex-Prime Minister Tony Blair's father-in-law, Antony Booth, is in it, too, playing Adam's mate, Gravy.

There is a well-documented difference between 'acting' and 'being a star'. In most of his performances, Laurence Olivier, for instance, 'acted', which is to say he changed his voice, his posture, sometimes the colour of his hair or skin and almost invariably the shape of his nose according to the character he was playing. He inhabited the part. 'Being a star' is what Paul Newman and Marlon Brando did. They found the character within themselves. The change from role to role was subtle. When you watch a Paul Newman film, there's never any doubt that it's Paul Newman on the screen but by some subtle psycho-alchemical-dramatic process this never impedes your ability to believe he's somebody else.

Adam was always a star. He had mastered the supremely difficult art – or craft, or knack or whatever it is – of looking like an ordinary person on screen, of relaxing, of doing as little as possible, of saying lines as though they were thoughts that had just popped into his head. The only difficulty one has with his performances – and the same occurred with Paul Newman – is that real people are never that good-looking. Thankfully *Mix Me A Person* is in narrow-screen monochrome. In wide-screen 3-D, those cheekbones would leap out and gouge.

Somewhere along the line, a couple of ho-hum songs are squeezed in: 'Mix Me A Person' by Johnny Worth and a cover of Ritchie Valens' 'La Bamba'.

The posh press was grudging in its praise.

"The young today are always with us," said the *Times* – as opposed to, say, five years ago when they were often kept somewhere else – "and no film can be blamed if it self-consciously and deliberately aims at holding the interest of youth." A key difference between 1962 and, say, 1965 is that, in 1962, "deliberately holding the interest of youth" was considered an unworthy act.

The review goes on to note some of the more surprising general points made by the film, for instance that Adam's "young friends who gather to express themselves vocally and otherwise at a Battersea coffee bar, are fundamentally decent people".

It concludes by saying that, "Mr Adam Faith has within him the urge and ability to act."[32]

And the *Times* always had the urge and ability to patronise.

One Friday night, John Barry, Adam's arranger, producer, mentor and friend, got a call from Noel Rogers, Head of Music Publishing at United Artists. They met the following morning and Noel told him that Cubby Broccoli and Harry Saltzman, film producers, needed somebody to do a fast turnaround arrangement on a main theme for a new movie, *Dr. No,* the first in what they hoped would be a series of films based on Ian Fleming's James Bond novels, to which Saltzman and Broccoli had acquired the rights. John would get £250 for the job and a promise of future work. He agreed and a few days later asked Vic Flick, guitar player with the Seven, round to his flat. John showed Vic a few musical sketches he'd made loosely based on a theme that the film's composer, Monty Norman, had suggested (One needs to choose words here carefully. Thirty-five years later the matter of who wrote what became the subject of a bitter legal dispute between Norman and Barry, during which it appeared that the only thing that John Barry and Monty Norman had in common was that, like Paul Simon, they both had two first names – as opposed to, say Harrison Ford who has two second names or Duane Eddy who has one of each, but the wrong way round.)

Among other suggestions, Vic thought that the guitar part might sound more ominous and more dramatic, if it was played an octave lower than John had written it, on the thicker, twangier, Duanier Eddier strings of the guitar. John made the changes and on June 21, Vic took his Fender Vibrolux amp and the Clifford Essex Paragon De Luxe guitar he'd bought in 1959 from fellow guitarist Diz Disley down to CTS studios and made history.

'The James Bond Theme' is the most recognisable film title music ever. Even punters who can't tell the difference between the themes from 'Star Wars' and 'Toy Story' will correctly identify 'The James Bond Theme'. Keen-eared punters can do it from that first little click of Vic Flick's pick.

But Mr. Barry's success in the film world had repercussions.

In August, the big news in the music papers was the split between Adam Faith and John Barry. It was portrayed as a purely amicable arrangement designed to enable both parties to develop alternative projects. Mr Barry told *New Record Mirror*'s Peter Jones:

"In the early days, Johnny Worth, Adam and I were concentrating on one thing, Adam's records. We were after bread. We wanted financial gains. When you've got those, you can relax and choose your work. It's a matter of sitting back and considering precisely what you want to do in your career. Do you want to be tied by the boundaries of pop music? Do you want to include all kinds of music? Or all art forms? As an artist, a musician, you can learn something from all forms. From literature, films and comedy."[33]

Up yours, Barry.

For the next bout of recording sessions, arranger Johnny Keating stepped into the breach. He and Johnny Worth had masterminded the career of Eden Kane, another of Eve Taylor's turns, whose 'Get Lost' and 'Well I Ask You' had brought growling anger to the British pop scene and whose brother, Peter Sarstedt, later had us all buying carefully designed topless swimsuits so we got an even suntan on our backs and on our legs.

John and Johnny's first session with Adam produced 'Don't That Beat All', a song which bears a distinct similarity to Eden Kane's 'Well I Ask You', both in its style and in its pitch, which puts Adam further down into the 'manly' parts of his register than usual. The arrangement features a Nashville fiddle. Some of the publicity hand-outs said the song was in the 'Hully Gully' style – although the fiddle made it 'Country Gully'. Whatever you called it, it was clear that Adam had left the pizzicato days behind him.

Johnny Keating could replace John Barry in the studio, but Adam also needed a band to back him on the road.

Chapter Fourteen

"You are a medium and have much work to do. Chosen by the Spirit World, you must not ignore the call. Please come and see me after the meeting."

Estelle Roberts, *Fifty Years A Medium*

Bob Henrit grew up in Waltham Cross, a leafy London suburb near Cheshunt, where young Harry Webb was living when he changed his name to Cliff Richard.

"I was in a little skiffle group," says Bob. "This would have been about 1956. I have no idea whether we were any good or not. Up and down from Hertford all the way to London there were thousands of places to play. That was our stamping ground and we could play every night. Everyone was very friendly. And nearly everyone we knew went on to make it – Mike Berry [of Mike Berry & The Outlaws], Chas Hodges [of Chas'n'Dave] – we were just a group of friends.

"Having mastered the washboard at the age of 12, I started to agitate to get a drum kit and started saving. My father and I went up the West End and I think we paid £5 15s 6d (£5.77) for a drum kit. It would now be called a bitsa [bitsa this, bitsa that], but for me it was wonderful. Then I was headhunted by Russ Ballard – I had grown up with him. He was in a band called The Rebels. He said: 'If you join The Rebels you can use our drum kit.' They had a proper Carlton Made-in-Britain drum kit. Everything was the same colour. My old drum kit had Fablon on it. You bought it in Woolworths and it was meant to go on shelves. It did *look* like drum covering. Anyway, that's how I joined up with Russ Ballard."

"I played the American bases. I wasn't old enough to be there officially. I was 13 or 14. I remember going into this bar – which was absolutely black. It was just as well that it was so dark because things were going on there that a 13 or 14-year-old shouldn't be seeing. Everyone was getting very drunk and – I don't know if I should tell you – they were all waiting for the Pig Bus to arrive. Now the Pig Bus was the bus that came from the local towns and picked up all the women to bring them over. A very detrimental term, I know. Different times..."

"Eventually we were backing the likes of Billy Fury – a whole slew of rock'n'roll singers. Michael Cox was one of them. Ricky Valance [Welsh singer of 'Tell Laura I Love Her' not to be confused with Ritchie Valens who died with Buddy Holly] was another. We would be booked to play with these people. There could be half a dozen of them on one bill and we would do our act as well, which meant that whoever was employing us would be getting a very good deal. We didn't care because we weren't in music for money. No one was. Except Larry Parnes.

"My brother-in-law to be [the bass player John Rogers] was offered the job with Adam Faith and, not long after he joined, Adam decided that the drummer he'd got was too much of a [big] 'band' drummer. He came from the Palais or something and didn't have the angst that I had. And also he wasn't as cocky as me.

"I was still in the sixth form. I got the call to join Adam Faith and I thought, 'I'll never get away with this.' My mother was a teacher, you see. But my parents said: 'Well, if that's what you want.' My old man was really into music. I didn't even have an audition – I turned up under the wing of John Rogers."

Bob soon guessed the real reason – at least from Adam's point of view – for the split with John Barry.

"John Barry wanted more money, and there were seven of them. There were only four of us."

Despite the savings, Eve Taylor was never Bob's biggest fan. "I survived in the band but only just. Evie was often heard to say, 'The drummer's too fucking loud.'"

The band was called the Roulettes.

"To work with Adam was a little difficult at first," John Rogers, the bass player, told *New Record Mirror*. "Not technically, you understand, but to learn how Adam reacts, his original ways. We never know exactly how Adam will sing. He is very conscious now about audience reaction and this means he will lengthen certain numbers, keep 'em going to whip up some excitement. Or he could chop one halfway through. And it's a little difficult when the man you are accompanying is trying to sing with a couple of dozen girls screaming and hanging around his neck... on stage!"[34]

Adam, or Eve, had secured the band their own independent recording contract with Pye. Unlike the Shadows, who approached the mic to open their mouths only in rare circumstances, the Roulettes sang as well as played. Their first record, 'Hully Gully Slip'n'Slide', indicated that Johnny Worth was betting the farm on the Hully Gully becoming the new twist.

"If you like your twist, then keep on twisting / If you like your rocking, keep on rocking / If you feel like a hully do a little bit of gully / If you feel like slipping do a little bit of slide."

The B-side was yet another version of 'La Bamba'.

The record did not do well.

"Eve used to push Adam," says Roulettes guitarist Peter Thorp, "but she was never a fan of the Roulettes. She never promoted us. We had a couple of good records but she didn't want us to be bigger than Tel." *

The Roulettes were featured with Adam in the six episodes of his big TV spectacular *Adam Faith Sings Songs Old And New*. Then on October 21, they flew off to Australia with him for an 18-day tour with John "Johnny Remember Me" Leyton. From Australia, they travelled to New Zealand and Hong Kong.

---

* Adam, Terry, Tel, Bill – different people called him different things – for significant reasons. See later chapters.

Back from the tour, Adam took up residence in his new house. Dennis had found him a mock Tudor pile in Esher – just up the road from the house he'd bought for his parents in Sunbury-On-Thames. It was called, appropriately if unimaginatively, Tudor Court, and it had leaded windows, heavy oak beams, a billiard room, many, many bedrooms and a ghost.

It had once been the home of Mrs Estelle Roberts, "regarded as one of the finest exponents of mediumship of the 20th century". Once, after a table-rapping session, the table grew so excited, it chased poor Estelle out of the room. So often did she assist the police in their efforts to find a mutilated corpse or a desperate murderer that tales of her exploits were almost a weekly feature in the Sunday Lurids.

She could also, if called upon to do so, locate lost budgerigars.

She conducted séances before 6,000 people at the Royal Albert Hall. MPs and peers of the realm attended her sessions at the Houses of Parliament. She had great success putting Lady Segrave back in touch with her husband, the late Sir Henry Segrave, motoring correspondent.

She was assisted – indeed enabled – in her work by Red Cloud, her Native American guide. Red Cloud was expert at reuniting punters with friends and relatives who had gone beyond the veil, but prediction was never his thing. Imagine the disappointment of those who had planned Austrian Alpine holidays on the strength of Red Cloud's reassurance that war would *most certainly not* break out in 1939.

There was no knowing whether it was Red Cloud, a mutilated corpse, an uppity table or a lost budgie, but there was most definitely a 'presence' at Tudor Court. Everybody noticed it. Cold spots. A general aura of spookiness.

Luckily Adam's cook, Angelina, and valet, Vincente, were always on hand making sure he was never alone in the place.

He was on the road most of the time anyway. After a week at the Birmingham Hippodrome with Chas McDevitt, Shirley Douglas and Norman Collier (the northern comic who invented the 'faulty microphone' routine), Adam & the Roulettes went on a long and winding tour. This time, to add to the usual dangers of touring – the falling safety curtains, the failing brakes, the toxic dressing rooms and so on – they had to contend with the company of Gene Vincent, a man who never travelled without a gun in one pocket and a bottle of whisky in the other.

November 24 saw the release of Adam's next single, 'Baby Take A Bow', a soppy confection of harps, glockenspiels and bassoons, aimed (unsuccessfully as it turned out) at the Christmas market. It stalled at number 22, his first failure to make the Top 20 since 'What Do You Want?'. Adam attributed its poor sales to bad weather. It was indeed an appalling winter, yet still, somehow, record buyers managed to struggle out and stock up on Cliff's 'Bachelor Boy', Frank Ifield's 'Lovesick Blues' and Elvis' 'Return To Sender'.

Adam released an album, too. Most of the 12 tracks of *From Adam With Love* are country tinged, perhaps trying to ape something of the success of Ray Charles' *Modern Sounds In Country And Western Music*, which had hit the album and singles charts earlier in the year: although beyond the odd chord change and a few steel guitar sounds there are no points of comparison between Ray Charles' sweeping, majestic masterpiece and Adam's 'some blokes in a pub in Colchester' sound.

For several months the Roulettes played musical chairs. The group (and they were always called 'groups' – 'band' in those days was used only in the context of 'big', 'brass' and 'elastic') that Bob Henrit joined consisted of John Rogers on bass, Peter Thorp on guitar and Alan "Honk" Jones on saxophone. Honk was soon replaced by a guitarist, Brian Parker, who stayed a week before being himself replaced by Norman "Henry" Stacey. It was only a matter of time before John and Bob invited their pal from Waltham Cross to play.

"John and Bob said, 'Adam wants to meet you'," says Russ. "He doesn't care what you play like, but he wants to meet you. I wasn't really into his music. I preferred Gene Vincent and tougher music. Adam was quite passive and sort of soft. He was on the soft side of Buddy Holly – all those strings and the pizzicato thing. Although I thought his records with John Barry were quite strong. Very well written by Johnny Worth.

"He said, 'Can you make next Sunday?' So we all jumped into the Thames 12 hundredweight Dormobile and went to Tudor Court. It was a mock Tudor house. I lived over a shop. And I wanted to live in a council house. And here's this kid of 22 living in a Tudor pile. It was a very spacious house. Years later, Adam said, 'You probably wouldn't be so impressed if you saw it now', but we were young then.

"Anyway, we walked to the door and we were greeted by a butler – yeah, this kid of 22 has got a butler. And he's got a cook. Impressive, eh?

"Vins – the butler – said, 'Adam's father is in the snooker room. Would you like to join him?' Actually it was a converted garage. We got to talking to his dad about football. Then Tel turned up. He was wearing a three-piece suit. He took off the jacket, threw it on a chair, unbuttoned the vest, took his tie off and said, 'Hello Russ, how are you?'

"Then we just made small talk and he said, 'Are you going to be staying for lunch?' So we all said yes. It was silver service. He was living the part – playing the part. I remember we had syrup sponge – syrup and cream. Tel had all these idiosyncrasies. He used to smoke a lot. When he was talking he would stand the cigarette up on its end and then he'd squeeze the tip: he'd pinch the filter together so it would look like a penny whistle. And he was always fiddling. He'd rip up pieces of paper and roll them up when he was talking. Always fiddling.

"Anyway, Tel was there at the head of the table and as far as my audition went he said, 'What sort of music do you like, Russ?' and I said, 'I listen to everything. I like stuff with a melody and stuff. I like Little Richard. Buddy Holly." He hadn't heard me play but he thought I looked cool. I wore shades but only because I was hit in the eye when I was a kid. And that was it. I was in the band."

Adam ended the year in panto again: *Aladdin* at the Pavilion Theatre, Bournemouth.

"It was a very interesting time," says Russ Ballard, the new boy. "We had to dance. Gracie Fields' brother was in it. And Sid Plummer who played Abazanar – he was a xylophone player.* And then there was us. We really didn't want to do this. Because we wanted to be a rock'n'roll

---

* The highlight of Sid's act was when he played "The Donkey Serenade" and his xylophone turned into a horse.

band. We listened to Radio Luxembourg. And we thought it should be like that. Not doing panto in Bournemouth."

Adam rented a house in Bournemouth and installed his cook, Angelina, and valet, Vincente, to look after him. An air hostess called Andrea whom Adam had started seeing when he was on holiday in the south of France earlier that year came to spend Christmas with him. So that was him sorted.

For now.

Chapter Fifteen

"The main focal point of the college life was the café 'over the road'. Tom had secured half the spaces on the jukebox for the students' use, the rest were for the lorry drivers that used the café too. So on this jukebox Frank Ifield's 'I Remember You', Pat Boone's 'Speedy Gonzales' and Cliff Richard's 'Bachelor Boy' would exist alongside Jimmy Reed's 'Shame, Shame, Shame', Booker T's 'Green Onions' and Slim Harpo's 'King Bee'."
Richard Barnes, *The Who: Maximum Rhythm & Blues,* 1982

People in Liverpool had known about it for ages, but it was a while before the rest of the country caught up.

In Birmingham, an O-level student who played bass in a group liked to listen to Radio Luxembourg while doing his homework. If a track came on that might be worth a second listen, that might even be worth the investment of 6s 8d, he made a note of it on the white top of his work table in his bedroom. One night in November 1962, in big letters, underlined, he wrote "Love Me Do – The Beetles". The next day he mentioned it to friends at school. Some of them had heard it, too. They'd all noticed; they heard the way the harmonica bent the notes; they heard the marriage of bass and kick drum, louder than usual; they heard the lazy harmonies sung back in the throat – Liverpool harmonies. And they thought, "Hullo". When they bought the record, they found the B-side was good, too.

Something about the record chimed with another, deeper undercurrent.

The trad revival and skiffle boom had both awakened an interest in what was later called 'roots music'. Folk clubs sprang up and Cecil Sharp House, where the English Folk Dance And Song Society keeps its definitive collection of source material, including field recordings of long-dead Suffolk drunks singing dirty songs their granddads taught them, became a cool place to hang. Imported American blues singers – Big Bill Broonzy, Sonny Terry & Brownie McGhee, Sister Rosetta Tharpe – played small but inevitably sold-out gigs. The British interest was matched in America by the release of a five LP set of twenties and thirties recordings of folk and blues songs curated by the film-maker Harry Smith. Folk and blues began to get big.

In November 1962, while the Beatles' 'Love Me Do' was struggling up the charts, Blues Incorporated, a British band featuring Alexis Korner and Cyril Davies, playing Chicago style electric blues, released an album, *R&B From The Marquee* – actually recorded at the Decca Studios in West Hampstead. It didn't sell well, and certainly didn't chart, but it led those who bought it straight to the specialist record shops in search of the source: the dirty, gritty world of swooping guitars, searing harmonicas, sodden voices, Blind Boys, Sleepy Johns, Black Cat Bones and Crawling King Snakes.

'Authenticity' became a quality to be admired and arguments would rage, often between men with bits of sandwich in their beards, as to whether this or that piece of music was the more 'genuine'. The argument continued to rage for the next 40 years or so, by which time frightened Mongolians with tuneless one-string banjos made of scrap tin could, on the right programmes, get airplay.

Whereas once pop had been a matter of a nice smile, good hair, a gimmick and some astute marketing, now it became an infinitely more complicated matter. One minute the word 'commercial' was the best thing you could say about a record, the next it was a damning condemnation. The trick in this new, difficult world was to sell shedloads of product while at the same time, by some sleight of hand, convincing the buying public that you were not, never had been and had no intention of becoming a "sell-out."

Adam Faith's career, it seemed, was doomed. His last record of 1962 didn't make the Top 20. His first release of 1963, 'What Now?' didn't even make the Top 30. "No arms to hold me tightly, no touch to touch me lightly," no lyric writ more tritely.

The follow-up, 'Walkin' Tall', released in July, with quacking brass, novelty bass slides and a tune that can't seem to settle, was even worse.

His album release for that year, *For You*, consisted of 13 covers of everything from Bobby Vee's 'Take Good Care Of My Baby' to Hoagy Carmichael's 'Lazy River', all delivered with middle-of-the road big-bandish arrangements. When you opened the inner sleeve, you could actually detect a faint odour of desperation.

By the summer of 1963, it was clear that the new big thing was 'the Mersey Sound' – more generically described as 'the Beat Boom' – and it filled the keen-eyed pop fan's field of vision like an Alp or the weather.

On June 13, The Beatles, Gerry & The Pacemakers and Billy J. Kramer & The Dakotas – all Liverpool bands, indeed, all Brian Epstein bands – were numbers one, two and three in the charts. The Searchers, the Hollies (from Manchester but close enough) and even Freddie & the Dreamers, a semi-comic group led by a man in glasses who sometimes pretended to pull a lavatory chain on his head, were doing better than old-established firms with haircuts and microphone technique. Cliff & the Shadows were just about hanging in there, as was Frank Ifield, from Australia, but apart from that, the Northerners had moved in, put their feet up on the *NME* and ordered cake.

What was very clear was that Dick Rowe, the man from Decca who had told Brian Epstein, "Guitar groups are on their way out", was wrong. All of the new acts – Beatles, Pacemakers, Hollies, Searchers, even Freddie & The Dreamers and Brian Poole & The Tremeloes – were guitar groups. In this new marketplace, The Roulettes, rather than being a cheap replacement for the John Barry Seven, were an invaluable, not to say essential, asset.

Adam's mouth kept working overtime. There were still a few years to go before John Lennon started putting Jesus in his place and ending war. In the meantime Adam remained the go-to Voice Of Youth.

On February 22, 1963, the *Daily Express* reported: "Doctors, teachers, social workers and Churchmen listened for an hour yesterday while Mr Adam Faith talked about his faith, hope – and chastity.

"The Faith Tells All session was at the invitation of a British Medical Association committee investigating teenage morals."

The session was private but when Adam emerged he spoke for another hour to the press assembled outside. Like any self-respecting youth faced with a bunch of doctors, teachers, social workers and churchmen who wanted to know intimate details of his private life, he lied his head off.

"My affairs have always been platonic," he said, "nothing more than a kiss and a cuddle. I'm not pure. I have lusts, but who hasn't?"

He confessed that he met his first and only love when he was 16 – it lasted three years then "we drifted apart".

"That girl is now married and has two children. Since we split up, I haven't fallen for anyone really. I'm lonely and still looking for the right girl."

He also told the committee: "Adults are to blame for the sex problems of teenagers because they don't educate them enough. They should start as early as you like – as soon as they get to an understanding age – eight, nine, 10 – I dunno. I went out with a girl when I was nine. It was just a stroll in the park.

"I'm not saying they should be taught to go out and get a woman and seduce her, but that the human body is nothing to be ashamed of or laughed at."

A couple of days later, Adam confessed to the *Daily Herald* that some of his remarks might not have been strictly accurate. "I wasn't exactly lying. It was a bit of a difficult situation. Our own sex problems are not easy to talk about in public. By hiding the fact that I had had sex, I realised that I had been guilty of a Victorian prudish attitude. I went home and thought about it for two days. I fought against my conscience all that time, but finally lost and decided to own up to my white lie. The worst thing in the world is for people to go on talking about their sexual successes. There is too much dirty thinking and bragging on this topic."[35]

In other words, he'd done it.

George Melly, in *Revolt Into Style*, saw Adam's owning up as a turning point in the history of pop, youth, society and the sexual revolution: "He was the first teenage idol to admit to premarital sexual experience, a banal enough confession you'd have thought, but it had an extraordinarily violent effect on those who preferred to believe that nobody ever fucked anybody until after they were married.

"Today the reaction appears almost incomprehensible; but it was pre the Ward Trial and a spiritual age away. It helped, however, to endear Faith to the newly emerging liberal establishment who, until that time, had ignored pop completely. [...] He became the tame teenager, the interpreter, the ombudsman. Faith opened up an entirely new possibility within pop, the idea that it represented more than noise or mindless sexual provocation. The first to admit that his ambitions went further than a home for mum and acceptance as an all-round entertainer."[36]

Melly had nearly as good a gob on him as Adam or Lennon.

In May 1963, another personnel change was forced on The Roulettes in the worst way imaginable. John Rogers, the bass player, happily engaged to Bob Henrit's sister, fell victim to the road.

The Roulettes were booked to play a week's variety with Adam in Sunderland.

"The last time I saw John was in the hallway of my house," says Bob. "I said, 'I'll see you at the station.' We always went on the train because we didn't want to drive with the nutter who used to drive the van."

The 'nutter' was their roadie Peter Cotter.

"And John said, 'No I'm not going in the van.' And I said, 'Why?' He said, 'Well, I'm saving up to get married, aren't I?' And I said, 'But that guy's lethal as a driver.'"

Peter Cotter had had five hours sleep before setting off from London. The theory is that he dozed at the wheel and ploughed into a stationary lorry on the A1 near Stoke Rochford in Lincolnshire.

"The next thing I know is this shrieking coming from downstairs," Bob says, "because the van had been involved in an accident. John was asleep on the back seat and had a guitar case fall on him. A corner of it broke his rib and punctured his lung. And that was it."

Cotter told the Judge at the Lincolnshire Assizes that he remembered stopping at a café and at a filling station near a roundabout but nothing more. He was adamant that he was not guilty of dangerous or careless driving; nevertheless, the judge fined him £100 and disqualified him for seven years.

"So we were on our way to do a week in variety in Sunderland. And I'm travelling up with Russ. We are numb. We are sort of expecting John to be there."

The "show must go on" mentality often makes no sense at all to people outside the business and sometimes precious little to people inside it either.

John died on the Monday morning. That night Adam & the Roulettes opened, as promised, at the Sunderland Empire. Adam dedicated the show to John.

More curiously still, either Adam, or Eve or the theatre management drummed up a little publicity for the Sunderland show by publicising their search for a new bass player in the local press and on TV.

Within days, the *Sunderland Mail* was able to report: "A 19-year-old Hartlepool bass guitarist and the youngest of 15 children left his home in Lumley Street today to join Adam Faith, pop singer and big recording star. John George Rogan worked in his sister's general shop yesterday. Tonight after making his first appearance on the professional stage – at the Sunderland Empire – he leaves for Coventry. The following week Adam and his group appear at Great Yarmouth and then leave for Singapore."

"It all happened so quickly," said John's sister, Lena, one of his 14 siblings. "On Tuesday John saw Adam on television and heard him tell the interviewer that he was looking for a bass guitarist. He wrote immediately and got an interview on Thursday. He was told he could join the group for a trial period and the starting salary will be £30 a week."

"We looked for a bass player," says Bob, "and we found John Rogan – John 'Mod' Rogan. His CV was extraordinary. Hilarious. He was a tap dancer, a trumpet player, a ventriloquist: we never saw him ventriloquisting but he really was a tap dancer. He was zany and crazy. He turned up in Denson Poynters. We were Mods, if we were anything. We had long grey crocodile-pointed shoes, but he had Denson Poynters and very tight-bottom trousers and he had a quiff. He was a Teddy Boy so we immediately called him 'Mod'."

Denson made a range of "fashion shoes for men" including Arrow Poynts, Fine Poynts, Short Poynts, Hy-Poynters, Chisel Poynts, Fine Chisels and Ace of Diamonds all priced between 49s 11d (£2.49) and 63s (£3.15).

Shoe prejudice was widespread in 1963. Attempts to stamp it out proved strangely counter-productive.

After they got Mod some new shoes and trousers and showed him how to degrease his hair with Swarfega, he fitted in a treat.

Adam & the Roulettes happened to be in Singapore at the same time as Noël Coward – playwright, songwriter, actor, singer, wit and raconteur. Noël was the Kurt Cobain of the twenties, frequently photographed in bed wearing silk pyjamas, smoking and speaking on the telephone – any one of which could be taken as evidence of drug addiction.

He made it his business to see everybody and everything, so of course he came to Adam's show at Happy World (then one of Singapore's top venues which, a couple of years later, changed its name, entirely innocently, to Gay World).

Afterwards Noëlly noted in his diary:

"Adam Faith appeared with a Jewish manager and four rhythm boys called 'The Roulettes'. I went to see his second performance in the Happy World Stadium. It was all so deafening that I wished to God that I had brought my earplugs. Adam is very attractive and has considerable charm. He wore a midnight blue Italian silk suit and rocked and rolled with the utmost authority to the ear-shattering accompaniment of the Roulettes. It was all most curious and I failed to hear one word. Apparently this is not important. It is only the 'beat' that is important and it is this that 'sends' the teenagers.

"I talked to him by the pool the following day. Simple, unaffected, a very nice boy. Like an island, he is always entirely surrounded by teenagers, photographers and the lint white Roulettes, who are uniformly hideous. By now he is back in London recording and rehearsing for a summer show in Bridlington."

At the pool, Adam asked Noël whether he'd enjoyed the show.

"Unbelievable, dear boy," Noël replied. "Unbelievable."

As Noël had mentioned, the 'boys' did a full summer season at Bridlington. The show was called "It's A Grand Night". As the name suggests, it was not the hippest show on the circuit.

In addition to their musical duties, the Roulettes were required to provide top quality entertainment for the ticket-buying public.

"The all-round entertainer thing was foisted on us, really," says Bob, "so we just got on with it. Tel wasn't a rock'n'roll singer. He really wasn't. But he was a very good entertainer. We used to do this skit – he would call me down the front of the stage. He would say, 'We've got a new drummer.' And the adoring crowd would say 'Aaaw'. And he would say, 'Do you want to hear him speak? He's French, you know." And they would go 'Aaaw' again. 'His name's Robert.'"

This would be pronounced in an Inspector Clouseau French accent 'Robaaaiiiiirrrr'. Adam and Bob would then pretend to misunderstand each other to great comic effect. Then Bob would start saying something like "Moet de Louan" to Adam's increasing confusion until eventually it's realised that he's not speaking French at all but merely has to go and "mow the lawn".

It usually took a good while to get the audience settled again after a punch line like that.

"It always went down well," says Bob.

"We would do a couple of numbers," says Russ Ballard, "and then we'd dress up and do 'Joshua, Joshua, nicer than lemon squash you are' – we were doing all that stuff – [sings a few bars of 'Spring, Spring, Spring' from *Seven Brides For Seven Brothers*] *'Oh the Farmyard is busy and…'* We hated it. I mean, I was 17 when I was with Tel and I felt old because we were doing summer season and all that stuff – but it was better than working in my dad's shop. And we were doubling up as well. We did two shows a night at Bridlington and then on Sundays we'd jump into the truck and do a Sunday concert at Blackpool or Scarborough – every Sunday we'd do a concert somewhere different. So it was a lot of work."

"One of these Sunday concerts we were playing on a pier somewhere with the Betty Smith Quintet and with Des Lane the Penny Whistle Man. Anyway, after we finished, Tel said let's go and have a cup of tea in the hotel. So we went into the television lounge and there was no one else there. Then the door burst open and in walked the four Beatles, straight off the stage, in their suits, followed by Neil Aspinall, their roadie. John walked in first, laughing and singing, '*It's my party and I'll cry if I want to. I'll cry if I want to. I'll cry if I want to.*'

"It wasn't a big room. John sat on the floor and Paul sat next to me. They were very funny and had incredible charisma. John was sat there on the floor and every time someone came in and said, 'Would you like a drink sir?' Paul would say, 'I'd like a chicken sandwich and a whiskey and coke and another one for my friend' and then John would pipe up with 'Mr Man? Mr Man?' He was very funny. The others had a lot of respect for him. You could tell John was the leader of the group then – they all wanted to please him."

While the others fooled around, Adam and George sat in the corner engaged in a long serious chat. Nobody overheard. Maybe Adam was telling George to buy Shell at 128. Maybe George was telling Adam about jelly babies (it was a bit early for sitars). Most likely they were talking about cars. Adam was in trouble at the time for driving his Jag (not the E-Type, a different Jag, he had a lot of cars so there's no point trying to keep up) into a Vauxhall. Nobody was hurt, but the Vauxhall was driven by a traffic warden and Adam was lucky to get off a charge of dangerous driving.

At some point, the Beatles, or at least Paul, must have caught one of Adam & the Roulettes' shows because several weeks later, Bob Henrit ran into them at Anello & Davide, the shoe shop where the stars bought their boots. Bob re-introduced himself, reminding them that he was the drummer in Adam's band. "That's funny," Paul said. "I thought you were French."

The Beatles had rattled most of the old school. "People keep asking me whether the Beatles worry me," Cliff Richard told the *Daily Express*. "They forget that practically all my career I have had people squeezing me out of top place. Presley, Adam Faith, Emil Ford ...

"What does upset me a bit about the Beatles is that people forget I attracted the same crowds in London two years ago. Three thousand people turned up for my premiere of *Summer Holiday* and I couldn't even get in to see it myself. I think the Beatles will ride high for maybe a year – then they will have to look to their laurels."[37]

Adam, as always, played his cards closer to his chest.

"He was very secretive," says Russ. "He'd never give anything away. Wouldn't give away any weakness. Everyone wanted to be the Beatles. Tel was sure that the Beatles wouldn't happen in America. I remember him saying: 'The Beatles won't make America. It's like taking coals to Newcastle. They do American songs! And they were done better by American artists – they won't break America.'"

The double-up gigs almost brought more fatalities to the ranks.

"During a Summer Sunday concert at Weston-Super-Mare we were playing on a half-moon stage," says Bob Henrit. "When the curtains went back and the guys moved to the front of the stage to start the first song, they put their hands to the microphones to adjust them like you do and the two on the left – John Rogan and Peter Thorp – went up into the air like rockets and collapsed on the floor. They were electrocuted. Tel ran on – he'd been having jujitsu lessons so he knew what to do – he kicked their feet, the soles of their feet, and saved them. Tel saved their lives."

Beatles one week, near-death experiences the next, and then it was back to Bridlington for more "Moet de Louan" and "*Joshua, Joshua sweeter than lemon squash you are*", in between which they played some pop songs.

Andrew Darlington, a kid at the time, went with his family: "By all the logics of showbiz the sudden unprecedented uproar of the Beatles, followed by the deluge of northern beat groups should have confirmed Adam's decline, as it did for so many others. Adam had recruited his own beat group backup. They did separate sets, then closed the show together.

The Roulettes were a smartly suited four-piece with all the essential attributes of the new thing. Lead guitarist Russ Ballard wore dark glasses and played a big red guitar. Pete Thorp and John Rogan carried – respectively – their rhythm and bass guitars at chest-height, like Lennon or Gerry Marsden did. Rob Henrit played drums. And collectively, they rocked. Adam's solo set was well stocked with hits. He had plenty to draw on – catchy pop, done showbiz light. Personable, radiating smiles, he sat on the edge of the stage, his legs dangling, to sing 'Lonesome' to the front row, investing the slight song with considerable intimacy. He'd always never quite fitted into the Brylcreem-slick bouffant template of the pin-up mag teenage idols anyway. The Roulettes' set displayed their easy mastery of group dynamics and close harmonies. Even my mother was impressed, 'They're just like the groups you see on TV'"[38]

Andrew's mum's comment wasn't quite as cute as it sounds. The Roulettes, at that point, weren't one of "the groups you see on TV". They'd done the *NME* Poll Winners Concert with Adam in April and appeared on his series in the previous year, but most of Adam's other TV appearances were him as a solo act, miming to his records. Until the release of 'The First Time' on September 29, the first single credited as "Adam Faith with The Roulettes", there'd been nothing for them to mime to.

At Bridlington, Andrew was treated to a pre-release preview of the new song: "The crashing guitars, the Roulettes' raucous interrogation – 'is it love, that you feel?', Adam protesting 'I don't know-oh-wow, cos it's the first time, I've felt this way'. His thin quavering vocals punched out by their more muscular backup, provided a reinvention of his career."

'The First Time' caused everybody who had written Adam Faith off as a dinosaur whose records should be hidden at the bottom of the pile to forestall the contempt of visiting Fab fans to think again. Salvation had come from a young, virtually untried songwriter called Chris Andrews.

As a performer, Chris, sometimes known as Chris Ravel of Chris Ravel & The Ravers, had been around since the 2i's, *Oh Boy!* days. But since then, rather than treading the all-round family entertainer, panto road to stardom, he'd been in Germany. He'd appeared at the Top Ten Club and the Star Club in Hamburg where The Beatles had learned their craft playing endless hours to drunken sailors. He drank the same stale beer and ate the same toxic sausages as Lennon and McCartney and, like them, had figured out that three-part vocal harmony doesn't necessarily make you sound like the Beverley Sisters, and those call and response backing vocals that you get on Tamla Motown records are the bee's knees.

"It came from Evie," says Russ. "Evie and EMI as well. They could see it was all going that way. Everything was slowly beginning to feel old fashioned. If you were there pre-Beatles, you were archaic. The Chris Andrews songs had a definite Mersey Feel. That was clever."

'The First Time' is a fine example of well-crafted 1963 new-wave pop. The intro, the "crashing guitars" – which recalls the opening of Johnny Kidd & The Pirates' 'I'll Never Get Over You' which, in turn, recalls the outro of The Beatles' 'Please Please Me' – the call and response vocals, the little triplet figure that leads into the stop at the end of each verse brand it so effectively that, if it hadn't been written in 1963, it could only be one of Neil Innes' Beatle parodies he wrote for *The Rutles*. The Roulettes can't half play and in Bob Henrit they had a superdrummer who could drive, inspire and energise. The group's pizzazz infects Adam, too, who sounds – for the first time in several releases – as if he's having a good time.

It entered the Top 40 in the middle of September and, a month later, buoyed itself up to number five. It was Adam's first Top 10 hit in more than a year – a lifetime in pop – and in a Top 10 that included 'She Loves You', Gerry & The Pacemakers' 'You'll Never Walk Alone', Roy Orbison's 'Blue Bayou' and The Crystals' 'Then He Kissed Me', getting anywhere was a triumph.

To the untrained eye it looked – and certainly sounded – as if Adam The Perky Popster had successfully made the transition into the new market and had reinvented himself as Adam the Beat Boom Big Wheel.

But Beat Boom fans knew different. It wasn't just the music that had changed. The world had changed. It was as if, between 1962 and 1963, a whole generation had come and another one gone. Adam was only a few months older that John Lennon, but even an uncle who's the same age as you is still your dad's brother. He might know the best people, go to the best clubs, wear the best clothes, talk the best new talk, but at, say, a family wedding, that's still your uncle there. Dancing.

The Beat Boom fans didn't say much. They didn't have to. They'd watch Adam and The Roulettes on *Ready Steady Go!* and afterwards say, "Good record, great band, fantastic drummer": and then they'd exchange a glance because... you know. It's not the real thing, is it? It's not *authentic*.

At the beginning of the year, Adam was still with the air hostess who'd kept him warm over the cold Christmas of 1962. In the New Year the two of them went to Egypt to take in the temples in the Valley of Kings before they were submerged when the Aswan Dam was completed. But, by the time they landed in England, the romance, too, had drowned and Adam was a free man again.

He cheered himself up with some more cars. He liked Jags. "He had the first Mark 10 I'd ever seen," says Russ Ballard. "It had the biggest back seat of any car in the world. I remember driving along the bypass to Esher and Adam was coming the other way. He was stuck at the lights. He had a starlet with him. She was beautiful. Adam made women feel... he made everybody feel... special."

Adam celebrated his birthday that year by taking Caroline Maudling for lunch. Caroline Maudling was the *Daily Mail's* "Travelling Teenager", stunningly beautiful, in the groove and on the scene. She was also the daughter of Reginald Maudling, the Chancellor of the Exchequer. Even if romance was off the cards, the government had recently sold off some £100m of its dollar holdings in Shell oil, creating an instability which had depressed Shell shares by sevenpence ha'penny. Should Adam sell or hold? And shall we have the syrup sponge with cream?

These were the days when unmarried couples still had to buy a fake wedding ring and pose as "Mr and Mrs Smith" to get a room in a hotel. Respectable hotels would keep a particularly close watch on the comings and goings of pop stars. "We'll have none of your British Medical Council ways in here."

Romantic endeavours during the long Summer Season in Bridlington were a matter of improvisation and initiative. "There were always a lot of girls to go around," says Russ. "I was 17 that summer and Tel was 23

– just turned. And he's got his Mark 10 Jag outside and these girls kept coming backstage at the theatre. Most of them get their autographs and then off they go, but at the end of the night these two girls were still outside the dressing room. So Tel said, 'Where do you live then, girls?' And they say, 'Well, we're on holiday.' 'Right – how far away?' And they say, 'We're staying on a caravan site just down the road.' So Tel said, 'I'll drop you off – coming, Russ?'

"So I get in the back with one of the girls and we go off to just outside Bridlington but not as far as Scarborough. And we get to this caravan site – his headlights hit these rows of caravans. It's dark. Everyone's in bed. It's a miserable place. Anyway, we get out and get into the caravan and Tel goes into the back with this girl and I'm in the front with this other girl.

"I'm doing all right – but I can hear the girl in the back going 'NO!' and 'DON'T!' and then 'DON'T DO THAT!'

"Hard to believe, but she's turning down the number one artist – apart from Cliff, of course – in the country. And suddenly I heard what I was dreading hearing. I heard Tel call out 'Come on Russ – let's go' and so we get in the car and off we go."

Oh, the glamour of the rock'n'roll lifestyle.

Chapter Sixteen

"But until then, I'll be a bachelor boy
And that's the way I'll stay
Happy to be a bachelor boy
Until my dying day."

Cliff Richard and Bruce Welch, *Bachelor Boy*

Cliff & the Shadows were doing their Summer Season at the ABC Theatre Blackpool that year. Cliff was in love.

"There is one girl I'm very friendly with," he told the *Daily Mail*. "A dancer called Jackie Irving. But she and I know that marriage is out of the question."

Jackie was from Manchester. She'd been a professional dancer ever since she lied about her age to get into an audition when she was 14.

"Obviously I like him a lot," Jackie told the *Mail*. "So does my mother. She's met him on odd occasions and has shaken hands with him. She thinks he's a nice boy. Neither of us is planning to get married. There's nothing like that. After dates he takes me home and says goodnight on the doorstep. It's usually pretty late and he has to get back to his hotel."

One Sunday, competition came to town. Adam & The Roulettes, guys who would never leave a girl on a doorstep, drove over the Pennines from Bridlington to play one of their Sunday gigs at the Queen's Theatre. They were having something to eat before the show...

"... when she walked into the cafe with Cliff," says Russ. "Jackie was one of the most beautiful girls I've even seen. Jet black hair and those high cheekbones. Cliff came over and said a couple of words to us and then went back to her and we all went, 'She – is – a – stunner.'"

"Cliff got up to go to the loo and left Jackie on her own. Tel turned to Bert Harris, his driver, and said, 'Go and get her number, Bert.'

"Bert said, 'I can't go and get her number – she's with Cliff!'

"Matt Monro was there too. Matt came over and had a chat – it was all show business then, not at all rock'n'roll.

"Years later, I asked Jackie, 'Jack, when I first saw you with Cliff in that restaurant, you had jet black hair, didn't you?' and she said, 'I used to wear a wig.'

"And I asked what happened that day. 'Did Bert come over and ask for your phone number?'

"And she said, 'Yeah he did'. And I said, 'You're kidding! Did you give it to him?'

"And she laughed and said, 'No'. Then I asked what went wrong between her and Cliff. And she told me that they had been together, but then he went off to make *Wonderful Life* with Una Stubbs, and when he came back he never spoke to her again. It was apparent Cliff and Una were an item. But Cliff always said if he could have married anyone it would have been Jackie."

Adam ran into Jackie the following April, again in Blackpool. He was there to guest star in Mike & Bernie Winters' TV show, *Big Night Out*. Jackie was on the show as one of the Lionel Blair dancers.

He chatted. She played hard to get. Only for a bit, though. Adam launched a sustained campaign on her indifference and by the end of 1964, she'd moved in with him at Tudor Court.

It took a while for Angelina and Vincente to understand first that the women they saw around the house every day were now not in fact women but one woman – the same one every time – possibly wearing a wig; and second that she was, in fact, mistress of the house. Once they were up to speed, though, everybody got on fine. It just took a bit of getting used to. Adam. Going steady.

The efforts of some of the old school popsters who'd taken the pathway marked "All Round Family Entertainer This Way" were being crowned with glory.

In March, Tommy Steele had opened in *Half A Sixpence*, the David Heneker/ Beverley Cross adaptation of H.G. Wells' novel *Kipps*. It was sold out for weeks in advance and there was talk of a Broadway transfer.

Eve – not quite understanding that Musical Theatre and Beat Boom couldn't co-exist in the same body, and if she tried to combine them they would cancel each other out possibly with a small explosion – looked at Tommy's success and wanted some of that for her boy.

Chris Andrews, composer of 'The First Time', had got involved with a promising-looking show based on Mark Twain's *Tom Sawyer*, written and scored by Tom Boyd. Adam was offered the lead, possibly with Joe Brown playing Huckleberry Finn.

Though there were sporadic mentions of the show in the press, in the end, as is the way of these things, it didn't happen, and Adam was allowed to retain whatever credentials as a Beat Boom contender he'd managed to acquire.

The year ended on a high. 'The First Time' was Adam's best single since 'The Time Has Come' and most successful since 'As You Like It'. 'We Are In Love', released on December 7, was even better. It's Chris Andrews' take on Beat Boom to its core. If the Fabs had released 'We Are In Love' that Christmas instead of 'I Want To Hold Your Hand' their reputation would have been undimmed and possibly enhanced. The production is crisp, the playing immaculate, the backing vocals tight, the drumming razor sharp, and Adam's in terrific voice.

Just don't listen to the B-side.

It wasn't the Christmas number one, but after Christmas it kept climbing, and peaked at a very respectable number 11.

The December *NME* poll placed Adam 14th Most Popular Male

Singer In The World, 25th Most Popular Musical Personality In The World and fourth Most Popular British Male Singer.

The *Record Mirror*'s Christmas edition had a large colour picture of him on its cover. He was in his sheepskin coat – hopefully not the same one he wore almost continuously in 1960 – over a sharp Italian single-breasted suit. He was lobbing snowballs at his fans.

"Christmas 1963," the text inside said, "and it's Adam-at-home with his family for the first time since he made his name in show business. 'Faith Castle' – which is what his mates call his fabulous new home – will be fairly bulging with all his relatives and family and friends.

"Said Adam, 'Normally, I've been working all over the festive season. And I've envied my friends who've been able to play Father Christmas to their families. Now I'm making up for it all by having a bit of a rest and a bit of a celebration.'"

"Films in the coming year?

"Says Adam, 'I'm dead keen on tackling some really big parts. Nothing definite yet, but I'm hoping.'"

What's more he was invited to appear on *Sunday Night At The Prince Of Wales* on December 22, and *Sunday Night At The London Palladium* on December 29 – his first appearance there for three years.'"

He was still a contender.

Chapter Seventeen

"Eastern Bluebird (sialia sialis) Bright blue above and on wings and tail; rusty throat and breast; white belly and undertail coverts. Female similar, but duller. Call a liquid and musical turee or queedle. Song a soft melodious warble."

The Audobon Society, *Online Guide To The Birds Of North America.*

Cliff's prediction, "I think the Beatles will ride high for maybe a year – then they will have to look to their laurels," and Adam's, "the Beatles won't make America – it's like taking coals to Newcastle," were both screwed up, kicked into some dirty bushes and laughed at.

On February 9, 1964, the Beatles' first US TV appearance on the Ed Sullivan show attracted 73 million viewers. By April, their records held the numbers one, two, three, four and five positions in the *Billboard* Top 10. Already their songs had evolved. Just after Christmas 1963, William Mann, music critic of the *Times* – a newspaper which usually kept a good selection of disinfected bargepoles to hand in case pop should chance to stray its way – praised their 'pandiatonic clusters': "But harmonic interest is typical of their quicker songs, too, and one gets the impression that they think simultaneously of harmony and melody, so firmly are the major tonic sevenths and ninths built into their tunes, and the flat submediant key switches, so natural is the Aeolian cadence at the end of 'Not A Second Time' (the chord progression which ends Mahler's 'Song Of The Earth')."[39]

Nobody ever said anything like that about 'Lonely Pup (In A Christmas Shop)'.

'If He Tells You', Adam's first release of 1964, was another, by now quaintly dated, Beat Boom pastiche complete with "Yeh, Yeh" backing vocals. It stalled at number 25.

His May release, 'I Love Being In Love With You', didn't make the Top 30.

In a different world at a different time, the 14 tracks of his 1964 album, *On The Move*, would have contained some delights. The strange intervals, and constant modulations of 'She's Smiling At Me' might well even have set William Mann's pandiatonic clusters a-jangling but, in this new world, the LP failed even to make the Top 40.

It was, it appeared, the beginning of the end for Adam Faith, Top Popster. He'd had a brave try at realigning himself to the Beatles' generation but his provenance had let him down.

In the spring of 1964, Adam appeared in a charity concert sponsored by Silvikrin Shampoo at the Hammersmith Commodore. The Hollies, The Swinging Blue Jeans and The Merseybeats were on the bill, too, and down in the small print was an act called Sandra & The Castaways. Sandra, just 17, had won her place on the show by coming second in a talent show at the Ilford Palais.

In her white catalogue dress that she was still paying for and her pink slingbacks, Sandra was too nervous to get through her whole set, but Russ Ballard liked what he heard and took her backstage to meet Adam in his dressing room.

"I was shocked rigid," Sandra said. "He [Adam] was so tiny." She was five foot ten inches. "Even in his Cuban heels and platform soles, he barely scraped my shoulder. But he was charming – the gentleman, even, in his cockney way."

Adam took Sandra to see Eve Taylor. She "entered the room, accompanied by John Bloom, the washing machine millionaire. Eve was an attractive, tiny blonde in her early forties, resembling Ruth Ellis [the last woman to be hanged in the UK]. She tugged on a cigarette and tapped her foot impatiently."[40]

Eve listened to one line, silenced Sandra with a look, whispered something to Adam and left.

"Adam reached up and patted my shoulder. 'Don't worry, luv. I'll fix it for ya. You're gonna be a star.'"

"Adam said she had a fantastic voice," Eve said. "I didn't think so myself but I thought if he said she was good she must be. I always listen to the young."

Eve's husband, Maurice, came up with a new surname for the new client (apparently after seeing her big feet, although the connection is obscure). Sandra was amended to Sandie and Sandie Shaw was born.

Eve took care of Sandie's image, having the good sense not to impose her own standards on her protégée. "We used to call her the Christmas Tree," says Peter Thorp, "cos she was smothered in diamonds – glitter all over her."

She advised Sandie to remove her glasses, sent her to Vidal Sassoon for a haircut and to the groovy new boutiques of Knightsbridge and Chelsea for a truckload of lacy frocks, turtleneck sweaters, cigarette trousers and pencil skirts.

Adam took her to see Tony Hatch, the 'Crossroads' and 'Downtown' composer who'd now moved from Top Rank to Pye records, and they planned a couple of demos. Sandie wanted to do something cool – maybe a cover of a Crystals song, or something by the Shirelles. Tony favoured an "uptempto version of Doris Day's 'Secret Love' and Susan Maughan's 'Bobby's Girl'." Sandie loathed both songs.[41]

The people at Pye didn't think much of the demos. Adam played them to Parlophone, then Decca, then anybody who'd listen. Nobody else liked them either.

Adam and Eve decided that better songs might help and commissioned Chris Andrews to come up with something. They also decided to put their money where their mouths were, and financed Sandie's launch with their own funds. Offered a deal which would cost them nothing, no advances, no studio fees, no risk, Pye happily signed Adam and Eve's new protégée.

Contracts were drawn up. The arrangement, as Sandie later discovered, proved particularly lucrative for her mentors, but cost her a fortune. "Dear Adam," said Sandie. "He may never have been a great singer, but he was always a fine businessman."[42]

Meanwhile, Eve started drumming up gigs. "I remember sitting in Eve's office," says Russ Ballard. "Tel was still being offered lots of work – miners' clubs and all these different places – earning big money. I remember Evie was on the phone one day and she was saying, 'Well, yeah, Adam will do it, but I want you to take one of our other artistes – Sandie Shaw. No, you won't have heard of her. But she's going to be big. Yeah.'"

Sandie's first single, Chris Andrews' 'As Long As You're Happy, Baby' was released by Pye but failed to survive in the wild.

On a trip to LA, Eve came across a Burt Bacharach/Hal David song that had been demoed by Dionne Warwick and had been a minor hit for Lou Johnson.

Bacharach & David, well recovered by now from debacles like 'Country Music Holiday', were on a roll, having clocked up major UK hits with, among others, Gene Pitney's 'Twenty-Four Hours From Tulsa', Cilla Black's 'Anyone Who Had A Heart', Dionne Warwick's 'Walk On By' and The Merseybeats' 'Wishin' And Hopin''. In 1964, no manager could do better for her client than connecting her with a Bacharach and David song.

Within days of Eve's return to London, Sandie had recorded the new song and at the beginning of October it entered the Top 40. Two weeks later, '(There's) Always Something There To Remind Me' was at number one.

Lou Johnson's follow-up to '(There's) Always Something There To Remind Me' was another Bacharach & David song that had been knocking about for a year or so in various versions and under various titles: 'Message To Martha', 'Message To Michael', 'Kentucky Bluebird' and in Marlene Dietrich's troubling German version, 'Kleine Treue Nachtigall'.

Eve heard the song on the same LA trip as she'd found Sandie's hit, and brought it home for her Golden Boy. The lyric is a request to a bluebird to carry a message to the singer's girlfriend who is working in a small café and has possibly changed her name.

Ken Woodman, who did a lot of work for Sandie's label, Pye, put together the arrangement: sparse, beautiful and featuring what is possibly the world's only recorded example of a jangle piano (or is it a harpsichord?), used tastefully.

Sometimes, when his back was up against the wall and the mood and the song were right, Adam could pull a standing-ovation performance out of the bag. So it was with 'Message To Martha (Kentucky Bluebird)', released at the end of November 1964. In the face of stiff competition from the Lou Johnson version released over here at the same time, it reached number 12. It was Adam's last ever Top 20 hit in the UK.

In the summer of 1964, while the Beatles, having won such a decisive victory over America, made themselves busy bringing the rest of the world under their suzerainty, Adam & the Roulettes did nine weeks at the Winter Gardens, Margate.

Jean and Peter Barbour, who tap-danced on stilts, were on the bill with him, and the comedian Bobby Dennis. Adam was headlining, but as well as closing the show he did three other numbers with "the company" and took part in a comic playlet called "Good Neighbours", playing one of "The Honeymooners". The programme cover is a cut-out photo of his head stuck on to a tiny cartoon body and gives the impression that new developments in graphic design stalled in about 1932.

But Adam had to keep grafting because it was expensive being Adam. At that time, he had about 15 people depending on him either partially or totally for their livelihoods, including Janice and Angela who ran the fan club, his brother Dennis, his road manager Bert Harris, Vincente his valet and Angelina his cook, Lesley his PR man, the Roulettes and Mrs Doris Askham, of the Roulettes fan club. He needed to clear at least

£20,000 a year – about 25 times the national average wage at the time – before he could pay himself a penny.

"Adam was pulling in £90,0000 a year," says Russ Ballard, "and he'd do pretty much anything for the money. I think that was probably Evie's influence. He played places like Imperial Hall at Waltham Cross when he was a big star and he shouldn't have done that sort of thing. Good management would say, 'You shouldn't be doing that – you have to be more selective.' Tel did big ballrooms like Nelson – a big hall up in the North West. He got £1,500 and that was 1963, but you didn't see him at his best because they didn't have a good lighting rig or a good sound system. Tel always used to walk around with his own mike in a little case – stupid really cos the mike wouldn't make any difference."

"Those variety tours – phew. You've got to feel bad for the conjurers and the like on the bill," says Pete Thorp. "All those girls screaming for Adam all through their acts. And all those kids sitting through their performances just for half an hour of Adam Faith."

"That Summer Season, he got a bungalow at Broadstairs – but my dad had to stand guarantor on a place for the band because we were all under 21. Adam never stayed in the same digs with us. He'd have his own place. He was the star. We didn't get resentful."

Adam blagged a free holiday that year: five days in Morocco all paid for by *Fabulous* magazine. ("*Fabulous Gets Away From It All*", "*11 King Size Full Colour Pin-Ups*", "*Dave C, Hollies, Beatles, Blue Jeans Etc.*", "*1/-*").

Journalist Keith Altham, the man who'd first met Adam backstage at the Albert Hall in1962, had risen to become "*Fab's* Keith". "Each year they [*Fabulous* magazine] would send a reporter and photographer on holiday with some pop star and write that up as a feature," says Keith. "Great idea. It was done by raffle in the office, I think, and that year I drew Adam and Tangier. Which was the pick of the lot.

"We went to Tangier for five days. We went with a photographer called Bill Francis. First we flew to Gibraltar where we had an overnight stay. When we got to the hotel in Gibraltar, they didn't have any rooms for us. I was tearing my hair out and arguing with the receptionist, getting nowhere when Adam's face suddenly appeared round my shoulder. 'Is there a problem, Keith?" and then it was all, 'Oh Mr Faith how lovely to see you. Of course we'll find some rooms for you, sir.'

"Adam turned to me and said, 'Cheekbones, Keith. Cheekbones. Means I always get recognised.'"

After the ice was broken, the two of them started laughing and basically didn't stop for five days – the way people do when they're having a good time. Everything was funny.

"We went in a terrible old biplane – it looked like you could take it to the top of the Rock of Gibraltar, push it off and it would just glide into Tangier. Adam was a nervous flyer. He took one look at the plane and started a routine about strapping himself in, jokes about Buddy Holly and stuff.

"One night, we went to see the dancing girls but we made the mistake of not specifying that we wanted to see dancing *girls*. We got in the car and the guide took us to this seedy little place down a narrow street in the Kasbah, but as we got nearer we started to get worried. There were no lights, no one around. It was deathly quiet and we were all going, 'Where have they taken us to?'

"Anyway the car stopped, the guide stepped out of the cab and clapped his hands. The lights went on and music started up. Obviously, it had all been put on for our benefit. We went to this room upstairs and there's lots of incense and candlelight and weird stuff going on. The guide clapped his hands again and in rushed a boy with a tea tray on his head with four candles balanced on it. And he proceeded to do a dance.

"And we said, 'This is not quite what we had in mind. Where are the girls?'

"The guide seemed astonished. 'You want girls? No, this is what the English want.'"

It was a time when people like Kenneth Williams, Joe Orton and Lionel Bart had discovered that temporary respite from legal censure could be found in cafés of the Grand Socco.

"'Maybe other English want it, but not us,' we said. So the guide took us to the proper belly-dancing place. And we had a lot of fun there. Dancing with the girls. And other things. That we will draw a veil over.

"It's hard to explain but everything was hugely funny out there – and we would start laughing at nothing. Everything would just crack us up. Adam always said that it was the five funniest days of his life."

By the end of 1964, the path that the Beatles had blazed from Abbey Road to Forest Hills Stadium in New York and the Gator Bowl in Jacksonville was well trodden. Gerry & the Pacemakers, Dusty Springfield, Manfred Mann, the Animals, the Rolling Stones, the Zombies, the Dave Clarke Five – everybody seemed to have had Top 10 hit in the US except Cliff & the Shadows and Adam Faith. Nevertheless the general impression, borne out by ample evidence, was that if it looked or sounded British, it would sell.

Jack Good, Adam's old mentor from the *Drumbeat* days, had become part of the British invasion. He was working for ABC in Hollywood, producing a fast-moving, energy-fuelled half-hour pop show called *Shindig!* which, understandably given the zeitgeist and Jack's input, became a showcase for British invasion acts.

The Beatles and Sandie appeared in the October 7 show. A week later, Adam made his first appearance, along with Roy Orbison, the Everly Brothers, Manfred Mann and Elkie Brooks. Rather than promoting his latest single, or even introducing some of his back catalogue to the American market, Adam did two B-sides, both rockers, probably suggested by Jack Good. He did 'Big Time', the Lionel Bart song that had been the B-side of 'Someone Else's Baby', and 'It's Alright', the B-side of 'I Love Being In Love With You', his flop from earlier in the year.

'It's Alright' is a belter of a song, vaguely reminiscent of the Contours' 'Do You Love Me', with wailing harmonica and overdriven guitar. On that first *Shindig!* appearance, Adam mimes to the record. He's nervous and at one point misses his cue.

All the same, Mr Good gave him another chance. And on the December 16 show, Adam does the same song again, this time live, with the Isley Brothers and the Newbeats doing backup vocals. He tears the house down.

Adam does not look like a British invasion act. The British bands – the top ones anyway – tended to make a virtue out of their unkempt hair, their sallow, spotty skin, their offbeat clothes, their sleep-deprived eyes. Adam has his hair combed nicely to the side. He's wearing a neat suit and tie. He looks as if he's auditioning for Vegas.

And he's got that look in his eyes, too. That 'counting the house' look. That cocky, irresistible, "I know exactly what I am doing, and what I am doing is making America love me", smile.

America did love him, too. A bit.

He made six appearances on *Shindig!*, on the back of which 'It's Alright' was released in the US as a single and rose to number 31 – Adam's only US chart entry.

But at least he didn't have to do panto that year.

Chapter Eighteen

"In South Africa, we could not have achieved our freedom and just peace without the help of people around the world, who through the use of non-violent means, such as boycotts and divestment, encouraged their governments and other corporate actors to reverse decades-long support for the apartheid regime."

Desmond Tutu

In the South Africa of the sixties, people were either "white", "black", "coloured" or "Indian". There were no grey areas. If you were a borderline case, the Race Reclassification Board would run tests. They might, for instance, put a pencil in your hair. If it stayed put, you were "black".

It was a criminal offence for the races to intermarry or have sex. The Reservation of Amenities Act specified which races could use which buses, beaches, benches, hospitals, schools and so on. The Black Self-Government Act effectively disenfranchised native Africans. Anybody who uttered a whimper of protest was branded a Communist and jailed. On June 12, 1964, one such, Nelson Mandela, was found guilty of "sabotage and conspiracy to violently overthrow the government" and sentenced to life imprisonment on Robben Island.

Getting round the Apartheid Laws was difficult and dangerous, but it could sometimes be done. There was, for instance, a degree of haziness about the regulations concerning multi-racial audiences at cinemas, theatres and concert venues because these came under the heading of something called "culture" for which a special case could, maybe, be made. This left a very limited possibility for wriggle room.

At the beginning of December 1964, Dusty Springfield flew out to South Africa with her band the Echoes to play seven dates. Aware of the situation, she and her manager had specified in her contract that she should play before multi-racial audiences at the majority of the concerts.

She completed five of her seven gigs, the last in front of a mixed audience at the Luxurama Theatre in Cape Town.

The Luxurama was owned by Ronnie Quibell, one of South Africa's biggest promoters. It was, he claimed in a later enquiry, originally built as a non-white venue, but when he started booking overseas pop stars to play there, whites wanted to come, too, and sometimes the whites outnumbered the non-whites. The result, just about, fulfilled Dusty's demand for a mixed audience.

Officials of the South African Government's Ministry of the Interior took a dim view of anything that transgressed their profound belief in racism. They didn't do wriggle room. They presented Dusty with an ultimatum – "Sign this pledge not to play before non-segregated audiences again or get out."

For a day and a half, the Men from the Ministry, three heavies, leaned on Dusty's manager, Vic Billings, encouraging him to sign. When he and Dusty refused, they were, in effect, deported from the country. The Ministry issued a statement saying, "Miss Springfield came to this country with the avowed object of defying the Government's stated policy with regard to multi-racial audiences and she was on two occasions warned through her manager to observe our South African way of life in regard to entertainment and was informed that if she failed to do so she would have to leave the country."

Back in the UK, 15 MPs signed a House of Commons motion applauding Dusty's defiance in the face of "the obnoxious doctrine of apartheid in South Africa". This leaves another 600 and something MPs who didn't sign.

Tito Burns, manager and promoter, cancelled forthcoming tours by The Searchers and The Zombies.

Eve Taylor, it seems, was largely oblivious to events in the wider world.

"She had no idea about wars and revolution," says Sandie Shaw. "Her knowledge of social unrest stopped at the Harrods sale."[43]

Adam had been booked to fly out to South Africa at the end of December. Cynical commentators, even at the time, suggested that when Eve saw the publicity that Dusty got out of her set-to, wild horses couldn't have stopped her going ahead with Adam's tour, but it does take an unhealthy dose of cynicism to believe that a manager – give or take a Don Arden or an Allen Klein – would endanger a turn's life and liberty for a few column inches. Besides, she wasn't just putting her turn's safety at risk. Eve's husband, Maurice, was going along, too, to look after Adam.

If Eve was genuinely not aware that Adam was flying into a hurricane, she should at least have gleaned some inkling when the Musicians' Union, which had a blanket instruction to members not to accept any work in South Africa, insisted that the Roulettes pull out of the tour. Defiance of the ruling would have resulted in their union cards being torn up, an act which, in those days of the closed shop, would have sent Russ, Bob, Peter and John down to the Labour Exchange looking for alternative careers.

Adam, however, as a singer/performer/actor, was not a member of the Musicians' Union. He was in Equity, the actors' union, and it dithered about South Africa for years.

A couple of days before Adam was due to leave, the South African authorities insisted that before they would issue a visa he would have to sign a letter giving assurance that he would play to segregated audiences only. As a sop, they would allow him to give, in addition to 42 performances to white audiences, two performances for non-whites.

Adam refused to sign. "I am prepared to lose a lot of money and four weeks in the sun."

It was a stand-off. Later the same day, the South African authorities withdrew their demand and granted Adam his visa. Adam also received a telegram from Ronnie Quibell, the promoter of the tour, saying that he'd sort out any problems with the government. Ronnie had sold a lot of tickets. If Adam didn't turn up he, too, stood to lose a fortune. Under such circumstances, any promoter would say whatever it took to get his artiste on the plane.

When Adam flew out on December 23, arrangements were still unsettled. Adam, however, remained determined to do what was right. "My contract states that I will appear before mixed audiences," he said. "If I am not allowed to do so, I will have no option but to return home"

He arrived to a Beatles welcome. Screaming fans endangered life and limb on the airport balconies; but opposition was building both from the South African government, who were determined he wouldn't play for mixed audiences, and from the press back home, who suspected his 'convictions' were no more than publicity-grabbing flim-flam.

The *Daily Mirror,* as a test, sent one of its journalists, who was Asian, to buy a ticket for one of Adam's shows in Johannesburg. The box office said he wasn't allowed. The cynics preened themselves.

At his hotel, Adam received anonymous phone calls warning him not to "criticise our politics". Adam and Maurice were never sure whether the armed coppers who stood guard over them 24 hours a day were there to protect or to intimidate.

Despite Ronnie Quibell's assurances, for the first two weeks, Adam found himself playing mostly to white audiences. Ronnie assured him that this was a temporary glitch and things would get better when they got to the more liberal parts of the country.

The crisis came at Ronnie Quibell's own Luxurama Theatre in the suburbs of Cape Town – where Dusty had stirred it up by playing to a non-segregated audience. In the intervening weeks – between Dusty's concert and Adam's – the authorities had clamped down. All the same, Ronnie said, there would be brown faces among the white.

Half way through a matinee performance, the house lights went up and two jackal-eyed police started stalking the aisles. Adam stopped singing and watched. An usherette pointed the way and the cops homed in on two pre-teen girls, sitting in the front stalls. The girls were not quite white enough. The police manhandled them out of the theatre.

Worst of all, as the police bundled the two little girls up the aisle, the rest of the white audience applauded their diligence.

Adam walked off stage.

Ronnie Quibell harangued Adam in his dressing room, telling him that he would sue the arse off him if he didn't honour every one of his engagements in South Africa – segregation or no segregation.

Adam and Maurice consulted with lawyers and even attended a meeting Ronnie had arranged with the Secretary to the Minister of the Interior. The Secretary was unsympathetic to the British sensibilities.

Arthur West, their lawyer, made preparations to smuggle them out of the country. Tickets were purchased, using the name of Terry Nelhams, for a flight back to Johannesburg and, from there, to the UK.

The first leg of the flight seemed to go well. Adam and Maurice landed at Jan Smuts airport in Johannesburg safe and sound, but, as they disembarked, they realised they'd been rumbled. The press were there to greet them.

"I've tried for 15 days to come to some compromise about mixed audiences," Adam announced. "But today the Secretary for the Interior, Mr G du Preez, told me finally the Government could not change its decision."

Even though they had first-class tickets, Adam and Maurice were denied entry to the VIP lounge and had, instead, to wait in the concourse where their white and almost universally pro-apartheid fellow passengers hurled insults and jostled.

Then the flight was delayed. Adam and Maurice learned from the attendant journalists that Ronnie Quibell had taken out a summons and now a warrant was out for their arrest. A Sheriff was heading to the airport.

The Captain of a passing VC10, probably an old *Drumbeat* fan, took pity. With cavalier disregard for bureaucracy and protocol, he hustled Adam and Maurice through immigration and onto his plane. Within minutes, he'd been cleared for take-off and was taxiing to the runway. Soon they'd be in the air and on their way back to blighty. Another order came over the pilot's headphones. Permission to take off had been revoked. The plane braked violently.

"The door flew open," said Adam, "and the next thing I knew, I was staring down the barrel of a rifle. A woman in a buff-coloured C&A dress was telling me to leave the plane."[44]

The woman was Mrs C. Malan, Deputy Sheriff of Kempton Park district. She had a Supreme Court Writ for Adam's arrest. Unless he could come up with 40,000 rand (around £20,000) to compensate Quibell for the broken contract, he was going to prison.

It was Friday. The banks were closed. BACS had not been invented. Prison was the only option. Adam was marched back into the airport and a wall of baying journalists. Though some of the journalists worked for the more conservative papers who believed that brutal torture followed by a sound hanging was the only language Adam's sort would understand, many – the majority even – were liberals, who, being able to see both sides of the argument, found it laughably easy to dismiss one of them. They defended Adam from the Sheriff's impertinence.

When a riot looked likely, Mrs Malan called for backup. Within an hour, the High Sheriff of Johannesburg had turned up, an old-school, knuckle-dragging, mouth-breathing, side-of-condemned-beef racist and professional hater. He set about the process of dragging Adam off to jail.

It was a Spartacus moment. One by one the liberal journalists stood out from the crowd. "If he goes to jail, you'll have to take me, too." "And me." "And me."

Some of them were able to persuade the High Sheriff that what he had on his hands here was not a run-of-the-mill-Commie-delinquent but potentially a major international incident.

The Condemned Beef backed down. Adam and Maurice managed to put through a phone call to London and contacted Sir Joseph Lockwood, Chairman of EMI, who arranged for an EMI representative in South Africa to bring the requested cheque for 40,000 rand to the airport.

Word, too, found its way to Gerald Croasdell, General Secretary of Equity, who did his best to foment the threatened international crisis by sending a telegram to Patrick Gordon Walker, the Foreign Secretary:

"Urgently request every assistance for our member Adam Faith now under threat of imprisonment South Africa."

The presentation of the cheque was, of course, no more than a token settlement because it could not be honoured until Monday, when the banks re-opened, but it did keep Adam and Maurice out of jail. All the same, they had their passports confiscated and were placed under house arrest at a hotel.

On the Monday, the cheque cleared, Adam and Maurice were escorted to the airport by security guards and hours later landed at London Airport.

Nell, worried sick, and Adam's sister Pamela were at the airport to greet him. So was an ITN reporter. Adam was in no mood to play the innocent "don't-know-nuffink-about-politics" pop star.

"Isn't it a fact that if you'd not spoken out about it before you went out, there is a good chance that you would have played before mixed audiences?" asked the reporter.

"No, because they definitely asked me to sign a piece of paper saying I wouldn't."

"In fact mixed audiences are barred by South African law but they are...."

"But there you are wrong, you see. You don't know South African law. There is not a law in South Africa that says that mixed audiences are barred in the theatres. There's no such law. It's not been put in the statute book. When they made the apartheid laws they left out the theatre. Because it was for culture"

"So they do endure mixed audiences?"

"They don't 'endure' them or anything, what they do... it's government policy. The Prime Minister there made a speech to say that he would not permit artists to go into the country and dictate who they want to play in front of. It's not a law, it's just a speech made by the Prime Minister."

A subsequent trial in South Africa found in favour of Ronnie Quibell in his demand for compensation and he was awarded the 40,000 rand that EMI had put up as surety to secure Adam's release. EMI deducted the money over the next few years from Adam's record royalties.

The Foreign Office seemed almost to agree with the South African government that visitors, especially pop stars, should shut their mouths and do as they're told: "If artists embark on foreign tours without first ensuring that the arrangements comply both to the requirements of local law and custom", such an oversight did "not provide grounds for government intervention on their behalf".

More shamefully still, Jimmy Edwards, handlebar-moustachioed star of TV's school sitcom *Whack-O!* and Honorary Chairman of Equity's sister union the Variety Artistes' Federation, said, "It is no part of the unions' function to thrust doctrinaire policies [like anti-racism] down the throats of its members. If they sign contracts to go to South Africa or elsewhere and break them, they ought not to involve the government. We regard South Africa as a very useful outlet for employment and it is not part of our function to deprive members of any outlet in any part of the world on doctrinaire grounds."[45]

Max Bygraves, of all people, wrote a piece in the *Express* saying that South Africans "do not expect rock'n'roll singers to arrive and start making laws to suit themselves". He followed this up with: "I feel sure that responsible men with an age of experience who make the laws know more about the situation."[46]

Adam presumably took a sharp intake of breath before telling the *Express* the next day: "Didn't people say the same sort of thing about the 'responsible' Adolf Hitler 30 years ago?"

Chapter Nineteen

"I always knew the sixties wasn't a revolution. It really was just a bunch of university students with wealthy parents having fun."

John Lydon

The Adam Faith product had never been designed to last. Over the years, tweaks had managed to keep it vaguely in line with the current trends in pop star design, but, as the sixties progressed, the fundamental flaws began to tell.

Tom Jones sang better, Marianne Faithfull was prettier, and The Who had a Demolition Derby stage act that made Adam's seem Sunday Afternoon Morris Traveller; even his own protégée, Sandie, eventually came to outshine everything Adam did.

At the end of February 1965, Adam went on tour with Sandie. By this time, at least when they were putting the package tours together – summer seasons were different – promoters no longer felt obliged to provide a "full evening's entertainment" by chucking a couple of jugglers and an escapologist into the mix for good measure. This time, other than Freddie Earlle, a comic Master of Ceremonies, the bill was straight pop. The Barron Knights, one of the other turns, were a crossover comedy act who specialised in parodying other groups, but they'd had a couple of novelty hits so counted as pop. Otherwise there was Eve's latest signing, Patrick Kerr, a singer/dancer who'd made a name on TV's *Ready Steady Go!* demonstrating the latest dance crazes, the Roulettes and the Paramounts, an Essex group, hired principally to back Sandie.

As the tour progressed, Adam's world began to go topsy-turvy and it became increasingly clear that the punters were turning out to see Sandie not Adam. She got the adulation: he got the polite applause. It rankled even more because Sandie's latest hit should have been Adam's latest hit.

Just before the tour had started, Chris Andrews had come up with a new song for Adam, 'I'll Stop At Nothing'. Eve heard it and thought it was more suited to Sandie so made the switch. Adam was miffed. His consolation prize was another of Chris' songs, a decent enough Bacharach and David soundalike, with a fine Ken Woodman arrangement, called, perhaps appropriately, 'Stop Feeling Sorry For Yourself'.

As the tour moved on from town to town, Sandie's 'I'll Stop At Nothing' climbed majestically towards the upper reaches of the Top 20 while Adam's record struggled to number 23 and fell back exhausted. On March 11, Sandie was at number four, Adam at 28.

The unthinkable happened. Their billings were switched. Adam Faith was a support act for his protégée.

Keith Altham, the journalist who'd taken Adam to Tangier had, by this time, graduated from *Fabulous* to the *New Musical Express*. He shared a car ride with Grumpy Uncle Adam, still trying to protect the increasingly wayward Sandie from the iniquities of life on the road.

"Sandie tapped our 'chauffeur' on the shoulder and asked for a cigarette," he wrote.

"'Certainly not,' replied Adam in his best for-your-own-good voice.

"Ten minutes later he gave in and she got the cigarette.

"'I want a tin of blackcurrants,' insisted Miss Shaw after we failed to locate a restaurant.

"'No,' was the ADAMant [*sic*] reply.

"Five minutes later we stopped for a tin of blackcurrants.

"'I want some ice-cream,' said Sandie.

"'Absolutely not,' decided Adam.

"Seconds later we stopped and got out to get the ice-cream.

"Later, while Sandie woofed her plateful of blackcurrants and ice-cream, Adam buried himself in his book of crosswords.

"'How's the stage act progressing? Is there anything new?' I asked.

"'He's changed the introductions I do for the songs. They're posher now,' said Sandie, somewhat reproachful but with just the right amount of respect." 'He' remained absorbed in 15-across.

"'Instead of saying, 'I'd like to sing my new record,' I now say, 'Thank you very much for making my latest record a hit and I'd like to sing it now for you.'" Adam nodded approvingly.

"'I only ever get mobbed outside the theatres when they can't get Adam,' said Sandie.

"'No boys waiting to pounce at the stage door?' I queried.

"'No,' grinned Sandie. 'No naughty men at the stage door. Shame isn't it?'

"The Lord Protector rose from his crossword in agitation: 'Don't you dare print that,' he quoth. 'She'll have the fans throwing naughty men at her on stage.'"[47]

Sandie had started laying down the law. "I don't stand for any nonsense," she said. "No birds about the dressing room. No drinking during performances."

It's uncertain whether these rules applied to Adam, and even if they did, a chaste life backstage as a support act on tour had to be better than a South African prison.

To compound Adam's humiliation, more dates were added to the tour in order to satisfy the insatiable demand of people who wanted to see Sandie.

The other acts on the bill were on the up and up, too. The Barron Knights had two Top 10s in 1965. Bob Henrit and Russ Ballard of The Roulettes had been moonlighting as the '+ 2' of Unit 4+2 whose 'Concrete And Clay' went to number one a month or so after the tour ended.

Even the Paramounts, Sandie's backing group, subsequently enjoyed chart success – once they'd changed their name to Procol Harum – with 'A Whiter Shade Of Pale', a track that still finds a place in everybody's "Top 10 songs to get stoned to".

But Adam Faith records didn't sell any more.

Nevertheless, EMI kept turning out the bits of plastic with his name on the label and his voice in the grooves. His next single, the oompah 'Someone's Taken Maria Away', almost made the Top 30.

In September, he released a 'live' album called *Faith Alive,* actually recorded 'as live' at Abbey Road studios in front of a hundred specially chosen members of the Adam Faith Fan Club. Among the 13 tracks are covers of Tommy Tucker's 'Hi-Heel Sneakers', Elvis' 'Heartbreak Hotel', Chuck Berry's 'Little Queenie' and Bruce Channel's 'Hey Baby'.

It does what a 'live' album should do – what Cliff's 1959 'live' album did, what the Rolling Stones' *Get Yer Ya Yas Out* did and *The Who Live At Leeds.* It generates something of the excitement of a live gig, the sweat, the thrill and the danger. The Roulettes are magnificent and Adam rises to the occasion. Had it been made in 1958, or maybe in the early seventies, when Dave Edmunds and Showaddywaddy were engaged in a rock'n'roll revival, it might possibly have been welcomed by the record-buying public. But this was 1965. The Beatles were more famous than anybody on the planet except Chairman Mao. Dylan had gone electric. The Beach Boys had gone mad, and if you didn't own a copy of the Rolling Stones' '(I Can't Get No) Satisfaction', people – even nuns – spat at you in the street. Nobody had the time to give anything but a cursory glance to an 'Adam Faith live' album. If Jesus and the Apostles had released product into that market, it would have needed a really fancy sleeve design to make an impact.

Adam's next single, 'I Don't Need That Kind Of Loving', was the last he made with the Roulettes. Russ, Bob, Peter and John had other fish to fry. Russ and Bob had commitments with Unit 4+2, but carried on working with the band as well, going on to make an album, *Stakes And Chips,* and a string of single releases over the next couple of years. The official announcement was made on September 29.

"Adam Faith and The Roulettes have parted company after three years together," the *Daily Mail* said, "because Faith's increased solo work has left the group too little to do."[48]

"We felt that we needed to be a fully-fledged band in our own right, not just a backing group," says Bob Henrit, "and anyway Adam was moving more into ballads."

The first of Adam's post-Roulette singles, 'Idle Gossip', was indeed a ballad in the mode of Perry Como. If it came near the charts, the charts must have backed shyly away.

Different versions of the next release, 'To Make A Big Man Cry', were released in the same year by Tom Jones and P.J.Proby. Both blew Adam's out of the water. In October, Adam tried another new tack. The folk thing was working out pretty well for Bob Dylan, Simon & Garfunkel, Peter Paul & Mary and the Byrds, so it had to be worth a punt.

'Cheryl's Going Home', a song by Bob Lind who'd had a hit earlier in the year with 'Elusive Butterfly', wasn't exactly folk but the lyric sounded like a poem that might be good enough to make the school magazine, so that was near enough. The record crawled to number 42. It was Adam's 24th single to make the Top 50 in seven years, and it was to be his last.

After 'What More Can Anyone Do?' and 'Cowman, Milk Your Cow', a vile piece of whimsy written by Barry and Robin Gibb out of the Bee Gees, Adam was ready to throw in the towel.

"If I make another pop record it will just be fun," he told the *Daily Sketch*. "I felt numb when suddenly my records didn't make it. I kept trying to figure out the reason. Maybe I was trying too hard or even not hard enough. I never worked it out. Luckily I survived. The only shadow in my life was my absence from the charts and I've learned to live with that."[49]

He later confessed that the live work he was doing in the working men's clubs and cabarets was less than rewarding.

"It was the lowest spot in my life, and it came at a time I was earning over £1,500 a week. I know it's hard to believe, but it's the truth. I'd been around the pop scene for about eight years or so and I suddenly found myself doing cabaret dates in the north. Well, the money was terrific, and everyone seemed to like what I did. Everyone – except me. I loathed the act and pretty soon I began to loathe myself for doing it. I felt a fraud and a phoney. There I was doing this rubbishy act with its cute patter and corny little dances, and not believing in a single second of it. The act was the dregs, and so was I. The experience, believe me, was horrible and degrading. All the more so because I was being paid so well for it."[50]

There were two more releases, then Adam decided to pack it in. He and EMI parted company.

But though it had moved entirely out of what was formerly its core business, the Adam Faith brand, thanks to versatility and diversity, was far from finished.

Chapter Twenty

"5 – 4 – 3 – 2 – 1 – Thunderbirds Are Go!"

Gerry and Sylvia Anderson,
Thunderbirds – Trapped In The Sky

At the end of 1965, ATV had started transmitting a show called *Thunderbirds*. Made by Gerry and Sylvia Anderson's AP Films, it followed the adventures of a secret operation called International Rescue, which essentially was in the business of rescuing people in trouble on land, sea, air or space using a range of specially adapted vehicles called Thunderbird 1, 2, 3. You get the idea.

The series was made using a technique called 'Supermarionation' which meant that the characters were not real people at all but marionettes. Nobody ever figured out what was 'super' about the marionation any more than they figured out why International Rescue had to be a secret organisation when *lack* of secrecy is one of the prime qualities responsible for the effectiveness of the present day Air-Sea Rescue.

AP Films already had a string of hits behind them with *Supercar, Four Feather Falls, Stingray* and *Fireball XL5*. For *Thunderbirds* they raised their game.

"We were looking for more natural faces, getting away from the earlier trend towards caricatures," said Christine Glanville, head of the puppet sculpting department.

One day, while browsing through the actors' directory *Spotlight* on the lookout for these more natural faces, she spotted Adam's entry. The chiselled features, the strong jaw line and the cheekbones seemed perfect for John Tracy, the "Space Monitor" who from *Thunderbird 5,* a space station in geostationary orbit, scoured the universe for SOS transmissions.

Look at Adam. Look at John Tracy. Can you spot the difference?

That Christmas, a poseable puppet was in the shops, distributed by Fairylite Quality Toys. Yes, it was branded not as an 'Adam Faith Doll' but as a 'John Tracy Doll', but that made no difference to diehard fans.

Cliff didn't get his own puppet, no Elvis doll was ever shown manning a space station on children's TV, no Beatle doll ever hitched a ride in a pink Rolls Royce with Parker and Lady Penelope.

But all the same, TV appearances in the form of a Supermarionated avatar could hardly be called a career.

"When I have lived down being a pop singer," Adam said, when he came back from South Africa, "I would like to become an MP."

The flirtation with politics remained a theme for the rest of his life. It was a natural choice. He could charm birds from trees, he could speak with conviction on any subject from God to the intricacies of South African law and his spending habits meant he probably did more to keep the British car industry afloat than Harold Wilson and Edward Heath between them ever managed.

He had the whole thing mapped out. "A first step will be standing for my local council at Esher – as an independent. I believe councillors and MPs should be independent. If they are tied to a party, they may have to vote against the people they represent."

Despite his experiences in South Africa, he said he had no intention of joining the anti-apartheid movement.

"I have never," he said, "joined organisations – not even youth clubs. I like fighting my own battles."[51]

Even now, local councillors don't make much more than £13,000 a year. By the time Eve had taken her cut, Adam wouldn't have had enough to keep him in lighter fuel. Besides, another trade was more accessible, more suitable, and potentially more lucrative.

In May 1966, Associated Rediffusion, one of the ITV companies, put on a series of dramas in its *Play Of The Week* strand based around the themes of the Seven Deadly Sins – sloth, avarice, gluttony etc.

The idea was that each particular episode's sin was supposed to remain a mystery until the last moments of the play. In practice it was often hard to guess even then.

"What was that one, then?"

"Wrath."

"You said last week's was wrath."

"Are there any more Murray Mints left?"

The last in the series, the theme of which was most definitely 'pride', was *The Erpingham Camp*, by the celebrated playwright Joe Orton.

The fifth was *In The Night*, a tense thriller by Anthony Skene, directed by Peter Moffatt. Best guess as to the sin actually *is* "wrath". Adam played the evil son of a dead blackmailer who is driven to murder. Derek Francis and Joanna Dunham were his co-stars.

The *Times* described it as, "A painless way of spending an hour," and added, "The play was notable for having among its cast Mr Adam Faith as the victim driven to murder but Mr Faith was asked to do nothing that might have demonstrated any outstanding acting ability. Miss Joanna Durham hovered tactfully on the verge on hysteria."

Not a great review but not a terrible one either – and anyway, acting opposite someone hovering tactfully on the verge of hysteria can be very off-putting.

At the Carl Alan Awards, an annual event to honour those who have excelled in dance and theatre, Adam – Tel – the lad from Acton, danced with Princess Margaret, the girl from George I, via Victoria on the female line. Simon Dee the disc jockey danced with her, too and, when the band played a rumba, Jimmy Savile tried to cut in. "I don't do this one," said the Princess and headed for the nearest exit.

It was 1967, bliss was it in that dawn to be alive, but to be young was very heaven! In the previous year, England had won the World Cup. This year, who knows? – maybe the Eurovision Song Contest.

Sandie's pop career had begun to go the way of Adam's. Sales had slumped. Her last release of 1966 only just squeaked into the top 50.

'Puppet On A String' had a jaunty, tick-tock, cuckoo-clock, Austro-Bavarian feel about it that made keen-eared pop fans wonder, sometimes aloud, whether this would have been the sound of pop music if Hitler had won the war. Sandie hated it. She saw it as her 'Lonely Pup (In A Christmas Shop)'. Eve and Adam, both of whom had a piece of Sandie, looked at the song, looked at the Eurovision market, looked at each other and noticed that their pupils had turned to pound signs. Nobody has ever suggested that a Luger was produced to help persuade Sandie, but all the same it's an interesting imaginative detail.

The Eurovision Song Contest was, that year – significantly – held in Vienna.

'Puppet' won by one of the widest margins ever and took twice as many votes as the song placed second (Ireland's 'If I Could Choose' by Sean Dunphy).

Adam was there in Vienna, thinking, no doubt, with each vote that came in, "that's next year's electricity bills paid", "there's the roof mended", "that's a Jag", "and that's a Roller".

When they came home, Adam was photographed carrying Sandie through London airport, like a groom carrying his bride over the threshold. But Sandie was, it must be said, very pissed.

The song then went on to storm the charts of Europe like a panzer division. Some hailed its all-conquering victory as a triumph for Swinging England.

"More like a triumph of the will," muttered the keen-eared pop fans.

By this time, Jackie and Adam had been living together for three years.

"Would you like to marry?" John Freeman had asked him in the 1960 *Face To Face* interview.

"Eventually, yes."

"But not yet?"

"Well, I don't feel prepared for marriage just yet."

"Have you thought – do you think of an ideal age that you'd like to marry at?"

"Well I think that 30 seems to be a good age to get married – I don't know – you can't tell about these things can you?"

"You wait – you'll find out."

Early in 1967, Adam was having problems with his voice and was advised by a throat specialist to maintain complete silence for two months. The absence of the usual distractions must have concentrated his mind. Using sign language he proposed to Jackie. At 26, he was four years ahead of schedule.

She said yes.

"Adam Faith To Marry Cliff Richard's Old Girlfriend," the *Daily Mirror* announced, tactfully.

They set the date for August 19, 1967 and planned to do the deed at Epsom Register Office, just up the road from Tudor Court, an essentially unprepossessing venue that had nonetheless been given the seal of pop approval the previous year when George Harrison and Patti Boyd had chosen it for their wedding.

Hello! magazine was still unknown outside Spain at that time, but Camilla Beach of the *Australian Times* was ahead of the journalistic curve in understanding that what the reading public want from their celebrity wedding interviews are details about the dress and the invitations and then as much information as can be packed into 1,000 words about their kitchen wallpaper, the plushness of their bathrooms and how much they paid for their antique pieces, expressed, as far as is possible, in the form of dialogue so that readers feel they're actually chatting with the celebs.

"'We are getting married at Epsom,' he [Adam] explained, getting up to turn off the television, which has pride of place in the kitchen.

"He sat down – and got up again to telephone about wedding arrangements.

"Jackie busied herself at the sink and talked about their reasons for not getting married in a church.

"'Bridesmaids? No. All those nasty, naughty little girls would make me sick,' she said, but not unkindly.

"'That's why I don't want to have a wedding in a church. Also there's always an argument in the family and before long the family's running the wedding.'

"She broke off to interrupt Adam, who was trying to organise the printing of their wedding invitations.

"'Nothing flash, darling,' she told him, smiling. He said that embossed invitations would take four weeks to print and would arrive too late to send out.

"'Five by four for size all right, Jackie?' he inquired, and she agreed.

"He returned to his phone conversation and said: 'What do you put on a wedding invitation?'

"'I know what to say,' she interrupted – and they began a long discussion on whether to have the invitations printed in black or gold.

"Adam wanted black.

"'Looks like a funeral card in black,' Jackie replied.

"The wedding is not going to be a big publicity attraction.

"'No mini mini-skirt for me,' Jackie said, now drying the silver. 'I'll wear something frilly and soft.'"

Having done the dress and the invitations, Camilla moved on to the subsidiary but nevertheless essential details about the kitchen wallpaper, the plushness of the bathrooms and how much they paid for their antiques.

"The kitchen [...] is big and spacious, decorated with quiet pop art wallpaper and hung with onions.

"They had put the finishing touches to two very plush bathrooms, equipped with sealed showers.

"The sitting-room is conservative and comfortable and they were especially proud of a Spanish-style bedroom nearing completion.

"Adam is a confirmed admirer of all things Spanish, to the point of spending two hours a day learning the language.

"The bedroom is small, with a painted metal four poster frame, and in the corner of the small gun-room is a large candleholder of the style found in some churches.

"'Isn't that beautiful?' Adam asked, pointing to a Jacobean writing desk. "I bought that for £6 in a little antique shop.'

"Obviously family matters were very much on his mind: in April he had bought a shop in Acton for his two sisters Christine and Pamela to run. It sold kids clothes and was called Minus Five."[52]

When they were married, the *Express* reported, "Jackie would give up her dancing career and probably breed Afghan hounds as she's been doing very well with them at recent dog shows. Adam himself, of course, will continue to make records and money, dabble in shares and property, and run boutiques and shiny cars."[53]

The venue was ultimately changed from Epsom Register Office to the more prestigious Caxton Hall in Westminster.

On the wedding morning, Terry O'Neill dropped in to take photographs of the happy couple.

Outside the register office there was a near riot. Police had to hold back the crowds of fans.

Jackie looked magnificent in a white caftan and little silver Turkish slippers. Her shoes were flat, Adam's had heels, but still she was an inch or two taller than him. They both look stunning; although the cheekbones (she has them, too) must have brought a flicker of anxiety that the "you may kiss the bride" moment could have turned into a bloodbath.

In lieu of a honeymoon they redecorated their bedroom. Regrettably, Camilla Beach was not on hand to record whether the large candleholder next to the gun-room survived the remodelling.

Tudor Court had been on the market for more than a year with Knight & Rutley. Adam was on record as saying it wasn't fair for Jackie to go on living in a house that was the scene of "so much of my carnal mileage".

"Close to the centre of Esher," Knight & Rutley's blurb announced, "Attractive detached house. Completely secluded position. Three receptions, billiard room, modern domestic offices, four bedrooms, two bathrooms, staff accommodation, full oil-fired central heating, charming terraced garden and water garden."

The asking price was £30,000.

The housing market was sluggish so it wasn't until after the wedding that they were able to move. The new place was in Cathcart Road, Fulham in London: a neo-Georgian townhouse that Jackie transformed into a Venetian palace, complete with glazed inner courtyard and tinkling fountains.

Adam became the good provider.

"I really do scheme for the future now," he told *The People*. "In a little while we'll have a family."

"Before I just kept myself busy making money. Totting up the profits on my stocks and shares. It was a pastime – but pointless. Now I have responsibilities to Jackie and the kids we'll have. Before I married, I just indulged myself – out of boredom as much as anything.

"I'd get a yen to take a few pictures and dash out to buy photographic equipment worth hundreds of pounds. Within a week, the lot would be locked in the attic. But the impulse isn't there any more. I don't have to spend money to kill my boredom.

"Lots of show business marriages are shaky because the couples lead separate lives. Even when we are apart physically – which is rare – we're together mentally."

"We came from the same backgrounds," said Jackie, "from ordinary families. We both truly appreciate what we have now but it's natural to us to live the way we were reared. The only difference is that we have money. Sometimes we kick our shoes off, gaze around and think: 'Well, look at us.'

"I want three children: ideally, two boys and a girl. If we have a girl first, she is going to be called Emma, which sounds so elegant and old-fashioned. No second names. And if it's a boy he'll be called Heathcliff – Heath for short."[54]

Early in their marriage Jackie suffered a miscarriage. Later she gave birth to a boy. His name, as they'd promised, was Heathcliff. He lived for just one and a half hours.

No words can describe grief like that.

Chapter Twenty-One

"I have noticed that one of the rewards of pop singing seems to be that as soon as you make a go of it, you are allowed to stop doing it. No doubt, for those prepared to spend the best years of their youth belting inanities onto wax, opening suburban shopping centres, and having their follicles dismembered by the faithful, escape is a perk every whit as desirable as a puce Corniche with smoked windows or a bungalow in Esher for Mum.

"The flight is usually towards the non-musical stage; and given the odds against success it is really rather surprising that so many singers have managed to pull it off.

"It may be that singers are natural actors: to put over trite mush with anything like conviction, you have to do more than hold a note and keep in step with the woodwind." [55]

Alan Coren

In July 1967, Adam was approached – through Eve Taylor – by Martin Tickner, a young theatre producer. He wanted Adam to co-star in a touring production of Emlyn Williams' 1935 thriller *Night Must Fall*.

He was offered the best part in the play: Danny, the good looking charmer, whose winning smile and fast mouth conceal the heart of a ruthless seducer and killer who keeps his victim's head in a hat-box.

"I'm a pretty little feller," Danny sings to himself from time to time, "everybody knows, don't know what to call me, but I'm mighty lak a rose. Their home addresses and their caresses, linger in my memory of those beautiful dames."

Adam knew the play. He'd seen in on TV in 1964 with Albert Finney playing Danny and thought, "I could do that."

In terms of an acting career, this was as big a break for Adam as *Drumbeat* had been for his singing career, not least because his co-star was to be none other than Dame Sybil Thorndike.

Dame Sybil was 85 and had been in the profession since 1902. In theatrical circles, her name was never mentioned without a slight lowering of the voice and bow of the head. George Bernard Shaw had written *Saint Joan* just for her. She had worked with Olivier, Richardson, Gielgud, Judi Dench, Brian Blessed, various Redgraves and Marilyn Monroe. She'd demanded multi-racial audiences in South Africa – and got them – as long ago as 1928 and eventually had a theatre named after her. In Leatherhead.

Adam had never worked with a Dame of the British Theatre before, but Sybil had done pop stars. She'd worked with Marty Wilde at Shepperton in 1959 on a film, *Jet Storm* ("good, conventional entertainment" – the *Times*). She could probably do a passable impersonation of Wee Willie Harris and belt out a couple of choruses of 'Whole Lotta Shakin' Goin' On' as well, because that's the kind of person Dame Sybil was.

To work with her – co-starring no less – was like being chosen to work with Leonardo Da Vinci on one of his inventions or Euclid on a bit of geometry. It was drinking from the very fountain of English drama.

And the honour was made yet more exquisite by the casting of Dame Sybil's husband, Sir Lewis Casson, in the relatively minor role of the Lord Chief Justice. This was like working with Euclid and Pythagoras simultaneously on the same triangle. The cherry on the cake was that this was possibly the first production in Adam's career in which his name would not be linked romantically with that of the leading lady.

This is not to say he didn't fall in love. His admiration for Dame Sybil was boundless. "It's women like that," he said, "who built the Empire for

England. They're the sort that would drive through the African jungle and get out the tea with all the silver."[56]

The play opened at the New Theatre, Oxford and toured Bristol, Birmingham and several points north. "Adam has a stab at his character," said *The Birmingham Post,* "without entirely persuading me that he is the cool, ruthless and impenetrable killer he is supposed to be."

Andrew Drummond was the production's designer. "Adam's performance was excellent," he says. "The play was met by good reviews and things boded well for not only the tour, but also for an opening in the West End."

But a West End opening was not to be.

"Emlyn Williams refused permission for it to come to the West End. 'The play is too old and it creaks,' he said. I must add, this was not the case but in spite of Sybil Thorndike constantly telephoning Emlyn at his home in Capri, a West End opening was not to be. I can remember at the first night party. Evie Taylor, Adam's agent was crying and saying, 'I've lost my boy, I've lost my boy.' She realised that Adam had a great future in acting and that he was going to move on from pop music."

On the opening night, Noël Coward sent Adam a telegram, the way he did: "At last you're legitimate; your mother will be pleased."

The experience and success of *Night Must Fall* convinced Adam that acting was his true destiny and singing had only ever been a diversion. It was the kind of switch he would continue to make for the rest of his life, mostly ringing the changes between singer, actor, manager and financial wizard. If he suffered a setback in one field, he would run to the next: a spectacular triumph here, a disastrous failure there, a blast of insane optimism here, a scream of discouragement there; round and round, back and forth, reinventing himself to suit mood and circumstance. Others might find these constant switches of identity confusing if not psychologically damaging, but not Adam. Terry made sure of that. Whatever Adam did, whatever Adam became, Terry remained the same – at least inasmuch as anybody does. Adam the brand, Terry the bloke: a useful demarcation enabling him not only to keep a sense of himself but also to settle moral and ethical conundrums. "I don't know what Terry'd think about that," he'd say when Adam did something dicey. It was also handy as a smoke and mirrors act to confuse others.

"A thousand times they ask me why, who am I, who am I?" he sang, in his 1961 hit. It was a question to which he might have replied, "That's for me to know and you to guess."

Terry enjoyed being Adam. Who wouldn't? And when Adam failed, when Adam was criticised, when Adam got in trouble, it was nice to be able to retreat into the safe familiarity of Terry.

Aware that if he was going to take the acting business seriously he needed to build a CV with credible grass-roots experience, Adam wrote to every repertory company in the country explaining that he had finished with singing and wanted to be a proper actor now.

He was ambitious. "When I've got a bit more experience, I want to try *Hamlet*," he said. "Why not? The theatre in Shakespeare's day was for ordinary people, wasn't it? Now, honest, I'm telling you the truth, I never even knew anything about *Hamlet* till a few weeks ago. I'm not kidding. Somehow I missed it. But I've just found it. It's a wonderful play. The quotes, all those famous quotes I've heard all my life, I never realised they came from a Shakespeare play."[57]

While working on *Night Must Fall,* he had confided his wish to play Hamlet to Dame Sybil. She was full of encouragement.

"When you play Hamlet, dear boy," she said, "I shall be there looking down on you from up above, cheering you on."

"Oh, no. Oh, no," said Adam. "We'll be playing in *Hamlet* together."

"Yes, why not? I've always said I'm going to live to be over a hundred. Perhaps we *will* play Hamlet together."[58]

Dame Sybil died in 1976, at the age of 93. She never played Ophelia to Adam's Hamlet, or even Gertrude.

"Adam Faith To Be Serious Actor," *The Times* announced. "Adam Faith, 27, is going in for a career as a serious actor, with a play being written for him by Anthony Burgess. Mr Faith's manager, Miss Eve Taylor, said yesterday: 'He is definitely giving up 'pop' and cabaret and concentrating on acting.'

"Mr Faith won approval in *Night Must Fall*, with Dame Sybil Thorndike, in a provincial tour this year. It was then that Mr Burgess saw him and decided to write a play for him – the life story of Christopher Marlowe."[59]

Anthony Burgess didn't get around to writing his Christopher Marlowe story until 1993, and then it came out not as a play but a novel – his last book, *A Dead Man in Deptford*.

But Adam had other offers.

The Citizens Theatre in Glasgow offered him the lead in *Billy Liar*, Keith Waterhouse and Willis Hall's rite of passage comedy – originally a novel, then a play, then a film and later a musical – about a young fantasist trying to break away from the grey boredom of a Northern town to travel to London and find work as a comedy writer.

Tom Courtney had played Billy in the 1963 film. He was stuck in people's heads as the 'real' Billy. All the same, something that Adam did impressed the *Glasgow Herald*: "Mr Faith is a remarkably good Billy. From the moment that he comes down the stairs with his hair flapping in his eyes, we feel both the splendours and the miseries of being Billy: commander of regiments, idol of the crowd, sought after friend of the rich and famous, the undertaker's clerk who never posted last year's calendars and has pinched the petty cash.

"Mr Faith gives us the superb effrontery of Billy ('I'm so glad you asked me that question' he says when cornered, nimble as any platform politician) and its pathos; he contrives most skilfully to make even the final scene of Billy's utter defeat – his gesture of independence exposed, creeping back home to empty his defiant suitcase and put the calendars back in the sideboard – into a kind of absurd triumph."[60]

A few months later, he did the same play again, this time at the New Theatre in Bromley, Kent. The hope was that Bromley might be close enough to London for West End theatre managers and impresarios to come out and offer a transfer but, although Adam played to packed houses, the transfer was not to be.

A reporter from the *Daily Express* wondered whether this was because the theatrical establishment could not take a former pop singer seriously. "Adam vigorously shakes his head. 'They all seem to have accepted me,' he says. 'Maybe I can thank Dame Sybil for that. She's the goddess of theatre and her recognition of me in that first production has served to convince others that I might have talent and above all that my motives are genuine.'"

The acceptance didn't lead to much in the way of prestige projects. He played Jingle in the musical *Pickwick* at the Billingham Forum, and was horribly miscast as Elyot to Susan Brown's Amanda in Noël Coward's *Private Lives*, but the Royal Shakespeare Company did not phone asking for his Hamlet and neither was Warner Bros planning a *Son Of Rebel Without A Cause* if only they could find somebody to play an older, wiser James Dean.

Theatre is a noble profession, but the money's rubbish. Adam's plans for financial security were coming unstuck. He and Jackie sold the house in Fulham for £42,500 and moved into a rented house on Weybridge High Street. Adam dabbled in an office furniture business, but got his fingers burnt.

There were more setbacks, too. Not long after the move to Weybridge, Adam's mother, Nell, died of diabetes complications. She was just 60. Adam felt her loss very keenly.

He took her ashes back to his house and put them on the mantelpiece. According to his autobiography, his sister Christine knocked the urn over when she was vacuuming the next day and sucked them up.

This gave rise to the immortal line.

"I've sucked up mum in the Hoover."

Adam started the new decade playing Feste in a production of Shakespeare's *Twelfth Night* at the Royal in Northampton.

Feste is a jester, a fool, a clown: Adam wore a costume of Harlequin's motley. It's a tough part. Most of Feste's gags – puns and the like – would certainly have had the Elizabethan groundlings wetting themselves with laughter, but don't do much for the modern sense of humour.

"I did impeticos thy gratillity," he says, "for Malvolio's nose is no whipstock: my lady has a white hand, and the Myrmidons are no bottle-ale houses."

Then he sings:

"O mistress mine, where are you roaming?
O, stay and hear; your true love's coming,
That can sing both high and low:
Trip no further, pretty sweeting;
Journeys end in lovers meeting,
Every wise man's son doth know."

On slow nights, the temptation to segue into a couple of choruses of 'Someone Else's Baby' must have been close to irresistible.

"People came to see if I was going to make a twot [*sic*] of myself," he said, "but I never got a bad notice. Not one."[61]

The boredom – a common occupational hazard of working in Shakespeare's comedies – got to him. Sometimes he fell asleep during the long speeches. This amused the audience, but didn't do much to endear him to his fellow players. Adam was on about £20 or £30 a week, probably about double what other members of the cast were making. The average weekly wage in 1970 – for people outside the acting profession – was £32.

His 30th birthday was looming. He'd been trying to make it as an actor for three years and he was working for peanuts, wearing tights, doing gags nobody understood, in Northampton. His savings were dwindling. But, he insisted that by this time, "I was so far into it I would have stuck to it forever."

All the same, the big break must have come as a huge relief.

Chapter Twenty-Two

"D'you know what your average punter wants these days when he wants a crafty drink after hours? He wants a bit of class, don't he, Charlie? Same as he gets round his doubles bar round the corner. I mean, he likes a bit of carpet on the floor. Some tartan wallpaper. Subdued lighting. Somewhere you can take a bird, shove a few scotches down her throat. You want some tables and chairs in here. I mean, jukebox over there. Table lamps. D'you know what I reckon, Charlie? I reckon we could serve toasted sandwiches down here."

Keith Waterhouse and Willis Hall,
Budgie, Series 1, Episode 5.

Just outside the fenced enclosure at the Isle of Wight Festival in 1970, a ragged assembly of English whingers, German nihilists, Italian anarchists and Swedish yippies had formed an encampment called "Desolation Row". They were proud to be the small minority that spoils it for everybody else. Their beef was that the organisers were expecting people – right? – *people* to pay – can you believe that? – *pay* to get in to see the bands. They daubed the fences with swastikas and obscenities and, when they could, tore a segment down and went once and once more unto the breach. In the end, the organisers gave in. The walls came down. "We put this festival on for you bastards with a lot of love," said Rikki Farr, the Master of Ceremonies. "We worked for one year for you pigs. Now you wanna break our walls and you wanna destroy it? Well you go to hell."

Elsewhere, the Beatles were suing each other. Drugs, which in 1966 had seemed such a jolly good idea, had turned out to have a downside. Everybody had gone, or had friends who had gone, nuts: acid-paranoia was the most common, but most of the other psychoses were well-represented, too. And all the fun was sucked out of student protest when police shot and killed four anti-war demonstrators at Kent State University in Ohio.

As the seventies unfolded, even pop went sour. The bands you'd come to know and love decided they could not possibly play without enough gear to fill every truck that Edwin Shirley could muster and, in a similarly megalomaniac spirit, kicked against the artistic constraints of the two-minute single, refusing to release anything shorter than a double album, usually containing just the one track.

Most of the rest of pop seemed to be based on the relationship – expertly commoditised since Adam and Cliff's day – between pre-pubescent girls and the objects of their obsession. The David Cassidy fan club was bigger than that of Elvis or the Beatles had ever been. During the few years of his reign, his handlers shifted half a billion dollars worth of Cassidy-related merchandise ($15,000 worth of which found its way into David's pocket).

Indeed, possibly the only incontestably good thing to happen in 1970 was the launch of the Curly Wurly.

Adam Faith was a name from the old days, remembered sometimes with an affectionate smile – like Muffin The Mule or Stanley Matthews. The kids would find one of his singles, with the old red Parlophone label, tucked away at the back of their Auntie's radiogram and put it on. It might as well have been a Bing Crosby 78 from the thirties, or John McCormack's 'The Garden Where The Praties Grow'.

He'd acquired a theatrical agent by this time and not just any theatrical agent: Dennis Van Thal was one of the most respected names in the business. As well as Adam, he represented Sir Alec Guinness, Franco

Zeffirelli, Dirk Bogarde and Roger Moore. Dennis arranged for Adam
to have lunch with Willis Hall, the co-writer, with Keith Waterhouse, of
Billy Liar. They had seen and admired what he did with their play and
wanted more.

Willis was a Yorkshireman from Hunslet in Leeds, 10 years older than
Adam. He'd served as a regular soldier in Malaya and put his experiences
into a play, *The Long And The Short And The Tall*, which won the *Evening
Standard* Award for Best Play of the Year and was made into a film starring
Richard Harris and Laurence Harvey. Then he'd teamed up with his
childhood friend Keith Waterhouse to write the novel *Billy Liar*.

Keith was an extraordinarily prolific writer who had started out as a
journalist on *The Yorkshire Post*. As well as the novel, play and film of *Billy
Liar*, he wrote the screenplay for Brian Forbes' *Whistle Down The Wind*,
produced a stream of novels, contributed columns to practically every
newspaper and magazine mentioned in the *Writers' & Artists' Yearbook*
and some that aren't, and wrote the definitive work on the theory and
practice of lunch.

Adam's lunch with Willis, at the White Elephant in Curzon Street,
Mayfair, was almost perfectly executed and extremely productive. Willis
told Adam about an idea for a TV series that he and Keith had had
hanging around for a while. It was to be called *The Loser* and followed
the exploits of a small-time criminal whose attempts to make easy
money always ended badly and who was plagued by a complex personal
life – a feckless ex-wife, a steady girlfriend who had borne him a child,
and a second girlfriend who was a prostitute. Adam, for whom playing
tearaways was second nature, said he was interested. It was, after all, telly
money, which wasn't movie money but all the same an actor on telly
money could hire an actor on rep money to clean his toilet.

They took the idea to Stella Richmond, Head of Drama at London
Weekend Television. She was interested, too, and passed it on to Verity
Lambert, a name greeted with religious awe by *Dr Who* fans for she
was the show's first producer. Verity had just moved over to LWT from
the BBC and was looking for projects. She reckoned that after years
of *No Hiding Place*, *Dixon Of Dock Green*, *Z-Cars* and *Softly, Softly*, a
cops'n'robbers show that sided more with the robbers than the cops was

well overdue. The project got the green light and went into production at the end of 1970.

The main character, Adam's character, "the loser" of the original concept, was called Ronald Bird, known as "Budgie". In the first episode, he's just out of prison but has no intention of going straight. He's a chancer, not too clever, always a little bit hard done by. His attempts to make a few bob are usually foiled by fellow crim Charlie Endell, a Scottish grizzly bear in a thick camel-hair coat and a thin veneer of respectability played, to the manner born, by Ian Cuthbertson. "There are two things I hate in life, Budgie, and you're both of them."

London Weekend Television had, in the previous couple of years, run into financial troubles enabling Rupert Murdoch, an upstart Australian media tycoon who'd just taken over the *Sun* and the *News Of The World*, to acquire a 30% shareholding. In February 1971, when *The Loser* was well into production, Murdoch became LWT's Managing Director.

At around the same time John Freeman, Adam's old pal from the *Face To Face* days, became the company's Chairman. "I expect many people are thinking I need my head examining, but I decided to take it up all the same," Freeman said. He was bullish about his appointment, though, and made it quite clear that he anticipated no interference from Murdoch when it came to decisions about programme content.

Fools' paradise. Within days, word came down from on high that Murdoch didn't think anybody would watch a show called *The Loser*. Change the title.

Keith, Willis and Verity Lambert obligingly did so. The opening titles were re-shot to show Adam chasing fivers which spell out the show's new title, *Budgie*, but then, in a sort of précis of the plot of every episode, a wind gets up and blows the cash out of his reach.

The new title was better for Adam – he was now definitely the star – but *The Loser* would have been a more apt description of the product. It is comedy tinged in every corner with regret, disappointment and disillusionment in which wide-eyed Budgie, hunched and worried, walks streets littered with broken dreams.

The series had the great good fortune to be blessed by a jaw-dropping "best of all time" production team: produced by Verity Lambert, written by Keith Waterhouse and Willis Hall, directed by Jim Goddard, Mike Newell and Michael Lindsay-Hogg. They did not disappoint.

Neither did Adam. He can do Budgie. It's possibly the stand-out performance of his acting career. He's inconsistent – few actors faced with the cold constraints of TV studio drama managed to shine every time – but when he gets it he doesn't half get it. The what-now anxiety, the bruised innocence, the feral six-year-old's sense of right and wrong are always present in his hunched little walk, his restless eyes, his quivering mouth. He looks damaged – as if some dietary deficiency had robbed him of the sense he was born with.

His screen presence had never been less than magnetic. Even in a turkey like *What A Whopper!*, he walks into shot and you wonder whether it might be worth watching for another five or 10 minutes after all. He's relaxed on screen, too. Sometimes – it has to be said – he relaxes a bit too much, doesn't listen to the other actors, doesn't listen to himself, gets the pitch wrong, makes nonsense of the lines and the scene, but when he hits the balance, the actor and the role meld. Adam was able to assume all the pathetic hopelessness of Budgie: Budgie assumed some of the glamour of Adam Faith.

It is, perhaps, an affront to his skill as an actor and a misrepresentation of the actor's art to suggest that Adam was so credible in the part because, with a slightly different shake of the dice, Terry Nelhams could so easily have become Budgie. One can point to a list of reasons as long as a copper's truncheon to suggest that something more than luck helped him evade the life of petty crime – his focus, his intelligence, his work ethic, his discovery of the Adam Faith brand and so on; but equally one can point to a list of people whose focus, whose intelligence, whose work ethic were rendered worthless by lack of opportunity, and melted away.

"Budgie is not really very much like me," he said. "But I've known a few people like Budgie. And we were born in the same sort of place in London. Acton for me, Edmonton for him. We are not trying to glorify a petty crook. If there were ever an advertisement for not being a crook, it's Budgie. He's such a pathetic little worm."[62]

Back in 1967, Adam's little brother Roger had been put on probation for three years. He'd been found breaking into Ealing Village Social Club with intent to steal. A condition of the probation order was that he should go into hospital for psychiatric treatment. The following year, he was in the dock again, this time for "loitering with intent". In his defence he'd said that, although he had been apprehended acting suspiciously in a Hammersmith street early one morning, he was merely "looking for some birds" who he thought lived round that way. "Roger has been very ill," Adam told the press, "and has not been able to work for some time. I shall do all I can to help him."

A few years later, Roger was in even more serious trouble, first for passing forged US $100 bills, then for a series of cheque book frauds. In court, he asked for 1,055 other offences to be taken into consideration. In his defence, his brief said, "Being the younger brother of someone who is a success can often have a considerable effect on someone."

Adam's older sister Pamela agreed. "Roger's problem has always been that he has to live in Adam's shadow."

Jackie and Adam had moved house several times since selling the place in Fulham. They fetched up, temporarily at least, in Henfield, a small village about 10 miles north of Brighton.

In the summer of 1970, Jackie had found she was pregnant again. After years of false starts, false alarms, miscarriages and heartbreak, they hardly dared hope that this time it might be OK.

Episode One of *Budgie* was in rehearsal when the baby, a girl, was born, two month premature, at St Theresa's Hospital in Wimbledon. She was just 3lb 12oz. The frail little thing was taken straight to the intensive care unit in Clapham. She thrived. Jackie had been reading Leo Tolstoy's *Anna Karenina*, so they called the baby Katya, after Anna's loving and courageous friend Ekaterina.

The demands of Budgie meant that Adam couldn't spend much time at home with the baby. New fathers didn't in 1971. He stayed in town for much of the time, in a flat just off the Kings Road, handy for the rehearsal rooms at the Duke of York's TA Barracks.

The plot of *Budgie* Episode One could not, in light of current, more enlightened, thinking, be considered a fit subject for comedy-drama or indeed any sort of TV programme other than a harrowing documentary. It involves the heist of a vanload of pornography and a 15-year-old runaway (played by Adrienne Posta). Charlie Endell takes the runaway under his wing – "I have a problem, Budgie. Myself. I am plagued with a heart of gold. That scrubber is stage-struck, Budgie, her heart is in show business." Accordingly, Charlie employs the runaway as a stripper but in the end she falls in love with a somewhat older lowlife and runs away with him to Manchester where, the plot seems to suggest, they live happily ever after. Budgie, however, is left feeling that a liberty (possibly a diabolical one) has been taken. "The scrubber belongs to Charlie!" he says.

It's a plot that these days would have writers, cast and crew having their laptops seized, but in those days – though a nipple on TV was a rarity, a penis possibly allowed in diagrammatic form and a medical context, and the word 'fuck' regarded as an absolute no-no – a 15-year-old stripper running off with an older man was apparently regarded as seamy but acceptable prime-time viewing. The casual racism, sexism and homophobia isn't much fun either, and might explain why, despite the show's popularity and influence, for the past 40 years it's only ever been repeated in a carefully framed historical context.

The first episode was transmitted on April 9 – Good Friday – 1971.

Leonard Buckley of *The Times* reviewed it in appropriate style: "There was this geezer just out of the nick, see, and he wanted to pinch this van outside this caff. But he got the wrong one, see, on account of his mate being a stupid bastard. So this bloke from the clip joint was going to carve him up and chop his mitts off..."

Buckley went on to say he didn't much like it.

"I was not myself shocked that it started on Good Friday, after all, there were thieves at Calvary. But I was sad that so much talent was put to such indifferent use [...] Adam Faith, in the steps of the old Groaner himself [a reference to Bing Crosby, a popular singer from a previous generation who could also turn his hand to acting] turns out to be a capable actor. He plays the reconstituted spiv, irrepressible, irresponsible, amorous and amoral. And he has the character off pat. So what goes wrong? The fault lies with the contradiction of the silly and the sordid. The silliness is not silly enough. The sordid is too sordid. The two become confused and the programme breaks up. As long as we do not have to take Budgie seriously we quite like him and he almost amuses us. But the dialogue turns sour, the irresponsibility becomes offensive and the Cockney Raffles is seen for what he really is – a nasty little squirt."[63]

George Thaw in the *Daily Mirror* dispensed with the religiosity and the pomposity and went straight for the jugular, describing it as a programme "dedicated to cheapness, nastiness and downright insincerity". "Budgie, a small time criminal who is played by ex-pop star Adam Faith is a character I found totally impossible to like…" blah blah "as much charm and vivacity as a dead weasel" blah blah "wondered why they bothered to put it on the screen" blah blah "contempt for the taste of the average viewer" blah blah "mindless and tasteless".

Budgie wasn't an immediate hit with the public, either. The first four episodes were made in black and white, not because colour equipment was unavailable but because industrial action prevented it being used. But by the fifth or sixth episode, the show had carved itself a devoted fanbase and by Episode 13 it had gone Top 10 in the ratings.

Even the broadsheet critics came round. "Two very solid acting performances have held together *Budgie,* the serial about the misadventures of a cockney petty crook which ended its present run last night," the *Daily Telegraph* said. "Adam Faith, who must now be recognised as an actor rather than a singer, has given Budgie a chirpy yet vulnerable tenacity and Ian Cuthbertson had brought to the part of the successful criminal a believable Scottish combination of ruthlessness and sentimentality."[64]

Adam Faith was news again. He was an actor. He was a star.

"What a transformation," the *Express* said, "since the day when he bounced, with a jolly upbeat tune." And went on to describe him as, "an accomplished dramatic actor".

On the back of *Budgie,* other offers came in. He played a Canadian killer in *The Protectors* – an ATV series starring Robert Vaughn and Nyree Dawn Porter – with a Canadian accent.

"Accents are things we actors have to learn,"[65] the newborn luvee told the *Express.* "I can't tell you what it's done to my life," Adam said. "In rep your reputation gets around on word of mouth. In TV you are able to make an impact so quickly."[66]

Life-changing events are like the buses of popular mythology. They come three at a time. Adam had had a daughter, he had been acclaimed as a "dramatic actor". Then came the third.

Back in Henfield, Adam discovered that he was living just up the road from an old acquaintance, David Courtney, a drummer he'd worked with in the past. David was now dabbling in, among other ventures, the used car business.

"For a laugh he came out on the road with me and we started buying and selling cars – just because he fancied it," David says. "But his idea of buying and selling was a bit different to mine. I mean, we'd buy the cars and bring them back, but muggins here would be the one who'd clean them up for reselling. Terry wasn't having any of that. But he was looking forward to some of the profits."

It was a laugh, though. Like it always was with Terry.

"Yeah, that's when our relationship was cemented. After that, he was the closest thing to a brother that I had. I had decided that I wanted to go into management – you know, look for talent and develop it. It had been in my mind for a while, so I thought right, OK, and I put an ad in the local paper for artistes – a bit like *Britain's Got Talent* really.

"I didn't even limit it to music – which was quite foolish because I got jugglers and people doing farmyard noises and all that. I had the auditions at the Pavilion Theatre, Brighton and narrowed it down to 50 acts. Out of the 50 really there was only two good acts. One was a guy with a blind pianist called Billy Jones. Don't know what happened to him. The other was this band called Patches. They had a singer – a little guy called Gerry Sayer. As soon as I heard, I knew. The music wasn't that great, but this voice was, like, unbelievable.

"I got Patches an audition at Air London Studios and sure enough they heard exactly the same as me and offered me a contract there and then. At that point I didn't know about contracts, so I went to Terry and told him I'd found this singer and I'd already been offered a record deal – what did he think? So he said, 'Well, let's have a listen to it.'

"I'd already got together with Gerry and started to write some stuff with him, because I knew then his material wasn't right. Anyway, Terry and I sat there and I played him the demos. I'd recorded them with Gerry in my apartment in Brighton: in the back room where I had a piano – which, oddly enough, was originally owned by Chris Andrews. It was the one he'd written "I'm Her Yesterday Man" on.

"The demo wasn't more than halfway through when Terry said, 'Turn it off.'

"So I thought, 'Oh, he doesn't like it.'

"Then he said, 'Where's this contract?' and when I showed him he said, 'Rip it up.'

"And I said, 'What do you mean – rip it up?'

"And he said, 'This is brilliant, what you've found.' He said: 'Never mind about the band – it's this kid's voice and these songs. Rip up that contract and you and I will manage and produce him.'"

Not long after that, they changed Gerry's name to Leo Sayer.

Chapter Twenty-Three

"Inga: I was sharing a flat with a girl in Hornchurch. A stripper who worked with a python. Doris.
Budgie: Was you really? I don't remember a stripper called Doris.
Inga: No, Budge. Doris was the python's name

Keith Waterhouse and Willis Hall,
Budgie, Series 2, Episode 12.

"The thing about Terry was," says David Courtney, "he was Adam Faith and every door was always open to him. Whether it be in politics or record companies or whatever, they all knew him. He was a household name. And if he picked up a phone, he got a meeting."

His newfound *Budgie* stardom had made his phone-picking-up superpower all the greater. No longer did the name and the face evoke no more than a nostalgic smile and an honourable mention in "Where Are They Now?" columns.

Everybody knew him. Traffic wardens would give him a chirpy hello as they wrote out his tickets. Coppers would ask him about the next series. Cab drivers would tell him of the Budgies they knew.

The second series of *Budgie* was blessed with a new sig tune, 'Nobody's Fool', by Ray Davies. The first series had ended where it had started, with Budgie in prison. The second begins, once again, with his release, and the 13 episodes essentially chart his decline. He learns that his wife is seeing another man, his mother dies, his father rejects him, he gets his girlfriend pregnant again, he gets badly beaten up and left homeless in the gutter. But he ends the series trying to start a new life with a stripper.

The series featured some impressive guest stars – Gordon Jackson, Derek Jacobi, John Thaw, James Bolam – and it exerted an influence on TV, on fashion, on behaviour and on the world.

Verity Lambert, the producer of *Budgie*, went on to produce, among others, *Minder, Fox* and *Widows*, so a strong case could be made that, just as Verity had hoped, *Budgie* spawned a genre of 'robber' shows to counter the prevailing predominance of 'cop' shows.

"In 1971, I'm a 12-year-old boy and I'm watching television," says Robert Elms, broadcaster, sharp-dresser and author of *The Way We Wore*, "and this character called Budgie comes on. This is when I first become aware of Adam Faith. Because of this jacket he had on. In school, the next morning everyone says: 'Did you see that jacket? Where can you get one of those jackets?' So we all ran to Shepherds Bush market to try and get one. But they didn't have one. Someone says: 'They've got one at Wembley Market.' So off we go. I bought one. It was purple and maroon leather with a great big tulip collar."

"Hero worship," said the *Daily Mirror*, "like lightning, rarely strikes in the same place twice – but it has for Adam Faith. For the second time in 12 years he has caused a storm with teenage fans. For as Budgie, the small-time TV crook, he has caught the imagination of a group of 14 and 15 year olds known as Smoothies and his clothes have taken on a definite cult meaning. The kids readily admit that they are looking for a trend to latch on to after the Skinhead scene ended. They found their new 'leader' in Budgie, the TV loser."[67]

In a couple of months, passion for the Budgie jacket – a shrunken-looking, zip-up, waisted, pilot-style garment with large 'rabbit ear' lapels (often with contrasting collars) in eight ounce duck cloth – had gone far beyond the preserve of Robert Elms and the West London fashionistas and was clawing at the hearts of the nation. Budgie jackets can be seen now in the Victoria & Albert museum – period pieces from Sterling Cooper of Wigmore Street.

Budgie's feathered haircut (created by Keith Wainwright of Smile) was also widely copied. By 1974, the haircut and jacket teamed with flares, wide-collared shirt and stack heels became the look for every working-class white male in the country who was dancing to Mud's 'Tiger Feet' with his thumbs in his imaginary braces. With tartan trim it was the look of the Bay City Rollers.

In the earlier episodes, Budgie had worn wet-look boots. Later he took to wearing lime green clogs. "When I met Adam later," says Robert Elms, "I asked him about Budgie's clogs. He said to me, 'Think about it. All Budgie does is run away. He's always getting caught out. I thought a lot about what he would wear. I grew up around Budgies and they always spent all their dough on clothes, cos that was all they cared about. Now, Budgie he's a bit stupid. But he wanted to be fashionable. If you've got to run away a lot, what's the most silly thing you could wear? So I put him in clogs."

As Series Two went into production, Adam told the *Daily Express*: "*Budgie* has given me a sense of commitment, something I never got out of being a pop singer in the old days. It was a bit of a laugh, I enjoyed myself, but I never felt involved. Now I am committed 110 per cent. I live and breathe being an actor."[68]

By episode two, the 110 per cent was down to about 80, by episode three maybe 60 – and so on as the daily routine of make-up, wardrobe, hit the mark, say the lines, reset, retake, say 'em again, reset, retake took its toll.

Boredom was probably the main issue, but money and control were a problem too. He always wanted more of both. He told the *Daily Mirror* that he reckoned the switch from singing to acting had cost him something like £30,000. He talks very frankly about his lack of influence on the writers of the series, Keith Waterhouse and Willis Hall. "Those two are princes among writers," he said, "so you don't try and shove your own oar in. I am but a mere player."

He says of Budgie, or maybe himself: "He's a loser that one. He'll still be nowhere when he's 50. Blimey, he's SAD."[69]

"I would like to do films," he said. "I could end up playing Budgie with a different name all my life if I'm not careful. I must avoid that."

During Series One, he'd said: "The actors are the ones who have to get on and do it. The producers, the writers, everyone else doing those jobs may think they are the ones who are doing the show. But they are nobody. Once that bleedin' light goes on they are nothing. Their job is done. Gone. Finished. The people who have their heads on the chopping block are the actors." It was intended as a general observation about the nature of film-making and though it's a refreshing inversion of the luvee's usual paean to the "supporting cast and fabulous crew without whom I am nothing", it does suggest that an arrogant and ungrateful resentment was festering.

As the transmission of the second series was winding up, he announced that if there was to be a series three, he would not be a part of it. He blamed censorship: "Budgie simply could not function properly within the strict censorship limits imposed on a TV show. He is a villain and as such associates with pimps and prostitutes and hangs out in a pornographic book store."

He still talked of the movie idea: "I'm not killing off Budgie as some people have claimed. If anything, I am making him into a bigger character because I intend to take him into film."[70]

If there was even a hint of a movie in the offing, it never became more than pipe talk.

Standing still and enjoying the view was not in Adam's repertoire. He had to be moving all the time, preferably in an upwards direction. He never thought the world owed him a living. He'd known since he was a kid that you have to work. Having decided to take acting seriously, he'd spent three years on tour, in Glasgow, in Northampton, night after night in jester's motley, waiting for his cue in a windowless dressing room or a fag-ash green room. Then he'd landed a starring role in a TV series. He'd made a success of it. But beyond, he knew, higher peaks were waiting to be conquered – more challenging TV roles, *Hamlet* with Dame Sybil at the National, multi-million dollar movies in Hollywood.

And if none of that was going to happen then he would instead complete his latest regeneration.

He was a big cheese manager in the music business with a star and a group to promote.

With David Courtney, he acquired an office in Brighton and a secretary. He booked time at Olympic Studios in London to record a single, 'Living In America', with Leo and Patches.

Adam bust a gut promoting the record and plugging Leo, introducing him to the movers and shakers, telling him how to act, how to stand, how to smile, what to say.

The record tanked.

"I think it sold 50 copies," said Leo Sayer. "But undaunted, and with Adam's great chutzpah, we were marching on to make the *Living In America* Patches album."[71]

Adam was flying to and fro between London and LA, fixing deals with Chrysalis in the UK and Warner Brothers in the US. He was, flying in the face of all industry wisdom, financing the project almost entirely out of his own pocket. He remortgaged the family home. He sold the paintings off his walls. He literally sold the family silver.

The Beatles had recorded *Sergeant Pepper* on two four-track tape machines. Since then, record production had become a more sophisticated process. Technology had turned the making of an album – an afternoon's work in Adam's heyday – into an odyssey that could stretch over weeks and months. And cost a fortune.

They began recording at The Manor, one of the first 'residential studios' where a band could live and work together for weeks or months "getting", as the expression of the time quaintly put it, "their shit together". Richard Branson had originally bought the place with a loan from his Auntie Joyce and subsequently installed a studio in the stable block/squash court. The grounds were extensive: the neighbours suspicious.

Adam quickly established his right to command and control.

Deciding that Patches weren't up to his exacting standards, he brought in various session musicians – including Russ Ballard and Bob Henrit from the Roulettes. Russ and Bob were, by this time, more successful than Adam had ever been. After Unit 4+2, they had joined Rod Argent, previously with the Zombies, and Jim Rodford, from the Mike Cotton

Sound, to form Argent whose 'Hold Your Head Up', sung by Russ, had gone Top 5 on both sides of the Atlantic. Adam had played the Winter Gardens, Margate: they had played the Municipal Auditorium, Atlanta GA and the Overton Park Shell, Memphis TN. Adam had shared a stage with Brucie and Des Lane the Penny Whistle Man: they'd played with B.B.King in Dayton, Ohio.

"We were midway through making the album," says David Courtney, "when Leo and I had a creative dispute with Terry – over exactly what I can't recall. Anyway, he threw a 'wobbly' and threatened to pull the plug on the album unless we agreed to do things his way. I remember sitting on the lawn outside with Leo, totally distraught and feeling like our world had come crashing down around us. Terry eventually cooled down, panic over, and we were back on line."[72]

And just as Adam had flourished under his mentors – Jack Good, John Barry, Eve Taylor – so Leo learned at the feet of Adam. "Adam was like a movie director, the way he made that record," said Leo. "I'd absorb his confidence. We were a great team: me, David and Adam."

"I would take care of the music side of it but Adam would be brilliant at getting the performance out of Leo," says David. "He would talk to him in a certain way to get him to perform. Those songs were very theatrical, so to see them from an actor's point of view could bring the poignant moments out much more.

"In the studio, Terry's musical instincts were good, too. He was brilliant. He was like George Martin was with the Beatles."

Keith Altham, formerly *Fab's* Keith, and *NME's* man on the spot, had become Press Officer and PR Guru to the stars. One of his clients was Roger Daltrey of The Who.

"Roger had built a studio in his home," says Keith, "because he was a bit pissed off with Pete Townshend doing a solo album. And he wanted somebody to be a guinea pig and try the studio out for him. So I suggested Leo and Adam. And Roger said, 'Bring it on. I love Adam, we were born in the same street.'" [close enough, anyway]

So, for stage two of Leo's album, Adam, David and Leo upped sticks to Roger's place near Burwash in East Sussex. Adam and Roger Daltrey found they had more in common than natural blond hair and fond memories of the Crown cinema in Mill Hill Place, Acton, with the double seats in the back row.

"Adam's on the ball," said Roger. "He's survived, kept in touch. Like when he wanted to learn golf he locked himself away for nine months then comes out a great player. And he wanted to learn the piano, so he gets a tutor to come and live with him for a year and now he can work his way round a piano. He's the sort of feller I like."[73]*

During breaks in recording, Roger outlined plans for his solo album.

"In the end, they'd heard me talk about the bloody thing so much," said Roger, "that they knew where I was at. So it seemed natural to say to Leo and Dave Courtney, who writes with him, 'Go and write me the songs and let Adam produce it.'"

For the time being, focus moved from Leo to Roger. Roger was given some of the songs that had been earmarked for Leo. Some of the best songs that had been earmarked for Leo. Granted, Leo had co-written the songs so he stood to gain financially, but all the same, it didn't seem right.

"I knew what I wanted to do and I knew by this time that it was my life," said Leo. "And don't forget, Adam was a tight bastard so there wasn't much money hanging around. So it was like, where am I going to live? I got fed up with sleeping on the studio floor at Roger's. It looked like it was never going to happen. You know, maybe Adam will lose interest, go off and manage Roger Daltrey and not be interested in me! But being a Gemini, I was able to see it from two sides. The artist in me was totally pissed off and angry, but the other side of it was this guy who was just a good bloke and loved hanging around with famous people. Roger would bring people like Jimmy Page, Paul Kossoff and Ronnie Wood to the sessions – so that side of me was like, 'No Leo, just hang on'."

Adam loved producing. He loved hanging with Roger and David and Leo and the superstars who were popping in to lay down a few tracks. He loved slipping over to New York or LA to finalise details on a contract with a couple of record industry legends. It certainly beat

---

* Adam, it should be said, might have learned to 'work his way round a piano', but he never actually learned to play it.

location filming in a Budgie jacket and green clogs on a cold wet day when camera breakdowns and aeroplanes flying overhead meant you had to do the same three lines 27 times.

But he was never home. He was spending far more time with Roger and David and Leo than with Jackie and Katya.

Jackie decided she'd had enough. When he could have been consolidating his reputation as an actor – the career path that she had supported for nearly seven years – he was instead giving every waking hour and risking every penny they had and many more they didn't have on a bubble-haired singer.

She kicked him out. He showed up at David Courtney's house in Brighton. David made up a bed in the spare room, then found himself slightly baffled, the way you did when Adam was around, sleeping in it himself.

One day, Andrew Tribe, a friend of David's who'd been in the music business for many years, popped round and found Adam in residence. "He was sitting in a peacock chair – remember those?" says Andrew, "with newspapers all over the floor. He'd been given the yellow card by his wife, Jackie, and was staying with Dave. That was the first time we met. He was very jokey – he always was – from day one. I spoke to him probably three or four times a day after that – every day. We used to think alike about a lot of things. We only had one conversation – which never stopped and never started – it just carried on. A bit later with the Vodaphones, you spent your life getting cut off anyway. Whenever and wherever we met, we never shook hands or hugged, we just carried on. Chatting. It was often me bollocking him about being daft about something or other and not paying attention to his career."

Whereas Adam's knowledge of the business side of pop was 50% bullshit, 49% bottle and 1% real, Andrew actually knew what he was talking about and tried to introduce at least a note of prudence into the project. "I did all the donkey work," he says, "because I knew what to do. I used to hide the cheque book. They kept buggering off to the Bahamas or somewhere to write. They'd go here, then they'd go there. I'd take care of the business side."

But nobody else seemed in the mood for prudence. "Terry had discovered a starting pistol in a cupboard," says David Courtney, "which was loaded and he proceeded to fire it down at his side in the control room. Well, as you can imagine, it gave out an almighty bang. The engineer, a guy called John Mills, rose to his feet in fury, refused to continue with the session and proceeded to storm out of the studio. Terry was outraged that John should up and leave and refused to have him back in the session."[74]

There was more madness when Roger's tapes were played to Chris Stamp and Kit Lambert at their offices. Chris and Kit, who'd managed The Who since 1964, were the founders of Track Records, slated to release the album, but by 1973 their relationship with The Who was hanging by a thread, not least because they were doing phenomenal quantities of drugs.

They decided they didn't like what they were hearing.

"Roger went into an almighty rage and the three of us promptly left the building," says David Courtney. "I remember standing outside with Terry watching Roger taking eight-track tapes from his car and hurtling them at the office window and screaming abuse at Kit and Chris."

Kit and Chris eventually decided to keep their opinions to themselves and in April 1973, the album *Daltrey* was released. It rose to number six in the album charts. Every track except two had been written by David Courtney and Leo Sayer. Even better, 'Giving It All Away', the single from the album – and a song that remains, in the face of indomitable competition from his Who catalogue, one of the best ever to exercise Roger's remarkable talent – went to number five in the singles chart.

The production credit on the album read "David Courtney and Adam Faith". Adam was back in the charts. He was a player, back in the game. He was Big Time.

> *"Let them all get lost*
> *I won't be double crossed*
> *I know the things I want*
> *I know the price they cost*
> *I'm gonna get my share*

While I've got my hair
I'm on the upward climb
Big Time"

He was back with Jackie, too. As had happened so often in the past and would happen again and again, she forgave and let him come home.

Then his car hit a tree.

Chapter Twenty-Four

"You can put almost any frail object in a box and provided it's held firm you can shake it about no end. But loose in a box, that's another matter. Clunk, click, every trip."
Jimmy Savile, *Seat Belt Public Service TV ad*, 1971.

On Saturday August 4, 1973, Adam went to a gig in St. Albans. Leo and Patches were on the bill with Procol Harum.

"While they were playing 'Whiter Shade Of Pale', I was sacking Leo's group," said Adam. "It was horrible: they wanted to be good, but they just weren't up to it."

After the gig he drove into London to drop Leo and his wife off at Victoria Station so that they could catch the last train to Brighton.

He was driving a rented Ford Granada. At around 3·20 in the morning, on the road into Henfield, just past the village of Cowfold, he ploughed the car into a tree.

Local residents heard the smash. They pulled Adam out of the car and laid him by the roadside. He was conscious, and kept muttering, "Leave me alone, please leave me alone."

By the time the police arrived, a small crowd had gathered. The general assumption was that Adam must have been drunk, although in fact he was practically teetotal.

Laurence Marks, who co-wrote *Love Hurts*, Adam's hit TV show of the nineties, has an alternative explanation, "Well you know what happened – he had been round a woman's house and he had fallen asleep – and he realised that he needed to get home, but he was very tired and he fell asleep at the wheel."

Adam had ruptured his spleen, perforated his bladder, split his shin, crushed his ankle joint, broken his left arm and all but one of his ribs on his left side, dislodged the lining of his abdomen and smashed his face. At Crawley hospital, surgeons spent eight hours putting him back together.

"I always feel a bit guilty," says David Courtney. "I mean, he had wanted me to go with him that night in the car, but I decided not to go. I remember him getting the needle because he didn't like being on his own. When I went to see the car the next day, the engine was sitting where I would have been. Literally, it was in the front seat."

Without the hefty engine of the Granada to absorb some of the impact, the crash would almost certainly have been fatal. But it was only a fluke that Adam was driving that car at all. "The day before his accident," says Andrew Tribe, "he had a VW [Beetle – a car with a rear engine] from Hertz. I told him to change his hire car and he got a Ford Granada. Thank God, because the engine took the blow."

Recovery was slow.

"Last Monday he started to come round," Jackie told the *Daily Mail*. "I knew he was going to be all right. His eyelids fluttered and he mumbled, 'Jack, you've got to get me a phone in here.' Then he dictated a letter and I pretended to take it down. The Savoy – God bless them – where he had dinner regularly, sent him a trifle, his favourite dessert, which impressed him beyond belief.

"He keeps weeping every time a card or flowers or a present comes. He slipped back a bit since Saturday when he really started feeling the pain. I couldn't bear it. He drove me insane. He said he wanted to give up fighting the pain and that really frightened me because he's such a fighter, such a toughie and I thought, 'That's it'.

"In the end I showed him a picture of Katya and I told him, 'That's what you've got to fight for. She's yours and she needs you.' We both ended up crying and I had to leave the room."[75]

Extreme pain wasn't the only suffering he had to bear. "One day when I was there, Jimmy Savile came to visit," says David Courtney. "This was the time when Jimmy was running his seat belt campaign with the catch phrase 'Clunk Click Every Trip'. He was dressed in a white robe like a Messiah coming to lay hands on the sick. He stood at Terry's bedside talking to him as if he was some kid on his *Jim'll Fix It* TV show."

The threat of a second visit from Savile was enough to encourage anybody to claim full recovery and demand discharge from hospital.

Jackie hired a nurse and organised a bed downstairs in the living room at Henfield. Katya, now three, loved having her father at home. Adam describes this as the first time, free from any distractions, that he really got to know his daughter. She made herself useful, too. Most of his body was encased in plaster but her arms were skinny enough to slip inside and scratch his arms and legs when they got too itchy.

As soon as he was out of plaster, having cancelled the Porsche that he'd ordered before the crash, he hired a physiotherapist to come every day and supervise his exercises. Obsessive personalities are good at this sort of thing. He would not be beaten. By November, just four months after the accident, he could walk without crutches. But the legacy of the crash – physical and mental – remained with him.

"I don't even complain about the pain I still feel in my leg," he said. "In a sense the smash was the best thing that could have happened to me. The pain is just a reminder I'm still alive.

"The accident brought me more into contact with reality than anything else. I'm an unbeliever, you know. When I die there's no after life for me. I only have one life to lead and I intend to lead it to the full."[76]

"Terry had come through it, but he wasn't the same," says David Courtney. "It changed him, yeah, it definitely changed him. He became more reckless... He was always reckless, but it also made him more self-centred. It would make a lot of people more aware of their vulnerability and how easily things can be taken away from you, but not him. He used to admit it to me that he always had this selfish streak, and I think it just brought more of that out in him."

The traits that had always been there – the obsessiveness, the fascination with money, the need to be in control of himself and others, the need to set himself sometimes pointless challenges simply to prove that he could do, that he still had it, the childlike inability to appreciate that other people had lives too, the capacity to cast off a friend or a project with barely a backward glance – they all, after the accident, seemed to intensify.

He had never liked being alone. He'd had a radio phone in his car since the early sixties and was first in line for any new innovation in car phones and later mobile phones. As we've heard, almost the first thing he asked for when he woke up in hospital was a bedside phone. Later, when his 'office' became a table at Fortnum & Mason, he famously had a phone socket installed and a handset laid with the knives and forks.

"He wouldn't consider what you might be doing at the time – eating dinner or whatever – he'd be on the phone to you," says David Courtney. "This was part of his selfishness. He'd be driving home and he'd call you and he'd stay on the phone to you until he was outside of his house and then he'd just pull up and say, 'OK, I'll speak to you later.' And hang up."

Much of the time this 'selfishness' could be seen as a charming idiosyncrasy, one of the things you had to put up with in order to access the fun, the laughs and the energy. But over the years it took on a darker edge, and was sometimes tinged with a ruthlessness that could appear downright cruel.

The accident changed the Adam Faith brand, too. Though a year earlier he could easily be seen as Budgie, a young tearaway, the new Adam Faith was a grown-up. Any sense of 'Poor Me' pathos was gone, at least in public. He was in control. He was The Management.

Andrew Tribe challenged him on several occasions. "I used to say to him: 'Have you ever been diagnosed with autism? Because that's what you are.' And he would just laugh. He wouldn't take any notice of anyone else."

Before he'd even left hospital, Adam was back at work, planning with David and Andrew the route by which Leo Sayer would achieve world domination.

'Why Is Everybody Going Home?', Leo's first single release as a solo artist, was a lush four and a half minutes of melancholia, a minute of which is taken up with the orchestral intro. It's an ambitious debut. Despite the long intro being a gift to a garrulous DJ, the song didn't get the airplay, or the sales, it deserved.

But, thanks to some innovatory marketing and image manipulation, Leo was getting noticed. The team got him a shot on BBC2's *The Old Grey Whistle Test* and a national tour supporting Roxy Music. For both, he wore a Pierrot costume, floppy white sleeves, floppy white trousers, black skull-cap containing the curls, white-face make-up with a red dot on each cheek and a tear beneath each eye. The costume was made by, and the make-up applied by, Leo's wife, Janice, but the idea, according to David Courtney, was all Adam's.

"Have you ever wondered," says David, "why we saw Leo, when he first appeared on *Top Of The Pops*, with all that make-up, the full white face? You can't see him at all. It was Adam who engineered all that. I asked Adam, 'Why, when Leo Sayer first appeared, did we not know what he looked like? Why did you put him in the white face and that Pierrot outfit?' And Adam said, 'It's simple. I was a good-looking guy who couldn't sing. Leo was the opposite.'"

As soon as he was up and about, Adam was working with his protégé, honing the stage act. "He picked up incredible visions from the songs that I wrote, and then managed to make them into landscapes," said Leo. "So the best thing about working with Adam was his vivid imagination; it was unstoppable. He was never scared of advancing everything that we were doing, all the time pushing the envelope, trying for more.

"Adam was telling me, 'You drop the jacket in the third number. If you do it in the second, it's all over.' You know, the parameters that Adam had were so exact. 'You stand on that mark. I've made an X on the stage, don't move from there.'"[77]

Leo regarded Adam, his Svengali, with something approaching religious awe. "My relationship with Adam was very intense, almost like a love affair," he said. "Short of sleeping with him, I would have done anything to be with him."[78]

'The Show Must Go On', the second single – a confection of spanking banjos and scat choruses – was as far away from 'Why Is Everybody Going Home?' as Gershwin's 'Summertime' is from Mungo Jerry's 'In

The Summertime'. But it was unquestionably more commercial and sat somehow better with the Pierrot image: instead of being a broken-hearted clown being wistful about his broken heart, he was a broken-hearted clown trying to keep things cheerful. Smiling through the tears. "Ridi, Pagliaccio" as Caruso used to say, "sul tuo amore infranto. Ridi del duol, che t'avvelena il cor."

'The Show Must Go On' entered the charts in December 1973. By January 19, 1974 it was up to number two. The LP, *Silverbird*, released around the same time, also made number two in the albums chart.

It was the early seventies. The hippy ideals of love and co-operation were still not quite dead. All the same, Leo had a two and a two. Roger had only had a six and a five. Nobody minded – what difference did it make? – but it was still worth a mention. In passing.

By the time 'One Man Band', Leo's third single, had been released, his music, the Pierrot look and the hand gestures that went with it had entered the national consciousness. He'd become a brand, every bit as celebrated as Adam Faith, Birds Eye Potato Waffles or Alan Bennett. Comedians referenced him. People in pubs did impersonations – just like they'd done with the "bay-be" thing 14 years earlier.

Leo was a hit. And Adam, like Lazarus, had risen from his bed and walked.

In retrospect nobody's sure where the next idea came from. It could have been the painkillers. Having never taken them, Adam had no tolerance for drugs, so there was no knowing what effect they might have had. It might have been the result of having his brains so badly shaken in the accident. Or it might have been some feeling of rebirth: the blessing of a second chance.

Whatever it was, it moved him to start singing again. He'd make an album: his first record in six years.

He and David Courtney decamped to the Bahamas. In the mornings they would borrow the hotel's piano to write songs. In the afternoons they would cruise the island on rented mopeds. In the evenings they would team up with 'Legs' Larry Smith, of the Bonzo Dog Doo Dah Band, and Terry Doran, manager of Grapefruit, signed to the Beatles'

Apple label, a former Liverpool car salesman immortalised as the 'man from the motor trade' in 'She's Leaving Home'. Larry and Terry Doran liked to party. They hit the casinos.

Somehow the work ethic still kicked in the following morning and the album got written.

Back in London, Adam and David booked time at Kingsway Studios and hired backing musicians. As always, Adam thought Big Time.

Paul and Linda McCartney hadn't been particularly busy since their 1973 Wings album *Band On The Run*. They'd spent some time in Manchester recording an album with Paul's brother, Mike McGear of Scaffold, and they'd been having to deal with a few personnel problems with their band, but, apart from that, and planning their next album, *Venus And Mars*, and bringing up the three kids, they were pretty much kicking their heels.

Adam had known Paul since they first ran into each other over post-gig cups of tea all those years before. He invited them out for dinner. Andrew Tribe joined them.

"Terry had arranged to have dinner with Paul and Linda," says Andrew. "And then we went on to the RAC club for drinks because Adam was a member there. This was in the old days, when the paint was still peeling off the walls and carpets all worn. After we had eaten, we went into the ballroom and had some tea. There was no one there. It was empty. There were two grand pianos on the little stage – no stools just pianos – and Terry said to Paul, 'It would be great if you would play 'Let It Be'.'

"So Paul started playing the chords and singing 'Let It Be' in full voice. Anyway, a little jobsworth came running in with a hat and uniform on and said, 'I'm sorry, sir, you're going to have stop that. You're going to upset the members.' So Terry said, embarrassed but furious, 'What are you on about? This is Paul McCartney. Fifty million yanks would pay 10 grand a piece to hear this.' And he says, 'I can't help that, sir,' and slammed the lid shut, nearly catching Paul's fingers. He locked it. We were crying with laughter."

In like manner, needing a photographer for the album cover, Adam went for royalty.

Lord Snowdon, formerly Anthony Armstrong-Jones, had done everything from high fashion photography to harrowing documentary to portraits of the great and the good. At the time, he was probably best known for being, as husband of Princess Margaret, the Queen's brother-in-law.

"I dropped Terry off at Kensington Palace," says David Courtney, "to meet with Lord Snowdon and discuss it. We met up later and he informed me that it was all agreed and that the Queen Mum was there at the time and asked him to stay for dinner, but he told her he couldn't cos he'd already made plans. The plans were him and me having a fish and chip supper at the Seashell on Lisson Grove."

For a while there were rumours that David Bowie was slated to produce, but he was busy regenerating from Ziggy Stardust to Hallowe'en Jack, so David and Adam produced. It was engineered by Deep Purple's producer Martin Birch. Russ Ballard and Bob Henrit played guitar and drums, joined by Dave Wintour, who'd played bass on Roger's and Leo's albums, and Ritchie Blackmore, popped in to raise the goblet of rock at the album's opening. Paul and Linda provided backing vocals on 'Star Song' and Paul also contributed keyboard fills on three other tracks.

Adam's voice is frail and thin, very like late period Ray Davies, but quite compelling. He's abandoned his old bag of tricks – the hiccups, vowel mangling and so on – and in doing so, seems to have acquired taste – a quality for which his early records were seldom noted. He can sustain notes. He can use vibrato. He can be a quiet, still, small voice.

The album was released in August 1974 and spawned two singles: 'I Survived' and 'Maybe'. Despite an appearance on *Top Of The Pops* and a generally favourable critical reception, though, neither album nor singles charted.

The collection of songs, as a rumination on the follies of the star system, midlife crises and the fleeting nature of life and love, worked very well and probably saved Adam a fortune in psychiatrist's bills. But he later decided he should never have made the album. "The car accident was quite serious," he said. "And you get terribly emotional after something like that. On reflection, if the accident hadn't happened.

I would never have made the album. It was valid for what it was, it just doesn't seem very valid now."[79]

Maybe it was all down to the painkillers, then.

"I thought I was seeing everything so much clearer than I ever had before," he said. "It's a bit like what I imagine it's like to be on acid."[80]

He added: "Given six months either way I would have not gone anywhere near a recording studio."[81]

Chapter Twenty-Five

"Sally Potter: Are you a Stray Cat?
Mike: No, I'm a roadie.
Sally Potter: Roadie sounds like some sort of vagrant. What is that
exactly?
Mike: It's like an army batman, only without the uniform. I make sure
there's enough beer, chips and rubbers to go round. I supply the birds, the
pills and the pot. And anything else that might be required to satisfy their
lust... carnal, or otherwise."

Ray Connolly, *Stardust,* 1974

Adam had spent nearly two years away from the acting business and several months recuperating from his accident. Scripts were piling up at home but he refused even to read them.

While Adam was working with Leo Sayer at Kingsway Studios on his second album, David Puttnam, the film producer, got in touch.

Puttnam had had a hit the year before with *That'll Be The Day,* a film about the rock business starring David Essex. He'd sent Adam a script for a follow-up, *Stardust.*

It was in the middle of the pile somewhere. Adam had barely glanced at it.

Not to be deterred, David brought the director, Michael Apted, and the writer, Ray Connolly, round to see him.

In the first film, *That'll Be The Day*, Jim MacLaine, the part played by David Essex, abandons lower-middle-class suburbia and the chance of a university education to pal up with Mike, a ne'er-do-well played by Ringo Starr. He gets a job at the fairground. In the end, Jim MacLaine increasingly finds himself attracted to a life in rock'n'roll.

As a result of the film, thousands of young men were given to assume that standing on the back of a dodgem car driven by a young woman and leaning forward from time to time to help the young woman with the steering would lead inevitably to meaningless sex, only to be disappointed when they learned that the strategy only works if you're David Essex.

In the second film, *Stardust*, Jim MacLaine forms a band, the Stray Cats. His old mate Mike becomes their manager and steers Jim to a troubled superstardom.

When Ringo decided he didn't want to repeat the Mike role in the second film, Puttnam, Apted and Connolly started looking for a replacement. Ian McShane was considered. Unbelievably, Keith Moon had already been screen tested for the part when the first film was being made.

"It turned out more like *Treasure Island*," said Ray Connolly. "Aaaaragh, Jim Lad! His eyes were all over the place. When you watched it, tears rolled down your face. And Keith, to his eternal credit, laughed too."[82]

Keith didn't get the part, but was given another role in the film, typecast as the insane drummer in the Stray Cats, the part he reprised in *Stardust*.

Initially Adam wasn't keen on playing Mike. He was still in pain from his accident. He'd left acting behind him. He was managing a superstar now.

David Puttnam had pester-power, however, to match Adam's. When he eventually got round to reading it, Adam realised that the script was excellent.

Production started in the summer of 1974 and, as the days rolled by, it soon became apparent that Adam did not play nicely with the other boys and girls. A particularly acute, but hardly surprising, animosity developed between Adam and Keith Moon.

Keith was drinking heavily during the shoot. His marriage was breaking up.

Adam needed to be in control. Keith preferred to be completely out of it. Adam needed order. Keith thrived on mayhem.

"I have never tried drugs," Adam said once. "Never even smoked a joint. Only ever taken Valium medically. It's not for any moral or health reasons, I just believe you should be able to carry on without any kind of crutch."

Keith loved a crutch or any kind of walking aid, especially if it was white and came in a little polythene bag.

Adam's lack of reliance on crutches was a matter of particular pride. It had been less than a year since he'd learned to walk again. He still had a slight limp which he incorporated into the role he was playing; a touch of vulnerability to round out what otherwise might have been an unsympathetic character.

Keith and Adam were, "like oil and water. One was fun, and the other was deadly serious. Two completely opposite poles."

Peter Butler, Keith Moon's driver and 'butler' was on the set, watching the whole sorry story unfold. "David Essex was OK. Adam Faith, I thought, was no fun whatsoever. He was the most unfun person I'd ever met. All he did was look in the money pages of the *Financial Times*, scouring for things. I thought he should lighten up. I never saw him smile. Even when Larry Hagman came on the scene, Adam Faith picked a row with him on the first morning, because Hagman had a Super-8 camera, and he was filming on the set, and Adam Faith didn't like it. He started in on Larry Hagman. He [Adam] was very unpleasant, I have no compunction about saying that at all."

Tony Fletcher, in his excellent biography *Dear Boy, The Life Of Keith Moon*, gives a vivid account of the problems. Dave Edmunds, who played the guitarist in the Stray Cats, quoted in the book, is vituperative: "We were on location somewhere at seven in the morning, and Keith ordered brandy. And Karl [Howman, another of the Stray Cats] got stuck into it. I think I got stuck into it as well. That was a hairy day. I told the director to fuck off in front of everybody, because I couldn't stop laughing. We were doing some scene where we had to mime in silence. They were doing a dialogue between Adam Faith and the club manager, and we had to pretend we were singing in complete silence in a room with 300 extras. I cracked up and so did Keith. Keith had a bottle of brandy hanging, like a drip. I have a photo with a bottle of brandy and a rubber tube coming down into Keith's mouth. I don't think a film has ever been made like that."[83]

"We didn't like [Adam]," says Peter Butler. "He didn't like me taking his photograph. He never socialised with us in the evenings. There was one particular time when we were shooting down south on a new motorway that was just being built. Keith and Karl Howman and the other boys were just having a laugh, messing around. Adam sent his driver over to us and he said, 'Adam's asked you to keep the noise down.' That's not what you want to say to Keith Moon. Keith turned round and said to the driver, 'You go and tell him to shut the fuck up. I could buy and sell him all day long. We are just having a laugh. Stop taking it so seriously.' We thought he was in it just to make money.

"Adam friended up with David Puttnam and the producers – we were like the riff-raff to him. Didn't have any time for us. We found him very big-headed – and in those circles – rock'n'roll – you can't do that.

"He didn't like us drinking on set. I used to put the brandy in an old Lucozade bottle just for a little tipple. We didn't used to get drunk or anything – it was just a little pick up."

The final scenes of the film take place at La Calahorra, a decaying castle near near Guadix, in southern Spain. On location, everyone stayed in a rat infested hotel – except of course for Adam who found accommodation in a swankier place some distance away.

In the early stages of filming, David Puttnam and Michael Apted were worried about Adam's performance. They thought he was sleepwalking through the scenes. But Adam refused to change his method. This was what Adam Faith the actor did: as little as possible. And he knew that, on screen, it worked. He was right too. His performance was widely praised.

"Adam Faith is first class," said Philip French in the *Times*.

Adam's "portrait of a rough diamond on the make could scarcely be more authentic," said Derek Malcolm in the *Guardian*.

He was nominated for a Best Supporting Actor BAFTA. Sir John Gielgud stole it off him for *Murder On The Orient Express*.

Adam hated watching himself on screen and eventually would refuse to do it.

"Whenever I see it, I only see myself, y'see. And any actor looking at his own performance isn't going to go into raptures. You always think, 'Christ that could have been better'. There were a few scenes I was really happy with."[84]

David Courtney had no trouble seeing where Adam's performance came from.

"You have to think – Terry was trained by Evie Taylor."

The shenanigans Mike gets up to in the script, the manipulations and double-dealings could, according to David, have been lifted directly from *The Evie Taylor Book Of Pop Management*.

"I remember watching *Stardust* – the bit where he's talking to Paul Nicolas about trying to get rid of him – where he says, 'You're too good for this band.' He put the words into your head to turn round your thinking and in the end you say, 'You know, you're right. I don't think I do want to do this any more'. So it's not on his shoulders, it's *you* that made the decision. It's a way of manipulating that could have come straight from Evie Taylor."

But Adam pours cold water on the idea that the film was in any sense a *roman a clef*.

"Please don't ask me if my own experiences as a singer were anything like what happens in the film cos I was out of that scene by '64, which is where the film really picks up from. When Cliff [Richard] and I were starting, we were playing a new sort of music, but the managerial side of things was still in the same old hands. It wasn't really till the Beatles came along that the old firms went out of business.

"I guess with Leo I'm now an 'amateur' manager myself – like Mike

Menary in *Stardust* – but we run things on a very different basis, we really do keep it like a family and very open.

"All the bribery and backstabbing that's in *Stardust* does go on in the music business, but I've never been involved in it [...] Very clean living lad, that's me."[85]

Chapter Twenty-Six

"Lost John made a pair of shoes of his own,
The finest shoes that even was worn,
Heels on the front, heels behind
You couldn't tell which way Lost John was gwine."

Lonnie Donegan, Lost John.

After filming was over, Adam went back to his 'amateur' managing with a vengeance.

He'd done well for his boy. Chris Wright, the joint chairman of Chrysalis Records, described the advance that Adam had secured from the company as, "a very big deal for a company like us. I'd rather not give the figure, but it was the largest amount of money we had put into a new artist and the largest promotional campaign we had mounted over a new act."

Leo's second album, *Just A Boy,* was released at the end of 1974. All tracks were written by Leo and David Courtney and it was produced by David and Adam.

The American magazine *Billboard* gave it the thumbs up: "There is no reason why the artist should not be able to score several hit singles from this set. Sayer is a stylist who is at his best when backed only by the piano of writing partner David Courtney."

Thanks in some part to the "largest promotional campaign" that Chrysalis had ever mounted, but mostly to the quality of the product, it went to number four in the British albums chart and, more crucially, to number 16 in the US *Billboard* charts. The single release from the album, 'Long Tall Glasses (I Can Dance)', went Top 10 in America.

Some very serious money was about to be made.

Adam decided to slim down the management team.

"Adam made a lot of money out of Leo," says Andrew Tribe. "He got rid of us before the money started coming through the pipeline – before the royalties came in. He knew it was coming."

Keith Altham had been doing Leo's PR. Even though he was a friend of longstanding, when the time came, Adam had no compunction about sacking him. "He gave me the elbow, then he left me standing in the pouring rain. It was a very poorly executed manoeuvre. He didn't have to do that. He didn't need to shut your fingers in the door when he slammed the door in your face. Adam made a lot of enemies around this time. He upset a lot of people. Money was his guiding light. He had a ruthless drive to get rich which was his undoing."

"Terry came to me one day a while after his car accident," says Andrew Tribe, "and said, 'We've got to get rid of Dave [Courtney].' I said, 'What are you talking about?' And he said, 'He doesn't do anything.' And I said, 'What do you mean? He wrote the songs, he produced him and he found him.' And he just said, 'Yeah, but ...'

"He wanted me to put my vote with his and get rid of Dave. And I just said no. And then he went to Dave and got rid of me instead.

"Then a few months later, Dave called me and said, 'You'll never guess what – he's got rid of me.'"

They learned that Adam had brought in a new face: Colin Berlin was a big time agent who'd been Eve Taylor's husband, Maurice's, partner in the old days. He'd since helped shape Tom Jones' career and knew the business inside out, on both sides of the Atlantic.

David was understandably confused and hurt at being, effectively, fired. "So, Leo was now on tour and was in America all the time," says David. "And when it got to time for a new album – well obviously Leo's out there and I was back here. Terry said, 'You'll have to send him the music on a cassette for him to work on.' And I said, 'I'm not doing that – that's not how it works. We write together. He stands next to me at the piano and we come up with stuff. This remote thing ain't gonna work because I need that feedback.'

"But he and Colin had already plotted to get me out of the picture. So it was a way of presenting me with a scenario where I would say, 'Well, I'm not going to do that'. Which made it *my* decision.

"Neither of them said, 'Well, why don't you go to America and be with him and write with him on the road?' because that wasn't what they had planned. And at that point I thought, 'Well, OK, if that's the way it is – I now feel confident enough to do my own thing.' I was at a crossroads, I guess. After that I didn't see Terry for about four years or something.

"But I discovered many years later, when Leo and I were reunited, that Terry had told him *I* didn't want to work with *him* any more which was totally untrue."

The wisdom of breaking up the writing team that had produced Leo's hits seems never to have been questioned by Adam or Colin Berlin. As Andrew tribe says: "Adam wasn't interested in Leo personally or musically."

"So suddenly he's taking me to America," says Leo, "with producers saying, 'Can I work with your boy?' – that sort of stuff. I had all these songs in my head and Adam said to me, 'Dave doesn't want to work with you any longer.' And I go, 'What?!' I'm about to pick up the phone and Adam says, 'Don't pick up the phone to him, it's all gone very strange.' So I'm thinking, 'Shit, what am I going to do?'"[86]

The main thing that had "all gone very strange" was Adam's obsession with moving the entire Leo operation to America – for tax reasons, contractual reasons, big bucks reasons, Big Time reasons – and clear up any remaining commitments, like an obligation to deliver an album to Chrysalis, as quickly and as cheaply as possible.

"Adam said, 'Just get the songs together. We've got to rush at this. We've got to deliver an album to Chrysalis, so let's just do it and get it out of the way.' I said, 'No, it's important. I've written some great songs.' And he said, 'Just finish them.'"

Adam told Leo that he'd brought Russ Ballard in to produce the new album. This was fine with Leo. He had a lot of respect for Russ.

"Tel wanted me to produce the new Leo album," says Russ. "But I was busy with my own album. He told me, 'Leo's album's got to be finished in two weeks.' Bear in mind it usually takes two months. He said, 'We'll split the money – you get half of what I get.' So I ended up playing on nearly every track on it, picking the songs, everything. I was working from 11 to seven at Island on my own album and then I jump in my car and drive round to Kingsway Studios and work from eight-thirty until about 11, and I'd get home about one or two in the morning. Leo's album was finished in 13 days. And mixed. We'd do two songs a night. I'd play piano and play guitar and marimba. He got me cheap."

The album, *Another Year*, released in September 1975, went to number eight in the UK albums chart and 'Moonlighting', the single taken from the album, went to number two. Neither were promoted in America.

Leo's next album would be a big budget affair, using the cream of LA's session musicians and produced by Richard Perry, the man who brought us *Nilsson Schmilsson*, Ringo's *Goodnight Vienna*, Art Garfunkel's *Breakaway*, with the stand-out single 'I Only Have Eyes For You', and Andy Williams' *Solitaire*.

Leo was iffy. "When Adam said I was going to work with hotshot producer Richard Perry, I said, 'What? He's boring!' I didn't want to do that. I wanted to work with someone groovy and funky!"

David Courtney could understand Leo's frustration. "You see, the trouble is, Leo walked out of the world of rock'n'roll into the pop world. That's what Colin Berlin did for him. I mean, Terry and Colin had him go to Vegas and all that and once you do that there's no going back. You lose the credibility. And Leo realised that."

Years later, Adam explained his thinking to Keith Altham: "'Leo's not a rock star, he's a pop star. Roger Daltrey is a rock star. Let me explain the difference to you. You would leave your girlfriend or your wife alone with Leo Sayer, but you would never leave them alone with Roger Daltrey.'

"I told Roger that," says Keith. "He thought it was very funny. And very accurate. Mind you, I wouldn't leave them with Adam Faith either. And he was a pop star."

As it turned out, rock or pop, *Endless Flight*, the first of three albums Richard Perry produced for Leo, went platinum in the US. Two singles from the album, 'You Make Me Feel Like Dancing' and 'When I Need You', both went to number one. Everywhere.

Between 1973 and 1977, Leo enjoyed a run of seven consecutive singles, all of which went Top 10 in the UK. The only UK artiste – as opposed to a group – ever previously to have achieved such a feat was... you've guessed it ... Adam Faith.

In many respects the story of Leo Sayer's rise to the top was designed from the same blueprint as the plot of *Stardust*: a shabby tale of backstabbing, double dealing and dark deceit by a ruthless, unfeeling manager, an everyday story of music biz bloodletting.

What, perhaps, makes it extraordinary is that the backstabbed – Andrew Tribe, David Courtney and Keith Altham – all ended up – after a space of months or years – back on good terms with Adam, working with him, socialising, laughing, playing golf.

Adam had appropriated – stolen – David Courtney's discovery. He had broken up his successful and creatively fulfilling writing partnership with Leo. He had denied him the chance of earning a fortune. Nevertheless, a few years later ...

"I was over in America on a trip promoting my album or something," says David, "and I happened to be staying at Le Mondrian Hotel when I bumped into a girl called Melanie Green in the lobby. She'd been Terry's PA for ages. She said, 'Oh my God, Dave, what are you doing here? Tel's here, did you know?' And I said, 'Oh really.' And she said, 'He would love to see you.' And I thought, 'Well this is going to be a bit strange, but at least we would be on neutral ground here.'

"So Melanie said, 'Look, he's gonna be down here in the lobby at six o'clock.' And I told her that I was going out to dinner that night, but would be coming through the lobby around that time. I remember standing in the lobby of Le Mondrian Hotel and the lift doors opening and when he spotted me his face lit up. It was like one of those things out of a chocolate box advert – we sort of ran towards each other in the lobby and that was it. And from that moment on it was like nothing had happened. He said, 'What are you doing over here?' And I said that I was going to be moving here. And he said, 'I've got to get you together with Leo because he's doing another album.' And... it... it was like nothing had happened."

Readers are not recommended to try this with their friends. In the same way as flirting on the backs of dodgems only works if you're David Essex, stabbing your friends in the back then making it up as if nothing ever happened probably only works if you're Adam Faith.

David did write more songs with Leo. And he produced his 1979 album, *Here* – "a return to Sayer's elemental rock style," as *Billboard* called it, "with r&b and bluesy overtones" on which he's "joined by cream of the crop session players such as percussionist Paulinho Da Costa, bassist Chuck Rainey and guitarists Fred Tackett and Steve Cropper." "Duck" Dunn, Jeff Baxter, Al Kooper and Steve Lukather are on it, too.

Adam was not always the bad guy. One night while having dinner with Paul and Linda along with Cher and Harry Nilsson, the talk turned to the old days and everyone around the table (well, probably not Cher. Or Linda. Or Harry) remembered how much they owed to skiffle. Adam had been in the Worried Men with Hurgy. Paul had been in the Quarrymen with John. In a sense, both owed everything they had achieved to the King of Skiffle, Lonnie Donegan.

In 1976, Lonnie, though still just 45 years old, had suffered a severe heart attack and three strokes. His survival – he lived another 27 years – was thanks only to timely intervention and quadruple bypass surgery.

It took a while to pull the idea together. The album, *Puttin' On The Style*, produced by Adam, was released in 1978. Adam was proud of the result, and hugely gratified by its effect on Lonnie.

As Adam told Radio Stoke in his last ever radio interview before he died: "Every time a new star came into the studio to work with Lonnie – Elton John, Brian May, Ringo Starr, Ron Wood, Leo Sayer,

Rory Gallagher – he was so surprised. He couldn't believe that he had influenced them so much."

The album introduced a whole new generation to Lonnie's work and led to further collaborations between him and Billy Joe Spears, Albert Lee and Van Morrison.

Chapter Twenty-Seven

"Gone are the days when, ... everything seemed possible.... We thought things were changing and all that romantic crap." Each of these characters is isolated by his ambition from warm personal relationships. As Caroline tells Kramer: "You don't believe in anything really do you – except your own ambition?"[87]

D. Keith Peacock, *The Fascination Of Fascism:*
The Plays Of Stephen Poliakoff

Stephen Poliakoff first came to the attention of the theatrical world in 1969 when, as a 16-year-old student at the exclusive Westminster School, he wrote and directed a play called *Granny*. It starred fellow student Nigel Planer, who later played Neil the Hippy in *The Young Ones*.

After its premiere at the school, he organised other performances at clubs and community centres and got the *Times* drama critic to come out and watch.

Pretty Boy, written when he was 19 and produced by the Royal Court Theatre, was followed by a prodigious and varied output. *Clever Soldiers* at the Hampstead Theatre was praised for its "destructive ecstasy". *Heroes* at the Royal Court was acclaimed for its "fire and anger which occasionally bathes the stage in a sulphurous glare". Few doubted that this *wunderkind* was the next big thing in British theatre.

His latest play, *City Sugar* ("a savage dissection of that pristine slagheap of Our Times – mass culture" – *Time Out*), had opened at the Bush, a pub theatre in Shepherds Bush, and was set to transfer to the West End. Adam was offered the lead.

The plot is as follows:

Leonard Brazil, a Leicester local radio DJ, spends all day in his grubby studio on a mission to "spin another circle of happiness and pour a little more sugar over the city", churning out papsongs for his audience while looking back in to the 'golden age' of the sixties, when pop culture had something to do with change and revolution. His life is contrasted with that of two shelf stackers in a supermarket, bored out of their skulls, bullied by the permanent surveillance of CCTV, but lulled into uncomplaining placidity by the supermarket's muzak substitute, Leonard and his papsongs.

Leonard comes up with a contrived "Competition of the Century" as a result of which he gets to meet one of the girls and tries, by various means, to get her to understand the fraud he's perpetrating. The girl is not to be convinced, so Leonard, now utterly disillusioned, accepts a job at Capital Radio in London: the politically confused implication being that this represents an abandonment of all ideals and an absolute sell-out.

"In the old days when I was working as a singer," Adam said, "I used to panic when I wasn't working. I used to be so particular about it all. Now I just work if something good comes up.

"This is the first thing that's excited me since *Stardust*. It's a coincidence that the two best things I've read happen to be connected with the entertainment business. I had a load of scripts sent to me after *Stardust* but they were all crap. I had offers for West End theatre but they were all rubbish".

In contrast, Adam thought that Stephen Poliakoff was "a fuckin' genius".

"Naturally I'm apprehensive about doing the bloody thing, but it is so exhilarating even though there is a gut-clenching tension about it."[88]

fought the law: with Ronnie Quibell and Sherriff C. Malan, 1965. TOPHAM PICTUREPOINT/TOPFOTO

And the law won: back in the UK with Maurice Press. REX FEATURES

Adam as the chairman of the board. DEZO HOFFMANN/REX FEATURES

"He barely scraped my shoulder." Adam and Sandie Shaw, 1967. BILL HOWARD/ASSOCIATED NEWSPAPERS/REX FEATURES

Adam and Jackie, a quiet wedding, 1967. PAUL POPPER/ KEYSTONE/GETTY IMAGES

"Sometimes we kick our shoes off and think: 'Well, look at us.'" ELLIDGE/DAILY EXPRESS/HULTON ARCHIVE/GETTY IMAGES

"Does money matter to you?" "Not 'alf." M. McKEOWN/EXPRESS/GETTY IMAGES

"Strange how potent cheap music can be." *Private Lives*, 1968. ASSOCIATED NEWSPAPERS/REX FEATURES

"It's women like that who built the Empire." Sybil and Adam. ASSOCIATED NEWSPAPERS/REX FEATURES

Billy Liar, Glasgow Citizen's Theatre, 1969. SCOTTISH THEATRE ARCHIVE, UNIVERSITY OF GLASGOW LIBRARY

Katya. DENNIS OULDS/CENTRAL PRESS/GETTY IMAGES

The many jackets of *Budgie*. ITV/REX FEATURES

"There are two things I hate in life, Budgie, and you're both of them." ITV/REX FEATURES

"Leave it out, Hazel." ITV/REX FEATURES

City Sugar opened at the Comedy Theatre on March 4, 1976. Adam had played the Palladium, he had co-starred with Dame Sybil Thorndike, he had been nominated for a BAFTA, but this was his West End debut as a straight actor.

"I have a routine when I work in theatre," he said, a luvee once again. "I get there an hour before and psyche myself into the character. I don't talk to anybody. I keep everybody away to keep the tension going. It's almost like going into a trance.

"For the last week I've been thinking this play's gotta be a success, must be a success. That's the tension you go under. I spoke to my wife about it and she said everything I've done – rep, films, records, – it's all the same pattern. And in the bath this morning, I thought to myself if this play isn't a success, if I don't come off well, there's no way I haven't benefitted from working on this play for the last few months."[89]

"Len is completely disillusioned with his life because he feels he's compromised himself. He's sucked into the whole idea of being a star. He didn't know when to quit. So he'll go on doing the same thing all his life. I could have gone on playing Budgie on TV but then I'd never be doing this."

Ian Christie, in the *Daily Express,* hated the play and Adam in it: "The play attempts to poke fun at the more obvious idiocies of the pop cult but it is written without much wit and misses most of its opportunities to attack its subject matter with satire. Any humour and subtlety that might have been in the script is flattened forcibly by Adam Faith, who gives a performance that is quite lifeless. It is the theatrical equivalent of the Tony Blackburn show."[90]

Other reviews were ecstatic.

Irving Wardle, in the *Times,* said it was "scathingly brilliant". "Leonard's commentaries are a tour de force, as a parody of the DJ style equipped with a ferocious sub-text, and Adam Faith puts them over with a savagery held in check by hard professionalism."

Michael Billington, in the *Guardian,* praised the play's "genuine animus against the brutalism of our provincial cities and of the society which treats its young as consumers ripe for exploitation."

The posters outside the theatre, though, mostly went with the *Sunday Telegraph's* assessment, "Very, very funny."

It ran until mid-May and won a "Most Promising Playwright" award for Stephen Poliakoff.

Adam "The Actor" Faith went into hibernation for three years after *City Sugar*, then woke up, knocked off three movies in fairly quick succession, and slumped back into somnolence.

The first, *Yesterday's Hero*, is a football flick written by Jackie Collins and is strenuously *not* anything to do with the life and times of George Best. Ian McShane plays an alcoholic footballer trying to claw his way back into the game. Suzanne Somers plays the woman he loves. Paul Nicholas plays the Club Chairman. Adam plays the Club Manager. The plot plays fast and loose with plausibility.

The characters have names like Clint and Cloudy. The clothes look as if they were made for the Man at C&A 'Rogue Male' range. The hair is tinted crazy-foam. Sometimes the characters smoke, sometimes they drink, but mostly they sit on velvet sofas and allow impish smiles to play around their lips. In some scenes, the curtains are quite elaborate which at least gave the audience something nice to look at. Paul Nicholas sang the theme tune.

Foxes was a proper Hollywood movie and a definite cut above. Starring Jodie Foster and Scott Baio, it was directed by Adrian Lyne, who went on to make *Flashdance*, *9½ Weeks*, *Indecent Proposal* and *Fatal Attraction*. It's a disco teen-flick with attitude. Adam only had a cough and a spit but he makes his presence felt. Just as he once specialised in tearaways, now he seemed only to play managers. This time, he's the tour manager of a rock band, and Jodie Foster's father. In the sense that it's a tale of crazy-mixed-up-kids-with-even-crazier-mixed-up-parents, it could be seen as the 1980 equivalent of *Beat Girl*, except that these crazy-mixed-up-kids are Valley Girls and thus have more money, booze, drugs and knowledge than Dave, Plaid Shirt or Dodo ever dreamed of. It has since been hailed as a prototype Generation-X movie, but at the time, when it was running at the St Martins Lane Odeon, you never had to book.

The third was *McVicar* – to be said in a defiant, threatening voice – *McVicaaaar.* This was a major British movie shot at Pinewood Studios under the auspices of The Who Films, a production company that was originally set up to make *The Kids Are Alright* – a history-of-The-Who-documentary, and went on to make the sublime *Quadrophenia. McVicar* would be their first non-Who-related film, though Roger Daltrey was in the title role.

John McVicar was an armed robber who had the honour for a while of being generally regarded as "The Most Dangerous Man In Britain". He was apprehended, sentenced to a long time in prison, escaped several times, was recaptured, then realised every social worker's dream scenario by taking an Open University degree in sociology and getting a first. When he came out he published an autobiography, *McVicar By Himself,* which he subsequently adapted as a film script.

"Being a thief is a terrific life," he said. "But the trouble is they put you in jail for it."

McVicar the movie was directed by Tom Clegg, who did the second *Sweeney* movie, so knew how to handle Britcrim Gangster Dialogue. "Bring in Gorran. I'm gonna beat the shit out of him and that scrubber of his." "But ..." "*Shut it!*"

Adam played Walter "Angel Face" Probyn, who, curiously, was not, and never had been, a manager. Instead he is "The Hoxton Houdini", McVicar's accomplice in his escape from Durham prison. Adam's hair is dyed a dirty brown for the part and he sports an impressive pair of sideburns.

"Oh Probyn," says the prison governor, "we ought to be seeing about your parole application."

"No, I don't think so, Mr Graham."

"Why not?"

"I'm planning to make me own way out soon."

The film had some snotty reviews: "The style of *McVicar* is mere TV show-off – loud noises, staccato editing, lots of rack focus," said *Movietone News.* Some critics felt that it let itself down by portraying all the convicts and felons as decent, down to earth blokes with great senses of humour while anyone in authority was inhuman, harsh and completely unsympathetic.

Others, however, saw this as its chief virtue.

"When Adam and Roger were working on films like *McVicar* and *Stardust*," said Peter Butler, Keith Moon's "butler", "they were just acting out what they would have been if they hadn't been rock stars. They would have probably nicked cars, done something bad and gone to prison."

Meanwhile Roger, Adam's brother – not Daltrey – had got into more trouble with the law. He was charged in Cape Town with dealing dagga – South African cannabis – although he denied ever seeing it.

Adam put up the £10,000 bail, but Roger, terrified of what life in South African jail might be like, jumped bail. He later surrendered to the police, but all the same, Adam forfeited the 10 grand.

Changing fortunes and Adam's increasingly transatlantic lifestyle kept the Faith family on the move.

Henfield was abandoned for Lindfield, a half-hour drive away, where they rented a place until Perry Press, estate agent to the stars, could find them something more suited.

For a time, Adam considered buying a psychiatric hospital. He took David Essex with him for a viewing: "After the sale, the inmates would be moved out," says David, "but they were currently still in situ. As we walked in, a patient welcomed us by smearing baked beans all over his face. But driven by sheer enthusiasm, Adam was oblivious to the confused souls surrounding us as he strode around the building, pointing out where the snooker table and the master bedroom would be."[91]

Eventually Adam discovered Warren House, a home fit for a king, and possibly even good enough for a discerning ex-popstar/actor/manager. Built for Countess Castle-Stewart in the 18th century, it was a Grade 2 listed Palladian pile overlooking Ashdown Forest (the 100-acre wood where Winnie The Pooh was said to live).

Adam bought it from John Paul Jones, bass player with Led Zeppelin, and it had featured as a location in Led Zeppelin's film *The Song Remains The Same*, the oak panelling, fine historic fireplaces and decorative plaster ceilings being shown off to excellent advantage as John Paul roams through the downstairs reception rooms on a horse.

Adam was barely there for more than a week at a time. He often flew back and forth from Los Angeles twice a month. Eventually it seemed more sensible simply to relocate the whole family to LA. They rented a house in Mandeville Canyon, just off Sunset Boulevard, but after three weeks of California sunshine Jackie was sobbing every day to go home – so back they moved.

They bought Heasman's Lodge Farm near Crowborough, but had only lived there for six months when another property tempted them. An agent phoned Adam while he was in California, and Adam cancelled a ski weekend to fly home for a viewing.

Crowhurst Place was owned by Sir John Davis, Adam's boss when he'd been a messenger boy at Rank. In Adam's eyes it surpassed every other house he had owned (and he had owned many by this time): a mediaeval manor house, possessing many fine features including, according to Pevsner's *Buildings Of England*, "a full height round oriel window bay inserted to Great Hall, jettied gabled porch to left of centre in spandrel and jowled chamfered posts and an irregular six bay facade with the first floor jettied on a moulded bressumer".

It came with 26 acres of gardens and parkland, a small lake, a tithe barn, a dovecote and an open air Elizabethan theatre.

Sir John asked for £250,000 ("You've done well for yourself, young Nelhams"); Adam offered £235,000. They shook on it. And if he'd built a bonfire and kept it fed day after day with handfuls of tenners, it could not have consumed his cash more quickly or effectively than did ownership of Crowhurst.

And so the eighties, the Thatcher years, began with Adam living in a medieval manor house, commuting to the fleshpots of California, skiing in the Alps, windsurfing in Antibes, and, when he could snatch a few moments from his busy schedule, enjoying family life with his beautiful wife and daughter. What could possibly go wrong?

Chapter Twenty-Eight

"In a helicopter, if the blades spin down more than 10-15% from their normal velocity, there is no way to convert potential or kinetic energy into spinning such that the helicopter will start to fly again. If you can't restart your engine, therefore, your helicopter can very quickly become a rock."[92]

Philip Greenspun, *Learning To Fly Helicopters*

A man and woman drop their child off at a posh looking boarding school, then drive home through idyllic countryside. The man turns to the woman. She is groomed. It is still early morning, so she must have been up all night having her hair done.

"Joanne," the man says, "there's something you ought to know. It concerns the house. And the kids. It's time to go it alone." There is a moment's intake of breath because she thinks and we think that he's broaching the subject of divorce. But it's not that.

"I'm starting my own business," the man says, with a face that could have won the Eurovision Smug Contest against tough opposition from French chefs and German engineers.

"John's with me," the smugger says, "Ian's with me. We've got the backing."

"David, that's fantastic," says Joanne in a voice that made Her Majesty the Queen Mother sound as if she was permanently auditioning for *EastEnders*.

When this little drama, a TV ad for the Renault 25, was broadcast in 1986, most sensible people wanted to burn down their televisions then strip off their clothes and, dressed in paint and feathers, form loosely organised mobs to seek out all Renault 25 owners and nail them to trees on the off chance that one or two of them might be guilty of displaying an iota of Joanne and David's toxic self-satisfied arsiness, then seek out David's cohorts, John and Ian.

The irritation has never subsided. Even today, to see the ad on YouTube, you have to search with the phrase "Die You Yuppie Bastards Die".

Sometimes, immediately after you'd seen the Joanne and David ad, you'd see a man go into a pub. The man would be approached by a second man who would thrust a phone number scribbled on a scrap of paper into his hand and hiss: "British Gas shares. It couldn't be easier to do. Phone this number and they'll send you information on how to apply. If you see Sid, tell him, won't you?"

This was what we were supposed to do in the eighties. We were supposed to get the support of John and Ian and form our own companies. We were supposed to pad our shoulders, roll up the sleeves of our suit jackets, clean our BMWs – or Renault 25s – with Perrier and drink in wine bars instead of pubs. We were supposed to purchase shares in the newly privatised companies that bafflingly, as tax-payers, we already owned, and buy our own council houses. This, it was argued, would bring an end to all the confrontations between bosses and unions – between capital and labour – that, according to popular mythology, had so marred the seventies because we'd all be capitalists. We'd have nothing to fight about any more. We'd all be on the same side.

"Enterprise culture" or "stakeholder culture" as it was called when Tony Blair took over from Margaret Thatcher and John Major as senior evangelist for the new religion, never really took hold outside a few selected postcodes in the South East of England and the fevered imaginations of headline writers. Admittedly, some perfectly ordinary people bought their own council houses. Some even bought the shares.

Then they sold them again when they lost their jobs and began to wonder whether the whole idea didn't contain some sort of flaw.

Adam had been an early adopter of enterprise culture. He'd been buying and selling Shell at 128 ever since he'd been able to rustle up the 128 to do it with. In 1971, when the patchouli mist of hippy lilies-of-the-field idealism was still fresh in the air, the *Daily Mirror* had asked him, "Does money matter to you?"

"Not 'alf," he'd replied.

At last, it seemed, the rest of the world was catching up with him.

In the summer of 1980, Adam decided that what he really needed was a helicopter. He found out that you could pick one up second hand for only £25,000. He cleared his diary for six weeks and booked himself a course of lessons at Bristow's Helicopter flying school at Redhill. He put down a deposit of £6,000 on a little two seater Bell G5 so he could practise, and started looking around for a Jet Ranger.

On his first solo flight, he encountered a problem. He had ascended to about 350 ft above the airfield and all seemed to be going well. Then the helicopter lurched and a voice in his headset said, "Mayday, mayday, Mike Yankee, going down."

Eventually he realised that "Mike Yankee" was him, that "Mayday" signified some sort of distress, and that "going down" wasn't nearly as much fun as it sounded. His helicopter was tumbling from the sky.

"Why me?" he said. "Oh, God. Why me?" To which a passenger, had there been one, might have replied, "Because you're in a helicopter and you don't know how to fly it properly."

At this point, either he did something sensible, or the helicopter – or God – took pity. It rose a little, just enough to clip, but not crash into, a stand of trees. Then it landed on its side in a field. Adam walked away unhurt.

It was later discovered that he had neglected most of the emergency drills and safety procedures he'd been trained for, including switching off the fuel cock and magnetos. In a less generous universe, Adam would have been charred in a fireball.

There was an important lesson to be learned here – a warning from

God, the gods, fate, or Icarus: if you try to fly too high using mechanisms you do not fully understand – be they workings of a helicopter, the wax on your wings or the financial markets – you will come crashing to the ground.

He never learned it. As he'd proved too often in the past, if he wasn't pitting his wits, his charm, his skill or his nerve against some fresh challenge, proving himself, he didn't feel alive. He said it himself: "'Always attack the thing you most fear.' Don't just sit there, in your armchair, letting life frighten you – go out and piss on your fear."

The experience didn't even put him off helicopters even though the fighter pilot's dictum – that when you've crashed and burned you have to get straight back in a plane before you lose your nerve – only applies if you get shot down. If you flew the plane into a tree because you forgot to pull back on the stick thing like you'd been told, it's probably best to ask to be transferred to a desk job.

"I used to go up in the helicopter with him," says Andrew Tribe. "We always got lost. He'd be flying low to look at the road signs to try and find out where he was. We always got lost – he was terrible."

The helicopter was kept in its own hangar in the back garden at Crowhurst, with the six trail bikes, the Rolls Royce Corniche and the Range Rover. On the lake were a pair of black swans and its water teemed with 900 trout.

"We used to get together to play golf at Kingswood," says Peter Thorp, guitar player with the Roulettes and friend forever. "He'd fly over in his helicopter. Adam'd ring up the Golf Club and say, 'Is it OK for me to land my helicopter on your practice ground?' And they'd said, 'Oh yes, Mr. Faith, no problem.' And they would close the practice ground for the day. We used to play a lot of golf. He was always intent on winning – he was *very* serious about it."

For ten years, Adam, Jackie and Katya had rarely stayed in one place long enough to bother unpacking the tea-chests. Crowhurst Place, the house that had seemed so perfect when they'd moved in, lasted no longer than any of the others. The upkeep was, indeed, laughably expensive. Floral carvings in spandrels, jowled chamfered posts and moulded bressumers do not, they discovered, maintain themselves, besides which, when the cold came, the house used up about a tanker-full of heating oil a week and two full-time gardeners were needed to keep the 26 acres in check.

They put it on the market. Rod Stewart came to look. He decided it was too small. Ridley Scott, the film director who'd just made John Hurt's chest explode in *Alien*, came to look. In the end Adam sold it to a French Canadian property dealer for, it was reported in the *Daily Mail*, more than three times what he'd paid for it.

The property market was booming. Jackie was a genius at remodelling and redesigning. They added a huge bank loan to their profit from Crowhurst and began to add to their existing property portfolio – by this time, among others, they had a complex of farm buildings they planned to develop, a factory, a small row of shops and, for themselves, Old Shoyswell Manor Farm, another historic building near Etchingham.

On May 11, 1982, the *Sun* reported that Adam was considering the purchase of Hever Castle in Kent, Anne Boleyn's old home that the Astors had made their own. It was on the market at £13.5 million.

A few weeks later, there was a mini-crash in the property market. The banks panicked and called in their loans. Working from what had become his base – a corner table in the Soda Fountain at Fortnum & Mason-Adam sold off their portfolio, but was forced to take a loss.

Finally he and Jackie put their own home on the market and moved to a cottage in the grounds – or rather three of the cottages which Jackie had converted into a comfortable five bedroom house, so the privation was only relative.

Adam also managed, eventually, to "squeeze £300,000 out of the bank" to buy "a pretty Georgian House" in Kent and send Katya to the fee-paying Croydon High School for Girls. The debts, however, continued to mount.

If such matters bothered Terry Nelhams, Adam Faith remained unruffled.

"He had this wonderful knack of making everybody believe he was a multi-millionaire," says David Courtney. "He taught me that when you walk into a big posh hotel you've to look like you belong. You don't walk in there and look down because people will spot it – like that! He always loved that thing of driving a Rolls Royce up to the hotel and getting out wearing jeans and T-shirt. He loved all that Acton Boy Made Good stuff."

"He was always wearing a pair of jeans, a T-shirt and a pair of trainers," says Laurence Marks, co-writer, with Maurice Gran, of most of the big TV hits of the last 40 years, including Adam's *Love Hurts*. "It was all he ever wore – which was usually fine except for the night I took him to the Reform Club. They said, 'You can't come in dressed like that.' So they took him downstairs and gave him one of the barman's suits and shoes.

"Often he would sit at his table and when the waiter would come over, he would say, 'I'd like two pieces of toast and a pot of marmalade.' Everyone else in the restaurant would be ordering big meals and Maurice and I just thought, 'God, he's so cool'."

"He was the only person I have ever met," says Keith Altham, "with the nerve to greet the *maitre d'* of the Savoy Grill with a cheery 'Got a table, cock?' It was the same greeting for kings, queens, popes and peasants. The *maitre d'* promptly instructed one of his waiters to find a table for 'Party of Cock'."

"In the eighties, I went to interview him after a matinee," writes Robert Elms. "There was a slight air of melancholy about him. I mean, he was a very big star and it hadn't even been a full house in the theatre, but he was still Adam Faith. So, he gets ready and puts on his camel coat – cashmere of course – and he says, 'Robert, let's do the interview in my office.'

"So we go out of the theatre and there is his canary yellow Rolls Royce. Now, you can't get louder than a canary yellow Rolls Royce. So we get in his Roller and we drive over town. We drive to Jermyn Street and he pulls up at the back of Fortnums. And he gets out of the car but he doesn't turn the engine off, he doesn't park it. So I said, 'Adam, what are you doing? We're in the middle of Jermyn Street.' And he says, 'Aww don't worry about that, Robert.' And we just walk into Fortnums. And I saw a guy from Fortnums rush out and get into the car and drive it off.' He didn't have an office – he just held court in the tea room in Fortnums every day.

"There's a table saved for him there, with his name on it, and so he goes in and sits down. He calls everyone 'cock – 'All right, cock?' he goes – and they all really love it. All the staff run over and they fuss over him. One of them brings over one of those old-fashioned phones and plugs it into a socket that they have had specially installed just for him. All just so Adam can carry on his business. And all through the interview he's ringing up people and saying things like, 'If I were you I'd be investing in...'

"He's selling a house somewhere and buying something else – it was just fabulous to watch – it was like a man conducting an orchestra. And all the time he's telling me these stories. So I'm listening to all this and I'm gently ribbing him – I say, 'Look, Adam, you've got the camel coat, and you've got the yellow Roller and the phone plugged in in the middle of Fortnums, but surely on the car shouldn't you really have one of those number plates – AFaith or Budgie1?' and he looks at me and he says, 'Robert, it doesn't pay to be *too* flash.'"

Throughout the eighties and nineties, the jeans, torn and used as a notepad, scribbled with reminders and phone numbers, the T-shirt, the trainers were his uniform. It was another little feather in his cap, another little challenge: proving the scruff from Acton who called everybody 'cock' could command tables in the finest restaurants and have cabinet ministers and rock gods at his beck and call. In the sixties he customarily wore the finest mohair money could buy. Now he'd only deign to get the suit and tie out of the wardrobe for an extra special occasion, like the time Mrs. Thatcher invited him to drinks at Number Ten in the run up to the 1983 General Election, along with other top celebrities like Jayne Torvill & Christopher Dean, Steve Davis, the snooker player, and Penelope Keith.

The Roller was part of the branding, too. "Terry had this yellow Corniche," says Andrew Tribe. "It was a horrible colour, really loud. He decided to sell it, and this guy, a Colonel, bought it. But two days after he sold it, Terry decided he wanted it back. So he kept phoning this colonel. It was over Christmas. He phoned him on Christmas Day, Boxing Day, all the way into New Year – drove him mad. In the end he said, 'All right. You have it back then'."

He was often in America at the same time as his old friend, the photographer Terry O'Neill. "We were all in Los Angeles at the same time," says Terry, "Parky [Michael Parkinson] and Trevor Nunn and Adam and me. Adam would be staying in the Beverly Hills Hotel and he used to keep Leo Sayer down in a little hotel down on the Santa Monica freeway – right on the freeway. Poor Leo. He put up with a lot.

"We would go out to dinner every night – swan about. He used to wear a fur coat all the time – even in the heat."

Everybody remembers the fur coat. "He called it Florence," says Andrew Tribe. "Ratty old thing. They kept it in storage for him in the Beverly Hills Hotel."

"A line of real A-list Hollywood celebrities are queuing up to get a table at one of the most fashionable restaurants in Hollywood," says Robert Elms. "And Adam just walks in and walks straight to the front of the queue. Adam is not a Hollywood star by any means. But all the staff run over and say: 'Of course, we'll find you a table – come this way.' And all the stars – Jack Nicholson and that – are looking at him. It turns out that he'd been in Hollywood for a couple of months and he'd heard that the waitress who'd served him before wasn't well and he'd gone to see her four times in hospital. He'd liked her and he thought he'd been given good service. And because of that, the staff loved him and got him a table over all the other A-list celebrities. Just because he'd taken time."

Though there is no hint of impropriety having taken place in this instance, it has to be said that Adam often took time for waitresses. His head was easily turned by a prettily turned ankle, a forgiving smile, a raised eyebrow, the right kind of skin. Marriage and family notwithstanding, he had never lost his taste for what he once described as 'carnal mileage'.

"He didn't have to go looking for women," says Keith Altham. "They threw themselves at him. I've never seen a man have such an effect on women – with one exception – George Best. They would just launch themselves at him. I think it was because first of all he was extremely good looking, but secondly he was small and non-threatening. So women felt safe with him – which was a mistake, but at the same time it drew women to him. And he had charm and charisma, and they fell at his feet."

"Although we were great mates," says Terry O'Neill, "he never involved me in his shenanigans, which I always appreciated. He knew I loved Jackie and I would have bollocked him about it. I didn't see anything. We never used to talk about it."

Such discretion wasn't always easy to sustain.

Chapter Twenty-Nine

"One might compare the relation of the ego to the id with that between a rider and his horse. The horse provides the locomotor energy, and the rider has the prerogative of determining the goal and of guiding the movements of his powerful mount towards it. But all too often in the relations between the ego and the id we find a picture of the less ideal situation in which the rider is obliged to guide his horse in the direction in which it itself wants to go."
Sigmund Freud, *New Introductory Lectures On Psychoanalysis.*

Adam was a tennis groupie. He knew all the players, their entourages and the officials, and they knew him. He was a face in the tea-rooms. Ever the ladies' man, he was a particular fan of the women's game. Given Cliff's later romance with Sue Barker, a monograph exploring possible causal links between the experience of having hits in the late fifties and early sixties and a subsequent fascination with women of powerful backhands might be a worthwhile endeavour, but one sadly beyond the scope or remit of the present work.

For the players, Adam – and Cliff – must have made a refreshing change from the fiercely focussed fellow-players and coaches they spent most of their time with: men who thought 'love' was followed by 15,

30, 40, and were prone to pausing now and then, even in the throes of ecstasy, for a quick swig of barley water and a towel-down.

On one of his flights to LA, Adam had met John Lloyd, Britain's brightest hope, for a while, in Grand Slam tennis. Subsequently, John slipped Adam the odd ticket for Wimbledon or, more locally, for the Brighton International tournament.

John was married to Chris Evert from Fort Lauderdale in Florida, one of the game's all-time greats whose record for competing in 34 Grand Slam finals, at the time of writing, still stands. John and Chris were known as tennis's "golden couple", "the perfect set", "the love match". The roundabout of the pro tennis circuit, however, meant their time together must often have been reduced to no more than the odd wave across a crowded airport concourse. And both realised that even when they were together there were problems. Some observers noticed that whereas Chris had the single-minded winner's mentality required by the professional game, John was British.

In 1982, Paul Dainty, an Australian rock promoter who had diversified into tennis, was staging a women's tournament at the Hordern pavilion in Sydney. Keen to make it a celebrity event, he offered Adam a first-class flight out to Australia and front row seats.

Mrs. Evert-Lloyd, as she was called, was playing in the tournament. It was a women's event. John wasn't around. Chris was tall, tanned, blonde, smart and funny. She had grown up in a tennis family, had been on court ever since she could remember and had been engaged to Jimmy Connors (a former world number one) before she married John Lloyd.

Spending time with a short-arse bloke from Acton who did not have a world ranking but who had done summer seasons with Des Lane the Penny Whistle Man and Joan & Paul Sharratt (puppeteers), who had launched Leo Sayer, starred with Dame Sybil and bent a helicopter, must have been a breath of fresh air.

One thing led to another and continued to lead to it – in secret and all over the tennis world – for the next couple of years.

People knew. They were seen out in restaurants and at matches. They socialised as a couple.

At the beginning of 1984, somebody snitched. The *Sun* said it was Teddy Tinling, the man who'd designed tennis dresses for pretty much every woman on the circuit ever since 'Gorgeous' Gussie Moran had scandalised Wimbledon in 1949 by wearing the frilly knickers he gave her. Teddy loved to gossip.

The story hit the headlines in January 1984. "Chris Loves Adam," the *Sun* said. The feeding frenzy began.

Sensibly, Adam's only comment was, "I have nuffink to say. I'm saying nuffink about nuffink."

All the principals involved have since put their stories on record. Inevitably the stories contradict each other in terms of who said what, when, to whom and what their intentions were. Trying to unpick the stories in the hope that some sort of 'definitive' account might result would be pointless and silly. People don't know what they're doing themselves half the time, especially in matters of heart and groin. They exhibit all kinds of irrational behaviour which, by definition, cannot be described in terms of sense and purpose, cause and effect, so let's cut to the chase.

The crunch came when Chris phoned Adam at home. Adam wasn't in.

After Adam's death, in an interview with Linda Lee Potter, Jackie said: "Terry would never normally give a woman our home telephone number and that frightened me. I thought, 'This must be serious.'

"I went ballistic that she had the audacity to phone my house. It's a despicable thing to do to another woman. Then Terry arrived home and he knew the minute he walked through the door.

"I tore into him, I smashed all our figurines and shouted, 'You rat'."

Adam was instructed to go to the end of the drive, phone Chris on his mobile and tell her never to call the home number again.

A line had been crossed, a sacred law broken.

"To me," says Laurence Marks, "he was always Adam Faith, the pop star but to Maurice (his writing partner Maurice Gran), he was Terry – the private person. Those two people – because they were two different people – lived very different lives. Adam wasn't real. He knew this and therefore believed as a consequence that he, Adam, could very much do what he liked – including commit adultery. Jackie knew what was going on and was happy – well, not happy – but she reasoned that what was going on was going to go on, and as it long as it was Adam that was doing it, it didn't impinge on her life. She was married to Terry and Terry lived at home, very happily. I went round there many times and there wasn't one sign of Adam Faith in their home at all – no posters, no gold discs – nothing. It was the home of Terry and Jackie. Adam didn't come into that home. And nothing Adam did came into that home until Adam's affair with Chris Evert.

"You only had to spend a few hours with Adam to know he wasn't a deep man, but neither was he shallow. He was obvious. He was a child. Adam hadn't grown up.

"I remember Jackie telling me about the night Chrissie Evert called him at home because she couldn't get him in London – Jackie went barmy. 'Don't bring Adam into the house. I don't want to know what Adam does.' That's what she said. Like, I'm not married to Adam – I'm married to Terry. It's not going on in this house.

"I don't think Terry liked Adam. I had this idea about him doing a one-man show. This nice family man and this complete arsehole who puts on a gold lamé suit or whatever he does.

"So Jackie threw him out. He went to live in a shed or a caravan at the bottom of the garden. She threw Terry out for being Adam. It was very weird. He was very much in love with Jackie – and he idolised their daughter, Katya. But that was Terry. Adam, as we saw it, was a very unreliable man and someone you wouldn't want to be in business with, let alone be married to, although he was, it has to be said, the most exhilarating company of anyone I have ever met in my life."

Freud defined three aspects of the human psyche: the id, the ego and the super-ego. Roughly speaking, the id is the wild side – all instinct and rutting. The super-ego is the constraints imposed upon the id by society, civilisation, good sense and so on. And the ego mediates between the two.

Men, on the whole, believe themselves, deep down, to be pirates, cowboys, mercenaries, studs, or gods of rock'n'roll. They cannot and will not accept that their failure to be a pirate, a cowboy, a mercenary, a stud or a god of rock'n'roll could have anything to do with a lack of talent, aptitude, courage or willingness to get off the arse. And, being men, they have nothing but sneering contempt for the constraints of society, civilisation and good sense. No, *somebody must be to blame.*

In other words, men prefer to externalise their super-egos. They decide that the only reason they're not pirates, cowboys, mercenaries, studs or gods of rock'n'roll is that some bastard's stopping them. Usually it's a mum or a wife gets the blame. "I'd have another drink, I'd fly with you on a diamond smuggling expedition to Lagos, I'd get the old guitar out the attic and have one last shot at the brass ring, I'd do all these things in a heartbeat if it wasn't for her indoors."

In cartoon Freudian terms, then, Adam was the id, Terry the ego and Jackie the super-ego.

There was nothing unconscious about the split between Adam and Terry. "The strength of being Adam," he told Jennifer Selway in 2002, "is that he has no history to deal with, no family or dependents. Being Adam is like playing a part in a film. Though Terry and Adam aren't at opposite ends, they run in parallel. On the whole I prefer being Adam."[93]

Jackie, as we've heard, certainly knew about the split and most of his friends did, too. "There's two very different people," says Andrew Tribe. "There was Terry Nelhams – the nice family man – and Adam Faith who could be a complete arsehole and was a ruthless individual."

Nell had been a strong woman who established clear boundaries as to what was and wasn't acceptable behaviour. When she died, in Adam/ Terry's head, the role had passed on to Jackie. It's a pattern common to many marriages: and since the whole procedure takes place somewhere deep in the wordless recesses of the relationship, people are rarely aware of the process taking place at all. They just fall into the pattern. They adapt.

"Jackie dominated him at home," says Andrew Tribe. "I used to call her Mrs Fierce. It was *my* nickname for her first – but he always called her that afterwards. If he'd done something bad, he used to try to get me to come home with him. I'd say, 'I'm not going to walk in to get a bollocking'."

Were they big transgressions? Infidelities?

"No. One day he'd let the dogs escape. They had two salukis, her pride and joy. And she went absolutely mental with him. You didn't mess with Jack. She'd just stick her head in the air and that was it."

"I think women are wiser and more mature," Adam said. "They don't compete and get all macho like men do. Men are always little boys at heart. That's why I'm glad I haven't got a son – I want to be the only child in my house, being mothered by all the women. Even our dogs are female. I do have male friends, but I'm more comfortable with women."[94]

Eventually, that time, Jackie allowed Adam back into the house.

Chris Evert and John Lloyd split up for a while. Then they were briefly reconciled before finally divorcing in 1987.

Chapter Thirty

"You know what? When I look back on my little life and the birds I've known and think of all the things they've done for me and the little I've done for them, you'd think I'd had the best of it all along the line. But what have I got out of it? […] That's what I keep asking myself. What's it all about? Know what I mean?"

Bill Naughton, *Alfie.*

On September 3, 1983, Channel 4 announced, "*Video, Video* a new series which reflects the video revolution now seriously damaging the cinema and reducing viewing audiences for many successful television shows. Presented by Adam Faith."

Adam would show clips from the new video releases and interview a guest star: Ned Sherrin ("that show-business man of many parts"), "Monty Python's" Graham Chapman, yachtswoman Clare Francis, Desmond Morris, Mary Whitehouse. The show ran at 6.00 on a Saturday evening. You had to miss the first 15 minutes of *Noel Edmonds' Late, Late Breakfast Show* to watch it, and only diehard video fans were prepared to do that.

More interesting, particularly in light of the soon-to-break Chris Evert story, was being offered the lead in *Alfie*, the Bill Naughton play about a conscience-free womaniser, adapted as the successful 1966 film starring Michael Caine and the less-successful 2004 remake with Jude Law.

The production, at the Liverpool Playhouse, was to be directed by Alan Parker, the film director. Despite a gobsmacking list of movie credits – *Bugsy Malone, Midnight Express, Fame* and *Pink Floyd The Wall* – and an Oscar-nomination, this was Parker's first crack at theatre.

"Adam Faith and I have been friends for a long time," Alan said, "but had never worked together. Over the years we'd bumped into one another in coffee shops in London and Los Angeles and spent many happy hours concocting plans, but great film ideas have a way of evaporating when the red wine wears off."

A young Celia Imrie played Ruby, one of Alfie's conquests, towering over Adam in beehive and high-heels. At the age of 10, she had written to the *TV Times* for a signed photo of Adam, "which I displayed on the dressing table in my bedroom beside my photo of Rudolf Nureyev."

"On the first day," she writes, "Alan [Parker] stood before us in the rehearsal room.

"'Well,' he said in his lovely Cockney drawl, 'I'm used to saying, 'Action' to get things going.' He looked round the assembled group. 'So what do I say here? Off you go darlings?'"[95]

The reviews were sensational but the money, according to Adam, didn't quite cover his hotel bill.

He was dismissive of his pop star persona these days. When Spencer Leigh, the writer and Radio Merseyside presenter, interviewed him and asked him to sign one of his albums, "he shook his head and said, 'Who buys this crap? The best British rock'n'roll record was 'Move It'. Do you think I even came close to that?'"

"By the eighties, he regarded his pop career as a little thing on the side," said Keith Altham. "He really looked down on it. He thought they were silly little tunes that he did when he was young."

At the beginning of 1984, BBC2 produced a series of one-off plays by new writers. Adam played a washed up jazz saxophonist in John Harvey's *Just Another Little Blues Song*.

"Just Another Dreary Little Play," the *Times* called it, "despite the attraction of Adam Faith in the lead."

Cheers was on the other side.

Budgie was repeated on Channel 4 over the slack summer period of 1985, but already most of the previews, even when praising it, suggested that its take on race and sex had to be viewed through a gauze of at least understanding irony.

And that Christmas, he had a cameo, alongside a host of other celebs, on a *Minder* full length TV movie, *Minder On The Orient Express*.

Public spiritedly, Adam also did a couple of charity films. In *Moving Away From Home*, a film made for Shelter, he played an affable but flint-hearted landlord. It was written by David Stafford.

A series of controversial 30-second adverts made by London Weekend Television with the Family Planning Association and The Brook Advisory Centre exhorting the young to use condoms featured Adam looking earnestly into camera and saying: "Any idiot can get a girl pregnant. If you're not man enough to use birth control, you are not old enough to have sex."

The films were eventually banned by the IBA on the grounds that they might inadvertently send out a message to young people suggesting that it's all right to enjoy yourself.

And then there was *Down An Alley Filled With Cats* by Warwick Moss, an Australian award-winning play produced at the Mermaid Theatre in 1985. It was a two-hander. Adam played Simon, a "dumb thug" with an Australian accent, who locks horns with a bookseller, played by David de Keyser. The *Mail On Sunday* described it as, "A deft, suspenseful play with more twists than a Rasta hairdo." Other reviews were less generous. The word "dull" was used a lot and Martin Cropper in the *Times* called it "neither funny nor thrillling".

A top selling book of 1977 was Jim Fixx's *The Complete Book Of Running*, which, it has been claimed, began the 'fitness' revolution.

By 1981, the washability of leg-warmers was a popular topic of conversation, HMV record shops had all but abandoned the sale of music in favour of celebrity fitness videos and records (Felicity Kendal's *Shape Up And Dance* went Top 30 in the albums chart), spandex had become a word and Olivia Newton-John a sex symbol. The fact that seven years after writing his book Jim Fixx died of a heart attack at the age of 52 changed nothing.

Adam, after years of committed smoking, had at last given up the fags. He'd never been a drinker and had kept himself in trim with golf, martial arts and any other sport that caught his fancy for an obsessive few months. In the early eighties, the obsession was running. He would often, he claimed – and none of his friends, knowing Adam, saw any reason to dispute the claim – do 12 miles before work. The running, the years of smoking, the fish suppers in Lisson grove, the trifles from the Savoy, stress, genetic predisposition – one, some or all of them nearly did for him. In 1987, just before he was due to leave for a holiday in Mombasa with Jackie and Katya, a routine medical check revealed a problem. His arteries were 70% blocked. The holiday was cancelled. At the Wellington hospital he underwent bypass surgery.

Like the car crash, the heart surgery changed him mentally as well as physically. Counterproductively for a man with a dicky ticker, the determination to 'cram it all in' became steelier and, as the sense of mortality took hold, a darkness came over him. "He became depressed after that," says Andrew Tribe. "It was never the same. We all felt it."

Leo Sayer's career was winding down. In 1983, his last Top 20 record, 'Orchard Road', climbed painfully to number 16, then relaxed.

In an interview on Australian radio, Leo said that the lyric was autobiographical, based on a phone conversation he'd had with his wife, Janice, asking for her to forgive him for an affair. Orchard Road is a pseudonym for Churchfield Road, Acton. Janice had fled to a flat there. Churchfield Road, Acton, was, as attentive readers may have spotted, the street in which Adam was born. It was also the street where Lionel Bart, creator of the musical *Oliver!* and of Adam's hits 'Easy Going Me' and 'Big Time', died.

Leo and Janice were divorced in 1985. At around the same time, Leo set in motion a professional separation from Adam Faith. The latter turned out to be infinitely more messy, acrimonious and litigious than the former.

"A lot of my royalties," said Leo, "were used to fund questionable 'business expenses' and it was only in the mid-eighties, when I was divorcing my wife Janice, that I realised I owned fewer assets than I imagined.

"For 15 years, I had no idea what was coming in or going out, nor did I have any say in it. I just recorded albums and flew to wherever I was supposed to be performing. It was like signing a power of attorney. The thing is, I have always been dyslexic with numbers, so I let it happen. In the end, Adam Faith made more out of Leo Sayer than I did."[96]

Trying to figure out the labyrinthine complications of rock'n'roll contracts and finance is a task that frequently defeats teams of forensic accountants. "Leo definitely blamed Terry," says David Courtney. "It was wrong what they did to Leo. I bumped into Leo years later when I was living in Australia. I hadn't seen him for ages so I didn't know that all this had gone on. He was furious and he said, 'I'm not gonna rest until I see them banged up for what they've done to me.' According to Leo, when he asked for the return of all his master tapes he was told that Terry had 'allegedly' burnt them in a temper. I don't like to think it was true but it wouldn't surprise me knowing how he could be when he didn't get his own way."

Out of court settlements were made. Some say a payment of £200,000 was handed over to Leo, but, since a condition of the settlement was a mutually binding confidentiality agreement, all Adam had to say on the matter was: "Speak to my lawyer, cock."

The world had meanwhile turned. Money, traditionally mentioned, if at all, in hushed tones by the British, like sex, religion or toilet troubles, and despised by the hippies who reserved a special circle of Uptight Fascist Hell for breadheads, had, thanks to Mrs Thatcher and the shiny-faced, power-suited City Boys and Girls, become something to celebrate. It was OK to like it.

Adam, of course, had always liked it, but now he could openly embrace it, he could, without shame or apology, indulge his obsession.

When City Boys were the new pop stars, there seemed no reason on earth why pop stars, especially ones who, back in 1962, were buying Shell at 128 and saying, "I've no time for anything but business at the moment", should not be City Boys.

And perhaps, in the way that women, as the years roll by, are traditionally reputed to turn into their mothers, Adam was turning into Eve Taylor. As a manager he had worked Eve-like magic with contracts and double-dealing: now, like Eve had enjoyed the company of people like Bernie Ecclestone and John Bloom the washing-machine king, he, too, wanted to rub shoulders with the high-flyers.

Jackie, furthering her skills as an interior decorator on a specialist painting course in Belgravia, became friendly with a woman called Karen Killik. She introduced Adam and Jackie to her husband, Paul, who was a stockbroker with Quilter Goodison.

Adam and Paul got on, to the extent that Paul and his fellow directors at Quilter Goodison asked Adam to start a joint company with them offering financial advice to 'high earners' in the media and entertainment business.

Adam saw this as an opportunity to put financial security and structure back into his life. With the help of his personal assistant of many years standing, Melanie Green, his new assistant, Jo Bowlby, and secretary, Juliet Parry, he set up a company called Faith Management with offices in Knightsbridge and proceeded to instruct the rich and famous in the art of turning fees and royalties into City gold.

Not everybody in the financial world or even in the show-business world was entirely convinced. Indeed, the company, in this initial phase, attracted just two clients.

All the same, Adam was full of it and babbled to the *Daily Express*: "Money is the biggest non-essential activity among humans. Everyone is interested in money and investing has become the new hobby."

He thought there should be more TV programmes devoted to the stock market.

"It's as if TV programmers feel business is like religion – they devote as little time to it as they can get away with."

The fourth regeneration of Adam Faith was complete: first pop star, then actor, then pop manager, then wheeler-dealer. Which is not to say he didn't still have time to indulge his former selves as a sort of hobby.

"Don Black [the lyricist] and I were having dinner on New Year's Eve 1985," he said. "Feeling maudlin and nostalgic, we decided we'd like to do a musical in the New Year. Apparently, it's in the nature of musicals that it takes three years to get them on the stage."[97]

Those three years had now gone by.

Don Black, from Hackney in London, is the most successful lyricist of the past 50 years. He's won an Oscar, a Golden Globe and two Tonys. He wrote the lyrics for: Elsa the Lion Cub's 'Born Free', Michael Jackson's 'Ben' (possibly the only romantic song ever written to a rat), James Bond and Shirley Bassey's 'Diamonds Are Forever', Lulu's 'To Sir With Love', Michael Ball's 'Love Changes Everything', Marti Webb's 'Take That Look Off Your Face' ... and so on and so on.

Mort Shuman, from Brooklyn in New York, is one of the most successful composers of the past 50 years. Usually in collaboration with Doc Pomus, he wrote Dion & the Belmonts' 'A Teenager In Love', the Drifters' 'Sweets For My Sweet' and 'Save The Last Dance For Me', Elvis' 'Little Sister' and 'Viva Las Vegas' and so on and so on...

After the New Year's Eve nostalgia fest, Don got in touch with Mort and Keith Waterhouse and Willis Hall, and together they made a musical version of *Budgie*. Of course, Adam would play the lead, and Anita Dobson, fresh from delighting the nation as Angie Watts in *EastEnders*, would co-star as Hazel. This dream team then confounded all expectations by producing a flop.

Budgie opened at the Cambridge Theatre on October 18, 1988 and closed three months later with losses reported to be in the region of £1m.

"When a musical doesn't work, it doesn't work," said Don Black, "and we never got the book right. It was too violent, and it was about abortions and the seedy low life in Soho. People preferred *42nd Street* and the big blockbusters."

But another crucial factor was the show's star. The world's finest songwriters, lyricists and authors had collaborated to put Adam Faith's name in lights, make him a star again and possibly even fill his boots with gold and, when it came to the crunch, he couldn't really be arsed.

"I always hated musicals," he said.

A few weeks before *Budgie* opened, Adam had been contacted by the *News Of The World*. Unusually, it did not want to speak to him about the forthcoming musical or about Chris Evert's divorce. Instead, it was offering him a job. It wanted him to become the paper's City Editor.

A few nights before, the paper had seen him on some TV show pontificating about business and was impressed by his flair. When word got around Fleet Street that the *News Of The World* was hiring Adam, the *Daily Mail* thought, "terrific idea", and put in a rival bid for his services. Adam accepted the *Mail's* offer.

He was a big-shot financial journalist and investment consultant now. Why would he want to be an ex-pop star in musical theatre?

More ominous still were the thoughts he shared with the press on the eve of *Budgie's* opening.

"I'm much less interested in performance than business," he said. "Acting, it's a shocking profession for a grown up person to be involved in. It's so silly, so daft. I had a great deal of reorganisation of my life to do for rehearsals. But once it opens it becomes an evening job. And I'm not interested in staying on if it's just ticking over."

"Adam Faith was not easy to work with," says Don Black. "He worked hard on the show. But when it came to promoting *Budgie*, Adam was difficult. He used to have this expression. Every time I asked him to do an interview somewhere, he would say, 'I run my life on the credo, "What would Marlon Brando do?"' And usually he concluded that, 'No, love. Brando wouldn't do it, would he?'"[98]

One day Don joked that Brando was on breakfast television. They both laughed, but Don was feeling the frustration.

When Adam did agree to a press interview, he usually did it while multi-tasking. When the *Mail On Sunday,* for instance, asked how he got on with co-star Anita Dobson: "'She's magnificent,' enthuses Faith, mobile phone pressed against one ear, elegant personal secretary reeling off a string of engagements into the other, 'Yeah, tell 'im I'll have breakfast with 'im in the morning, if the poor sod can get up. These people with one job beat me.'"[99]

The problems reached fever pitch one night during previews. Tension was riding high and the pressure of getting the word out about the show was immense.

A charity night for Princess Anne was a much-needed fillip for publicity. However, when the cast lined up on the stage to be introduced to Princess Anne, Don was told that Adam would not come out of his dressing room. It was not an anti-Monarchist statement, he just didn't like the idea of waiting in line to meet Princess Anne. "If she wants to see me," he told Don, "she can come to my dressing room."

Don was forced to make up an excuse. He told Princess Anne that Adam had had to be rushed off to hospital.

The following day, *Today* newspaper reported that Adam had broken a tooth and been rushed to an emergency dentist.

In a way, the heat was off Adam, anyway. Anita Dobson had just been spotted holding hands with a married man and father of three. He was the guitar player with the band Queen and his name was Brian May. They're still together.

Things didn't get better when the show was up, running and in its stride. Actor/musician/composer Julian Littman, who played Wossname and was Adam's understudy in the show, found himself unexpectedly busy.

"Adam lost interest in the show very quickly," he says. "To be honest, even on the nights he turned up, he was phoning in his performance. He seemed to have a lot of other stuff happening in his life at the time, and a musical that had failed to set the West End alight didn't really engage him."

"Why bother at his age to kid himself he can be a musical star?" said Maureen Paton in the *Daily Express*. "It must be a case of blind Faith. The opening number is a cacophonous shambles in which Mr. Faith as wide-boy Budgie hardly makes himself heard above an orchestra sounding as if they are moonlighting bricklayers on a musical YOB opportunities course."[100]

The *Times* was a little kinder, but not much, and the reviewer did have the kindness to quote one of Don Black's more delightful couplets, a little bit of perfection floating away from the shipwreck of a show, the survival of which somehow should have made all the effort and expense worthwhile:

"I'd like to sprinkle Malcolm," he quoted,

"From head to toe with talcum."

Chapter Thirty-One

"Adam Faith is to financial advice what Frank Bruno is to English literature."

Michael Winner

Adam was not getting on with his editor Andrew Alexander at the *Daily Mail*. Even though he'd managed to blag a Budget Day interview with the Chancellor's wife, Therese Lawson, when the time came the *Daily Mail* didn't renew his contract.

So he jumped ship to the *Mail On Sunday*. It was a happier berth. His column there dispensed advice for three years.

On November 5, 1988, Adam opened the *Money Show* at Olympia in London. He told *The Guardian* that day: "The big problem with selling financial products to the public is that they perceive them to be excruciatingly boring. We must try to encourage people to think of money as an exciting and profitable hobby. We must keep the message simple and make it sound fun."

Like so many others, he was deal crazy. He headed up a multimillion pound consortium to take over Queens Park Rangers, along with Rangers' former manager Terry Venables who planned to turn Loftus Road, the club's ground, into a multi-purpose stadium with a plastic bubble roof and an ability to stage tennis, boxing, hockey and pop concerts. It nearly happened, too: the referee was already looking at his watch when a rival company scored with a better bid.

The 'fun' of which Adam had so fondly spoken, took a bit of a dent when weeks after having started his column in the *Mail*, Adam got wind that Quilter Goodison, his partners in his investment advice business, were about to be taken over and were pulling the rug from under him.

"We didn't see it as an ongoing business," said a spokesman. "It didn't really get off the ground with Adam as the frontman. It had two clients. There wasn't enough new business to keep the home fires burning."

The plush offices in Knightsbridge were cleaned out and closed up.

By December 9, Adam had found a replacement partner to back in a new company. This was to be 50% owned by Adam, who was to be responsible for introductions to the financial advice service, and 50% by the Levitt Group, run by Roger Levitt, which was providing the backup. The business was to be run from Levitt's West End Offices.

Adam was bowled over by Roger Levitt – a consummate showman and a brilliant salesman. The deal was good, too. For a 50% share in the company, Adam would get an option to buy 5% of the Levitt Group for two and a half million pounds. He felt it couldn't fail. He was made for life.

Others weren't so convinced.

"Adam introduced me to Roger Levitt," says Andrew Tribe. "He said something to Terry and walked out. I said, 'Is that him?' And Terry said, 'Yeah, great isn't he?' And I said, 'I wouldn't let him take my dog for a walk.' He said, 'What do you mean?' And I said, 'He's got lying eyes.' You could see it straight through his eyes. But he didn't want to hear it."

Essentially, Adam acted as a highly paid greeter for the company, oiling the wheels, fixing introductions, giving lavish lunches, pulling the punters in. As well as a handsome cut, Levitt supplied Adam with a chauffeur-driven Bentley, a swish office suite and full time assistants.

It's not clear whether Adam was entirely comfortable with this role. It certainly caused uneasiness in some of his old friends. "I pulled away from Tel a little when he got involved in the money side of life," says Terry O'Neill. "He wanted to involve people like Eric Clapton. And because I used to know everyone – I was the king of doing everything – he'd ask me for contacts. I didn't like that bloke Roger Levitt. So we didn't see each other much. I didn't want to get involved in that side of things because I didn't want to ask people like Eric to meet him, mainly because I didn't know what he was up to."

The shit hit the fan in 1990.

A Japanese bank expressed an interest in taking over the Levitt Group. Adam, with his 5% stake, anticipated a huge profit.

But no sooner had he put the vintage fizz on to chill than Levitt declared bankruptcy and the Fraud Squad moved in.

One of Adam's clients, Michael Winner (film producer, gastronome and director of *Death Wish*, *Hannibal Brooks* and *Won Ton Ton, The Dog Who Saved Hollywood*) had, on Adam's advice, invested with Roger Levitt, and was quoted widely as saying that: "Adam Faith is to financial advice what Frank Bruno is to English literature."

In 1991, Winner told the *Times*: "Adam Faith rang me in late 1988 or early 1989 and told me how he had met this genius. According to Adam, he was the most wonderful thing since sliced bread. I knew Adam well. I had lost money in his first company, but he is such a charmer when he wants to be."

In the same article a "leading City figure" said: "Adam took me to lunch and gave me a big sales pitch on why I needed Levitt. I told him I wasn't interested but he was irritatingly persistent."[101]

The company collapsed with debts of around £34m. A number of high-profile investors, including *The Day Of The Jackal* author Frederick Forsyth, were left with hefty losses. Michael Winner managed to retrieve around £1m of his money but gave no indication of how much he lost. The only assets left when the receivers had done their work were an executive box at Arsenal's Highbury Stadium and an interest in the boxing career of Lennox Lewis.

In the wine bars of the City, wags were renaming Adam's big hits: 'Poor You', 'Someone Else's Money', and, without changing a word, just adding a note of heavy irony, 'Big Time'.

Roger Levitt went to trial at the Old Bailey on a charge of fraudulent trading. Michael Winner gave three examples of 'serious irregularities' in Levitt's dealings with him and stated that they were all known to Adam. He claimed that he had warned Adam to stop recommending Levitt to his friends and to get out of any arrangements that he had made with Levitt.

After eight days of evidence, Levitt changed his plea to 'guilty'. The Serious Fraud Office agreed to drop 21 other charges, including forgery and obtaining property and services by deception.

The judge described Levitt as "thoroughly and markedly dishonest", but gave him a sentence of what to many seemed a surprisingly lenient 180 hours community service.

No charges were brought against Adam.

A year or so afterwards, when the dust had settled, Adam spoke about Levitt with Barbara Cox, one of the writers on his nineties TV series, *Love Hurts*.

"Over the lunch, we started talking about how he'd been ripped off by Levitt and how everybody in the City that he dealt with were public school type guys. I asked him why he thought nobody had warned him about Levitt and he said, 'Well, they did warn me about Levitt, but I didn't understand what they were saying. It was just little things, little asides, little comments, stuff like, "Are you sure about this, old thing?" I thought they were just being snobbish, but it was just I couldn't read properly what people were saying.' It seemed clear that the fact that this Levitt character was also from a working class background had pushed them together."

Adam was shaken and bruised by the experience. He had lost a business, the chauffeur-driven Bentley that Levitt had supplied, and, perhaps worst of all, his reputation as a man who knows about money was looking decidedly dodgy.

Chapter Thirty-Two

"Love hurts, love scars,
Love wounds, and mars
Any heart
Not tough, nor strong enough
To take a lot of pain,
Take a lot of pain..."

Felice & Boudleaux Bryant – *Love Hurts*

In 1989, ITV showed an odd series of 15-minute "gumshoe yarns" called *Shady Tales* – written by Richard Ireson, starring Adam as a South London private detective and co-starring Sue Scadding as his girlfriend – but not with any confidence. They were batted around the schedules, always in a late night slot, disappeared in London when only five of the 13 episodes had been transmitted, after which they could be glimpsed from time to time in the regions, usually after midnight.

But there was better just around the corner.

In the early eighties, Witzend, the production company, was planning a new TV show written by Laurence Marks and Maurice Gran. The show, *Shine On Harvey Moon*, concerned the trials and tribulations of an East

259

End family just after the Second World War. Adam, it was decided, would be perfect casting for the dad.

"We went to see Adam, just off Berkeley Square where he had an office on the top floor," says Laurence Marks. "He was very nice and very pleasant and he made some very good suggestions, not least that Harvey, the dad – who in our first draft was not the central character – should be centre of the story. Adam was very excited by the script. We read it through with him and he was very good. It was all going well. Linda Robson and Lee Whitlock were cast as his kids, Stanley and Maggie, because they were the same colouring as Adam. It was all going along famously and then about a week before we were due to record the pilot, we were told by Tony Charles, the producer, that Adam had pulled out.

"We didn't know why. But if ever a show fell into place by people pulling out it was *Shine On Harvey Moon*."

Tony Charles took the script round to Kenneth Cranham, an actor of extraordinary talent who accepted the part, showed up for work diligently and made a huge contribution to the show's success.

"Adam was a very nice guy and we liked him a lot," says Laurence, "but then he let us down. I know that when *Harvey Moon* was a mega hit he was thinking that he had really buggered his career up. He could have been a major TV star again."

Ten years later, when the Levitt business had gone belly up and Adam was, once again, looking around for his next buzz and a few quid in his pocket, Alan Field, who was now Adam's agent, got in touch with Laurence and Maurice.

"He asked if we'd consider doing a television series for him again," says Laurence. "We said no, we wouldn't. He's unreliable – why would we want to waste our time?"

By this time Marks and Gran were two of the biggest names in British TV. *Shine On Harvey Moon* had been a major success. Two other series they'd created, *Birds Of A Feather* and *The New Statesman* – both running at this time – were top-rated shows, showered with critical acclaim and awards.

"Alan said, 'He knows he made a terrible mistake and let you down over *Harvey Moon*. He wants to apologise. Will you meet him?' So we said, 'Yeah, sure we'll meet him. But really how would we know that he wouldn't do the same thing twice?'

"We met Adam at the Savoy and he said, 'I'm surprised that you even bothered turning up. Honestly, I wouldn't have turned up if I were you.'

"We asked him to tell us what happened. He said, 'I lost my nerve. I couldn't do it. I just couldn't do it. I thought it was too big for me.' And I said, 'But you'd been in *Budgie* – why did you think it was any bigger than that?'"

In 1980, Adam had been a jet-setter, in funds, living high on the hog. Losing his nerve would have been one of the reasons he'd backed out of *Harvey Moon*. Being arsed would almost certainly have been another.

"Anyway, he said what he wanted was for us to create a series for him. We spoke to him and said, 'What sort of thing do you want to do?' He had no idea. We said that what we wanted to write was a love story. What we had at the back of our minds was the story of a man who's never been in love before meeting a woman who never wants to fall in love again."

The series was to be called *Love Hurts*. Patricia Hodge was to play the woman who never wanted to fall in love again

"We brought Patricia to lunch in the Savoy with Adam and we discussed the sort of thing we wanted to do and everyone was very excited, not least the controller of BBC1 [Jonathan Powell] who was hugely hung up on Patricia Hodge. He was absolutely potty about her. When we mentioned that the drama series we wanted to write had Patricia in it, he just said, 'Do it.'

"We didn't at that time mention Adam Faith because we didn't think that Adam would cut any ice with the controller of BBC1 even though he done *Budgie*.

"Then Patricia got pregnant, even though she must have been 43 or 44 years old, and she knew she couldn't do it. We were stuck then with Adam and nobody else. Jonathan Powell had backed the commission on the promise of Patricia Hodge and we had to go back – well, the company had to go back and say that Patricia was pregnant and she can't do it."

The search for a replacement began.

"One evening I went to the National to see *The Crucible* – the Arthur Miller play – and came back and said to Maurice that I'd seen an actress who would be great for Tessa – Zoë Wanamaker. She wasn't very well known – not known on TV at all."

Laurence and Maurice brought Adam and Zoë together over lunch at the Savoy.

"I was very wary," says Zoë. "Adam was so naughty. He did this thing of actually looking me up and down – which was very sexual. It was very amusing, unnerving and flattering at the same time. I was being vetted.

"I didn't really want to do *Love Hurts*. I was in *The Crucible* at the National at the time. I wasn't confident about the script and I wasn't sure about the premise.

"I was wary of Adam because he was an icon. We used to dance to his records in the biology lab at school. But would we be able to work together? But as we did work together it was obvious that he was extremely bright and very much in touch with his feelings.

"I always called him Bill. One day he told me that was what his mother called him. God knows why. But it did suit him.

"I found him a complete delight. When I didn't feel like slapping him."

Love Hurts went into production at the end of 1991.

"From day one," said Adam, "I loved being back on the telly. I realised what I'd missed. It's a great life. The first few weeks took some doing – it was like getting on a bike after not riding it for 20 years. I was a bit rusty. But there was one scene where it clicked and I thought: now I am back in the saddle."[102]

"When we had written the first episode," Laurence says, "the producer had said, 'I'm not really happy with this. Adam doesn't come on the screen for 18 minutes.' We explained that everyone who turned on that television knew Adam. What we've got to do is get them to know Zoë.

She needed the first 18 minutes. The minute *he* came on the screen –
well, he was Humphrey Bogart."

Tessa Piggot, played by Zoë, is a high-flying City executive whose
heart is broken when her boss, with whom she's been having a longstanding affair, dumps her. She quits her job, gets a new, poorly paid one
with a charity and downsizes. When the defective bath at her new flat is
in danger of flooding the place out, she calls a plumber.

Frank Carver, played by Adam, an ex-plumber, now a millionaire,
happens to answer the phone. He goes round, fixes her bath and flirts.
She's haughty. Frank's amused.

"Most posh birds, you see," says Frank, "they like a little bit of the old
working-class badinage."

And they're off on a will-they-won't-they odyssey of love, class,
education and money.

"Adam never acted," says Laurence. "Adam was Adam playing Frank.
There were lines that we wrote that could have come out of Adam's mouth."

"As an actor he was incredibly bright," says Zoë, "and it was a pleasure
to discuss and wrestle through the scenes together.

"When we started, he was still writing the Money Page for the *Mail*
so he was exhausted by having to get that done every week. He was
supposed to have learnt his lines before filming, but as it was when we
came to scene he was struggling. It was difficult for him to do two things
at once. But once involved in the scene his instincts were fantastic and
that's when we really got on because we connected. Which was exciting
and fun.

"Occasionally I would get irritated with him. I thought he was being
lazy and didn't care. He had a lifestyle that I knew nothing about. It
seemed to me to be so glamorous."

The series took off from the first episode.

"I was away when the first one went out," says Laurence, "but when I
got back to England, I remember someone gave me a folder of reviews.
They were incredible. One of the reviewers said that Adam Faith and
Zoë Wanamaker were Spencer Tracy and Katharine Hepburn. You never
once didn't believe that these two people weren't real. You were rooting
for them. They were quite magnificent.

263

"I remember on the night of the preview of the first one at a viewing theatre. Adam came along in his T-shirt and his trainers and everyone filed in to watch the first episode of *Love Hurts,* but not him. He just walked around outside.

"When it finished, everyone was wowed by it and I said to him, 'I think you're going to be in a really big hit show.' And he said, 'Is it good?' and I said, 'Yeah, it's terrific.' And it was. He never saw it but he knew it was a big hit."

Adam never saw that first episode – or indeed any of the subsequent episodes.

"Whether a psychiatrist would say that it was because Terry didn't like Adam, so he wasn't going watch him....?"

Chapter Thirty-Three

*"Past performance of shares is not an indication of their future performance.
The value of shares or income from them may go down as well as up"*
Statutory warning issued with
Financial Products and Services

A dam's debts were piling up.

In the early seventies, he'd met a man at a party in LA who told him a corking wheeze for making money for nothing was to become a Lloyd's Name.

Lloyd's of London, founded at Lloyd's Coffee House in 1688, is not an insurance company like other insurance companies. In fact, it's not a company at all. It's propped up by investors, known as Names, who share the profits when there are profits – which is most of the time – and the losses when there are losses. Their liability is unlimited. If a claim worth billions is found to be valid, they have to reach deep into their pockets.

In money circles where people care about such things, there's a certain cachet attached to being a Name. People whisper as you walk past in your Jermyn Street cuffs and your cloud of Trumper's Cologne – "He's a Name, you know." It's like being a Face at the Marquee in 1964, or going to trainspotters club in 1957 with 34 of the 35 A4 Pacifics underlined in your Ian Allan.

In 1991, Lloyd's declared losses of half a billion pounds. Initially, Adam had to find getting on for £60,000, but he knew that it might be a while before the Lloyd's books revealed his full liability.

Then the *Mail On Sunday* column crashed and burned, a victim, in a sense, of its own success.

In May 1992, under the headline, "Do You Want To Be A Millionaire?", Adam announced a scheme by which readers prepared to invest £6,000 could make a million in 10 years.

"Raid Granny's mattress," he wrote in the column, "pawn your Sony camcorder but please don't get carried away and borrow the cash."

Basically, the wheeze involved punters setting up their own Personal Investment Plan then buying and selling shares recommended by a 'top City analyst'. The analyst was Robin Griffith at James Capel Stockbrokers.

On the Monday after the column appeared, 28,000 people got in touch wanting to know more.

Adam called the scheme "Faith In A Million". Others later called it "Budgiegate". A senior executive at the *Mail On Sunday* called it "the biggest cock-up in the history of the paper".

The Securities and Investments Board, the City regulatory body with a brief to protect the interest of small time investors, was up in arms because Adam's scheme was almost certainly not in the interest of small time investors. "Are all the details explained?" they asked. "Can the consumer be sure his money is being looked after properly, and is he aware that shares can go down as well as up?"

The City was up in arms because a mass of small investors all following the same tips would distort the market.

James Capel was up in arms about his firm being named, which could possibly put him in breach of the Financial Services Act.

Lord Rothermere, owner of the *Mail On Sunday*, was up in arms because everybody else was up in arms.

Adam wasn't fired. His column continued to appear for another three months before he announced that he was giving it up because he wanted "to make acting his priority".

He missed it. "I loved doing it," he said later. "If they'd asked me to write a gardening or fishing column, I'd have said yes. I love newspapers. I even love the way newsprint makes your hands dirty."

A few years later, he decided he liked newspapers so much he wanted to own one. He arranged a lunch with his friends Bob Henrit and Russ Ballard and a man called Richard Desmond, a keen drummer and a friend of Bob's who also happened to be the owner of Northern & Shell, a media group with a portfolio of top selling titles including *OK!*, *Asian Babes* and a string of hobby magazines. At the time, he'd also recently taken over Express Newspapers.

"Tel wanted to edit the *Express*," says Bob Henrit. "He just thought he could do it. Me, Russell and Rick Desmond, we all sat there and Tel laid out his stall. 'You've got to have me – I'm great!'"

As Russ says, "Tel was never short of ambition."

On Christmas Day 1991, the Union of Soviet Socialist Republics was formally dissolved. At the Kremlin, the Soviet flag was lowered for the last time and the Russian tricolour raised in its place. Eighteen months later, Adam, Zoë and a BBC crew invaded the country.

In series two of *Love Hurts*, Frank has problems with a Russian girlfriend, Frank and Tessa are kidnapped by Russian gangsters, there are shenanigans with a Russian oil deal and it ends with the pair of them shepherding a group of Russian orphans.

"We landed at Leningrad, but by the time we got to the hotel they had changed the sign – it was then called St Petersburg," says Zoë. "It was a standard joke in Russia – did you go to Leningrad or did you go to St Petersburg? Adam was not at all keen on the hotel, which was basically a sort of fifties block, and moved himself to a more expensive and cooler hotel on the River Neva, run by Finns. I was very happy with my river view in the crummy hotel."

Laurence Marks' wife, the actress Brigitte Kahn, was cast as Frau Louise Arnheim. "My wife went away filming to Russia for two weeks with Adam and she said, 'I never in my life had such an incredible time.' She did not stop laughing from the moment they touched down in Russia to the moment they took off. 'We went everywhere,' she said.

I said, 'But there was nowhere to go. I know because I did a recce six months ago.' But she said, 'Well, Adam knew everyone and we went everywhere – he took us everywhere.' I asked her how they got around and she said that he had a chauffeur-driven car. I mean – how? Where did it come from? When I told Maurice, he wasn't at all surprised. Of course Adam could find a chauffeur-driven car in St Petersburg. It was an inevitability."

Adam tried to buy a flat in St. Petersburg but never made clear whether he saw this as an investment opportunity or as a chance to start a new life in a newish country where the word on everybody's lips was "oligarch". The negotiations dragged on for weeks, during which time he was heard frequently to rail like a Gogol character against the iniquities of Russian bureaucracy until the scheme had burned itself out.

Back in the UK, Adam's affability began to wear thin. It was partly down to health problems. His stents – the cardiovascular tubes he'd had inserted to strengthen the walls of his arteries – were playing him up.

"He was having terrible trouble with the stents," says Zoë. "Much later, he had some new Japanese stents put in that he was very proud of."

Money was another worry.

"The other members of the cast got a bit frustrated with Adam," says Laurence. "We would say, 'Adam, we need to shoot this scene now.' And he'd say, 'I'm just on the phone to my broker.' And of course, with filming, time is money. In the end we forbade him to bring a phone onto the set. He had, to an extent, been doing it to exercise his power. This is what Maurice and I always say success is – the shortest line between gratitude and contempt."

It was the old problem, when there was a challenge, something to prove, the working-class work ethic kicked in. But then...

"He was a star again and that made him intolerable in the making of the second series. He'd done it. He was number one. It was his 'What Do You Want?'. So now he was bored. In fact he was bored during the filming of the first series.

"Things started to get difficult. He'd want changes made. It was, 'My character wouldn't say this.' 'Frank wouldn't be like this.' And in the end we'd say, 'Look Terry – we know what we are doing. Just act. Just do it.' But that was never his way. He wanted the changes because he could. I spoke to him a lot about this.

"You have to go back to the beginning. He wasn't your average pop star. He was a very intelligent man, always knew what he wanted. But there was some gene in him that always pulled him back at the last moment. For example when he managed Leo Sayer, everyone wanted him to manage them: Elton had asked him and Roger Daltrey particularly, and he said, 'No I can't be bothered', because it was hard work. Adam's idea of success was to do nothing and earn lots of money. He always said that. And, of course, acting was really difficult and it demands a lot of your time. In the old days he could have gone into the studio and made a hit record in an hour or an hour and a half. We were demanding nine months of his life. He was bored. Even when we were filming the first series, he was on the phone to 10 other companies about 10 other projects. The producer said, 'Look, you are booked to do this so bloody well get on with it'."

Whatever he did, Adam was on the lookout for perks and extras. At that time, few people had mobile phones. Adam, of course, had the latest model as soon as it came on the market, if not before.

"He said, 'You should ask the producer to get you one'," says Zoë. "So I asked the producer and I got one. I never knew you could ask producers for that sort of thing. But I got one. Size of a house brick. But I got one."

"At one point we – well, *he* really – we had a big fight with Alamo [the production company] about getting more money. We made a little sign with, 'Please can we have some more money' and when we were filming on London Bridge we sat with the sign and our hands out."

Not until series three, the one in which Frank and Tessa were married and had a baby, did Adam's truculence begin, slightly, to affect Zoë. There were never big rows or animosity but ...

"We had arguments about the script. He didn't like the fact that we got married in the third series but I'd always felt that there should be a third act. He was resistant to do a third series. He thought once the couple got married then that would be the end of interest. The race was off. The pursuit was off. But I thought that – because at the time, in the early nineties, it was all about thinking that women could really have it all, running a business, bringing up children, having a relationship – I felt that it was an interesting aspect that we could get into. But Adam didn't like that. He thought that should be the end of the story."

Barbara Cox, who wrote the last but one episode in series three, thinks that Adam had a good point. "An on-and-off romance story is very hard to keep going. And they made a total and utter error – which basically killed the show – which was to make the couple get together and have a baby. And, of course, once they had a baby then you couldn't have any sympathy for them at all. It was, 'Why don't you two just shut up and get on with each other and bring up your kid?' Basically the show collapsed. There is only a certain amount of time that you can run those."

There was no fourth series.

Barbara Cox, it should be added, is exceptional inasmuch as she found herself, even up close and personal – Adam took her for lunch – immune to the charm. "He turned out to be quite a chilly soul," she says. "Not nasty but quite cold."

Hunter Davies, the writer and journalist (usually described as 'Beatle Biographer' for his first and arguably most intimate 1968 portrait of the Fabs at work and play) remained calm in the face of smile and cheekbones, too.

In May 1994, a couple of months after the last episode of the last series of *Love Hurts* had been aired, he interviewed Adam for the *Independent*.

"I used to think he looked a bit misshapen as a pop singer," he wrote. "His head too big for his body. Now, at 53, he has come into his looks. In fact he has been called stunning, in an Essex sort of way."

Adam received Hunter over lunch at the Savoy.

"He clearly loves being here," Hunter wrote, "meeting people, swapping stories, making appointments. Just as one might imagine a financial dealer would.

"'What are you talking about?' he says. 'I've given all that up. I've decided at last on the person I am. It's taken me 25 years to find out. I've been denying myself for too long. It's like coming out as a gay. I now know what I am. I am an Artist.'

"I didn't snigger."

Chapter Thirty-Four

"Trying to make some sense of it all,
But I can see that it makes no sense at all"
                    Joe Egan & Gerry Rafferty, *Stuck In The Middle*

Adam's first venture as an Artist was to direct and star in a new production of *Alfie*, the Bill Naughton play he'd done in Liverpool with Alan Parker, and take it on the road. Then he planned to take the play to the USA, where Katya, who had just graduated from Harvard, would co-direct an American production.

"He is proud of Katya," said the *Daily Express,* "now studying film production and direction at Harvard who, Adam says, is partly responsible for the way he has thrown himself back into showbiz after his years in the city. 'Because she's set for a showbiz career, it made me realise that's what I really want for myself. I've got a passion for acting and singing that I have never had before and I feel that I'm dealing with my own career properly for the first time now.'"[103]

Adam could do crinkly, twinkly womanising *Alfie* till the cows came home. His age – when he began the tour he was a few weeks shy of his 54th birthday – and the fragility he seemed to acquire in middle age, added resonance to the part, making the character's plight all the more pitiable.

But a 54-year-old Alfie was not, he insisted, a reinterpretation of the part. In the movie, he told the Scottish Herald, "'they had to lower his age to suit Michael Caine. But Alfie is really a middle-aged man. In the play you get the feeling from the end that if you went back in 10 years' time he wouldn't have changed, but in the movie you felt that he was young enough for some girl to come along and change him.'"

"Well, people ask me if it's outdated. But it is about men's attitude to women and their attitude to themselves. If you talk to the women like I do when they come round to ask for autographs, they say, 'I've got an Alfie outside in the car'. Or 'I've been sitting with one all evening'."[104]

An interview with the *Mail On Sunday* gave him a chance to share a few thoughts on feminism. "Since Alfie was written 30 years ago, I don't believe men's attitudes have changed. Women's attitudes have changed incredibly – they perceive themselves in totally different ways. They have more self-determination, more self-worth, more strength and the confidence to take a slice of life on their terms.

"Look at men, only the language has changed. They wouldn't dream of calling a woman 'it' or a 'bird' to her face these days because of political correctness. But Alfie is lurking in almost every man. You only have to look at who laughs the loudest during the performance – it's the women. They recognise Alfie in their men."[105]

"People forget it's an upsetting play," he told Hunter Davies. "The Michael Caine film version missed out the tough stuff. You get laughs for an hour and a half, then I describe this woman having an abortion in my room. That's what gets them. I can't bear it myself. In the sixties it was women who collapsed. Now it's men. Guilt, I should think. People think it's a sexist play, but it's not. It's how men shouldn't treat women. There's no redemption for Alfie."

When the play opened at the Churchill Theatre, Bromley, for the most part the finer points of the drama were forgotten as *Love Hurts* fans, many of them people who, like Zoë, used to dance to his records in the biology lab, smashed the sexual energy at him, just like the old days.

"Alfie's arch asides to the blue-rinsed matinee audience, packed in jowl to jowl, were greeted with throaty cackles which visibly swelled

Faith's self-esteem," said the *Daily Express*. "They adore him, and he adores being adored. At the stage door he smiled gamely into the lens while an hysterical fan directed her friend to cuddle ever closer to Alfie's – aka Frank Carver's – blazer. 'I'm a happier, nicer person to be with when my acting's going well. It's a very pleasant life I lead anyway. This is just the icing on the cake.'"[106]

From Bromley, the circus moved on to Brighton, Birmingham, Oxford, Richmond, Poole and anywhere else that ladies eager to cuddle a blazer could be located.

Then, in October 1992, a new production, co-directed with Katya, ran for a month at the Tiffany, a boutique theatre in Los Angeles.

The *LA Times* called it a 'serviceable revival' and suggested that, "Faith needs a stronger directorial hand to draw out the subterranean impulses that motivate Alfie's behaviour" but did not record any incidents of blazer-cuddling.

He was an Artist with a "passion" for both acting and singing.

"I retired from singing 20 years ago so I could be an actor," he told the *Daily Mail*. "I had begun to hate my pop association because I so wanted to act. In those days you couldn't really do both [?]. Now I realise that the two things I do best are singing and acting. I'm only sorry that it has taken me so long to combine the two."[107]

Laurence Marks was not alone in being somewhat astonished by this turn of events. "We asked him if he wanted to sing the theme song for *Love Hurts*," he says. "But he didn't want to. He said, 'No, I'm a not a singer.' He wouldn't do it."

"He wasn't very confident in the strength of his voice as he got older," says Russ Ballard. "He could have earned 80 grand a week touring at that time. We talked about it a lot, but he chickened out."

Confidence was restored, it seems, when Adam sang at Jackie's 50th birthday party. Katya, he told the *Daily Express*, was gobsmacked.

"She may be 21 years old, but she had no idea that I could play the guitar because I had never done it around the house. That got me thinking about how it would be fun to return to the studio. I would like to go back to the music which inspired me as a kid, like American blues and country. People put too many restrictions on themselves. You can do a lot more than you think if you are determined."[108]

He got in touch with David Courtney, who introduced him to Brian Berg at Polygram records. A deal was struck.

"We recorded the album, *Midnight Postcards*, at Advision studios and it was great to be back in the studio together after so long – it was just like time had stood still."[109]

The album included seven original tracks written by David and Adam together with Bob Dylan's 'I'll Be Your Baby Tonight', the Who's 'Squeeze Box' and Stealers Wheel's 'Stuck In The Middle With You' – which Adam sang as a duet with Roger Daltrey and was later released as a single.

"We had a lot of laughs filming a video with Terry and Roger performing the track on Brighton Pier and on top of a Brighton double decker bus," says David. "It was fantastic for the three of us to be working together again after 20 years."

The production is magnificent, the songs are terrific, but Adam, it has to be said, sounds like a man with stents in his arteries. He sounds old. On the duet, Roger Daltrey, just four years younger, comes across like a singer who has every right – more right than anybody else in the world – to be fronting a band. But Adam is an elderly financial advisor who thinks he can still get down with the kids; an uncle at a wedding.

The album wasn't well received. One critic came particularly close to the mark when he drew comparisons with a karaoke session. All the same it went Top 50 in the albums chart – for one week anyway – making it Adam Faith's last ever chart entry.

Adam dedicated *Midnight Postcards* to his wife and told the *TV Times*: "I've been lucky to meet someone like Jackie. If I hadn't been married to her, I'd be like Henry VIII, with six wives. You should never think that you've cracked it, though, because the moment you become complacent about marriage, problems can set in."

Chapter Thirty-Five

"At its centre is the disastrous meeting of Terry, a Cockney rogue who leads a high-profile militant campaign for open government, and Hilary who is meant to strike us initially as a prim and dedicated civil servant. […] But Terry himself has a secret or two, since he is also a philanderer with a strong interest in not being caught out wearing glass trousers."[110]

Patrick Parrinder, *Review of Michael Frayn's novel,*

Now You Know

A few months later, the marriage hit the rocks. Adam moved out of the family home and into a flat in Chelsea.

Adam and Jackie continued to see a lot of each other, but Adam saw a lot of other people as well. "Jack's problem had been his womanising," says Peter Thorp. "All the way through their marriage, she had a pretty poor deal. He adored her but he was just the way he was. She must have known about it."

It had been a long time since he'd been a 19-year-old Adam, "smashing all that sexual energy" back at a theatre full of baying teenage girls. Now he was a 54-year-old Alfie trying to prove he'd still got it. Which is not to suggest for a moment that he hadn't still got it. He had. And he could prove it.

"I was watching the telly on a Sunday morning once and I phoned Terry up and said, 'Are you watching this?' It was a programme about France and it had a very pretty French girl talking about the English living down there. So we chatted and both agreed how pretty she was and the rest of it. Anyway, about a week later, he phoned me up and said, 'What are you doing for lunch?' And it's like quarter to one and I said, 'Not much'. So he said, 'Why don't you come down to San Lorenzo's, then?' And, wouldn't you just know it, when I walked in, he's sitting there with the same French girl we saw on telly. He did it just because he wanted to take the mickey out of me."

"Tel was a star fucker – before anyone knew anything about that," says Peter Thorp. "So he had all these girls that he courted. There was one wonderful story – and I'm too much of a gentleman to name names – but she was a news reader and he had been with her the night before and he said to her, 'If you want me tonight, when you are reading the news, do something with the papers on your desk when you are on air.' So anyway this reader was reading the news and she started shuffling the papers – I ask you...."

"He bought one young ditsy blonde who couldn't have been much more than 18 for lunch once," says Laurence Marks, "and we were sitting on the sofa and he was regaling us with stories about what actually happened the day that he found that he was number one for the first time, and he said that things were great for three years and then the Beatles came along and everything changed. And this girl said, 'Tell me again, Adam, who the Beatles were?'"

And on another occasion...

"We all went to a restaurant," says Laurence. "Four of us were sitting there – Maurice, Alan Field, Adam and me – and the young waitress came over and asked to take our order. Adam started chatting to her – which was a common occurrence. He said, 'Where are you from, kid?' 'Poland,' she said. 'Where in Poland?' 'Warsaw' 'Been here long?' 'No'. And he said, 'Where do you live?' She told him and then he said, 'Do you like Italian food?' – doing a number. And she said that she did but you couldn't really get it in Poland. So he said, "The best Italian food you get is from San Frediano. What's your night off?" So she told him and he said, "Give me your address and I'll pick you up and I'll take you to San Frediano's for dinner." And then she took our order. Anyway, she kept coming over and smiling at him and he smiled at her and that was that. And at end of the evening, Alan said to Adam, 'You're not really going to take her out to dinner are you?' And Adam said, 'No, I'm not, but I wanted to prove to myself that Terry could still do it.' Because he knew the waitress didn't know he was Adam Faith. He needed to prove himself."

In July 1995, Adam opened in a Michael Frayn play, *Now You Know*, adapted from his novel of the same name, at the Hampstead Theatre. Robert Hanks, writing in the *Independent*, wasn't impressed.

"The pace constantly founders around Adam Faith, beautifully miscast as Terry. While everybody else in the office has their little secrets, it's essential that Terry should be big, blustering, rhetorical, determined to show that he has nothing to hide; whereas Faith inevitably projects inward canniness and discreet charm – the wrong qualities for the part."[111]

Few other papers, however, mentioned the merits or otherwise of Adam's performance, mostly because he shared the stage with Louise Lombard, the 24-year-old star of TV's *The House Of Eliott*. Adam and Louise were photographed rollerblading together in Hyde Park. Implications were subtextualised by the *Mail On Sunday*. Miss Lombard issued a statement "denying any 'personal involvement'".

Rumours were fed however, when Adam and Jackie confirmed that their marriage was over: "Friends said he and Jackie had been living apart for the past 10 months."

Jackie spoke to Linda Lee Potter in the *Mail:* "'I don't think my husband is looking for a wife. He's got a wife – me. I don't think he wants to marry again. We are not divorced and we have no plans to divorce – it has never been discussed.'

"'When you've been with someone for 30 years, they are your family. I know young women find Adam incredibly sexy. But when you've tidied up for someone, picked up their socks and looked after them, you see them differently. He knows I love him absolutely, but whoever he decides to see is his business.'"[112]

A few days later, Jackie suffered a heart attack and was taken to the Kent and Sussex Hospital at Tunbridge Wells. She recovered well. Adam spent all the time he had with her, leaving only to fulfil his obligations to *Now You Know*, still running in Hampstead.

The *Daily Mail* reported that "a hospital spokesman said Jackie was sitting up in bed and looking good. Mr Faith and his daughter have been in constant attendance since she was admitted,'" But nonetheless couldn't resist mentioning "24-year-old *House Of Eliott* actress Louise Lombard"[113].

"Although a photograph publicising the play was released showing them with their arms around each other, both strenuously deny they are romantically involved. They insist their friendship is platonic." And just to keep spirits up around the sick bed, the piece also drops in a mention of Chris Evert.

Two years later, when Louise Lombard spoke to *Miss London* magazine, the rumours still hadn't died. "'To suggest we were having an affair was absolute rubbish,' she says angrily. 'It was an absurd experience – because the more you protest, the more guilty you look.'

"'I mean, I did a job with someone and all of a sudden my name is linked with his for ever more!' she exclaims. 'All I did was take a theatre job I got paid peanuts for and I got my name associated with someone I don't particularly want to be associated with. Oh! I didn't mean it that way – but you know what I mean.'

"'We got on, like you get on with anybody you're working with. It was no big deal. But all of a sudden I had people camping on my doorstep. I had to move out. It was absurd. I said quite clearly at the time, 'This is absolutely rubbish.' But the more I protested, the more I sounded as if I had something to hide.'"

When Jackie came out of hospital, Adam moved back into the family home for a while, but it didn't work out. Meanwhile, the paps and the gossulmnists declared open season. Now when you opened your paper in the morning and saw Adam grinning back at you, in was rarely in connection with financial shenanigans, a new play or even a record.

While driving his silver Mercedes, he noticed an attractive woman driving alongside him. She was Sky Sports presenter Helen Chamberlain.

A "friend" told the *Mirror*: "They were both going along the motorway in their cars when he noticed her. He pulled up alongside Helen and kept smiling at her. In the end, he signalled for her to stop and they met up in the motorway service station for coffee. They got on really well immediately, exchanged phone numbers and arranged to meet up again. They went out for a few romantic dinner dates – but it was nothing heavy."

The *Sunday Mirror* was pretty sure it had caught Adam at it again with Emma Tremlett (who they identify as Henrietta Tremlett), who was helping him write his autobiography. "Adam has told friends that he and his pretty co-writer Henrietta Tremlett – who often arrives for their meetings on a mountain bike – have had to work late into the evening to catch up." [The mountain bike detail is, of course, a dead giveaway. Many of Casanova's conquests would ride to his palazzo in Venice on a mountain horse.]

"The pair have been inseparable lately, sometimes collaborating into the early hours. In between chapters, they have spent their time shopping for wine and food and chatting together at coffee shops. She has even been seen driving Adam's luxury J-reg Mercedes sports car."[114]

And so on, with each irrelevant detail presented as if it's some sort of salacious wink – 'coffee shops?', 'J-reg cars?' – we all know what that means, don't we, guv'nor?

He took a holiday in Hua Hin, Thailand, with 26-year-old Henny Frazer. The *Daily Mail* reported that Miss Frazer was: "A former debutante and, according to an old school friend, 'cool and fun-loving'.

"A fellow hotel guest said Miss Frazer and 56-year-old Faith seemed obsessed with each other throughout their five-day stay.

"'I've seen them each day at the pool and at dinner and breakfast together. They appeared to be very much in their own world'."[115]

Adam never lacked intelligence and he was blessed, sometimes, with the gift of self-awareness.

"Me living on my own has nothing to do with Jackie," he told the *Daily Mail*. "It's because I'm 56 and I'm going through the male menopause. I'm a f★★★★★★ [*sic*] idiot."

Some might argue that knowing you're an idiot, in some small way, makes you less of an idiot. Others argue that knowing you're an idiot but doing nothing about it makes you a wilful idiot, wallowing in your own idiocy. It's a moot point, because either way you're still a fucking idiot.

"I live in London and Jackie lives in the country," Adam said. "I don't know if she's angry with me – nobody will ever know except her. She's a beautiful, strong, exceptional woman. The marriage is broken, yes. We're not together now because I'm a stupid, immature, bloody idiot."[116]

Chapter Thirty-Six

"Throw me a rope to grab on to.
Help me to prove that I'm strong.
Give me the chance to look forward to sayin':
"Hey. listen, they're playing my song."

Marvin Hamlisch and Edward Kleban,
The Music And The Mirror, from *A Chorus Line*

At the end of 1996, Adam became a star of musical theatre again, in a revival of the 1975 hit *A Chorus Line.* This required him to hone his American accent ("accents are things we actors have to learn") and learn to dance.

The accent wasn't a great challenge. He'd spent his formative years watching Hollywood movies and listening to rock'n'roll. Katya, the Harvard graduate, coached him.

He was, however – or so he told the press – a klutz when it came to happy feet, snappy rhythm and jazz hands. "I have never danced before," he said. "Even when I got married, I got Lionel Blair to do the first waltz for me."

He was being modest, as ample evidence of him executing a choreographed watusi with a line of go-go dancers on *Shindig!* in 1964 will testify. He moves well, gets the steps right and looks relaxed, like good dancers do, as if no choreography is involved and he's just moving to the music the way he feels it.

In *A Chorus Line,* he was playing Zach, the hard-arsed choreographer who spends much of the show as an unseen voice on the PA, putting the poor auditioning dancers through their paces. It's not one of the principal dancing roles, but all the same Adam had to learn to move and to carry himself as if he'd been a dancer all his life. So, being Adam, he threw himself into lessons and exercises.

"I wish I had learned 36 years ago," he said. "The physical sense of well-being is better than Prozac."

The show opened at the Theatre Royal, Plymouth on February 27, 1997, ran for a couple of weeks there then embarked on a gruelling 22-city tour. There was talk of a West End transfer, but it never happened.

And inevitably, gossip linked his name with one of the young dancers in the company, Maria Laura Baccarini.

Ho hum.

When Hunter Davies, in 1994, had suggested that Adam was some sort of 'financial dealer' Adam had bristled. "What are you talking about? I've given all that up." He wasn't interested in money or business any more, he was an Artist.

However, in the same year, he became one of the presenters on the BBC business programme *Working Lunch,* and later, when London Weekend Television asked him to present a money programme called *Dosh* for Channel 4, it revived a grandiose plan he'd first hatched 10 years earlier.

Paul Killik, his stockbroker friend, had suggested, off the back of Adam's *Mail On Sunday* column, a TV channel devoted entirely to financial matters. At the time, the technology available for new TV stations – cable or satellite – made the launch of such niche channels economically unfeasible, but at the end of 1998, the advent of digital TV brought the costs down to more manageable levels.

"We couldn't afford it back then and the figures just didn't stack up," Faith explained in *Accountancy Age.* "When digital was announced it suddenly opened up a window of opportunity. The costs came crashing down." Relatively.

Adam was on a mission to explain. As he'd said years before, "TV programmers feel business is like religion – they devote as little time to it as they can get away with." He was going to put all that right.

Putting the business plan together cost Adam and Paul £400,000.

Using it, they set about raising their start-up costs of £6.5m. As well as money, they needed expertise. Working in a film cutting room and singing 'What Do You Want?' in front of a bank of TV cameras is all well and good but ...

"He needed people who knew how to set up a TV channel," says David Courtney. "I introduced him to these two guys down here in Brighton that were running cable and wireless television."

When Victoria Moore of *Metro* magazine interviewed Adam about the project on the phone, he was, as ever, bullish. "You've had financial catastrophes," Victoria said. "Did you ever worry people wouldn't want your advice?"

"Well, wouldn't you rather have somebody with experience telling you the whys and wherefores of money? You wouldn't want to go into battle with completely green people, would you? Paul Killik, the chairman of the Money Channel, has been massively successful in his business. Between us, we cover a lot of the areas, good and bad, about how to make, lose and invest money. [...] If this works out, I'd like to buy myself an island in the Far East or Africa. [...] Are you dark haired? Blonde?"

The keen-eyed social observer might, at this point, want to say, "Oh, Christ, leave it out Tel, will you?"

But he doesn't.

"So," he says at the end of the interview, "can Paula my assistant ring you in about three minutes and see when you're going to come over for lunch?"

The Money Channel was launched at the beginning of 2000.

Paul Killik was justly proud of their achievement: "In the last eight months, we have built our own studios, recruited 140 staff, developed 24-hour programme content and launched on time. Considering that we raised the money for the venture only last June, this is a fabulous achievement."

Other start-ups might have been a little more modest in their approach – perhaps, for instance, renting studios in the initial stages until the financial prudence of a custom-built studio of their own had been established.

David Courtney was not alone in expressing his misgivings about the venture: "They had raised all this money, but it had a terrible location in Wapping, which meant it wasn't easy to get to. And they'd spent a fortune on building this full blown television channel – their own studios. Everything you could think of was in there. All off the back of the idea of Adam's *Mail On Sunday* column, transferring that onto TV and broadening it out into a whole channel."

The location of the studio remained a problem. Piper Terrett was a 23-year-old researcher at the channel: "I remember we used to have to walk past lots of burnt out cars to get there. And we weren't in the City. We were just outside the City, so we had to send cars to anybody – any guests or interviewees – they always had to have a car and it all costs money. It was all very high tech for the time because everything was computerized, so that must have cost a fortune."

The press release made much of Adam's reputation as a man who had "spent more than 30 years investing in the stock market" with TV experience that included "the highly successful BBC2 programme *Working Lunch*; two series of the much-acclaimed Channel 4 programme *Dosh* and a highly popular money advice page called *Faith In The City* which he edited for *The Daily Mail*."

It was widely reported that, at the launch, the channel's share price had soared. Some estimates reckoned Adam's holding was worth as much as £40m. But outside the business pages, the coverage stuck to the personal angle.

"When Adam Faith opened champagne to celebrate the launch of his new television channel," said the *Daily Mail*, "Jackie, his wife for almost four decades, was by his side.

"'I couldn't have done this without her,' Adam said. "'No way. I keep saying that to her, and she keeps shrugging it off. But I could not have survived at all without Jackie.

"'I don't think there's anything more gratifying than to meet someone when you're a kid and to love them and be best friends nearly 40 years later. It's remarkable to get that lucky.'

"More remarkable," adds the *Mail*, unable to resist sticking the knife in, "is the catalogue of betrayal that undermined a marriage he is eager to paint as idyllic."

A year before, Adam had met a waitress in an Italian restaurant. He did his usual number. Her name was Tanya Arpino. She was 18.

"The first time he came in, he had a terrible flu and I asked if he was OK," she told the *Mail* years later. "We got chatting and he asked where I got my big brown eyes from. I told him my mum was Croatian and my dad Italian."

"I had no idea until he left that he was famous. His hits were long before my time. I wasn't attracted to him at first – that came later."

In the earlier stages, the relationship was so innocent that Adam felt comfortable taking Tanya home to meet Jackie. She helped in the kitchen.

He returned regularly to the restaurant.

"My parents were dining and my mum recognised him," Tanya said. "She told me Adam was looking at me all night with real tenderness. One day, in June, he came in and asked if I wanted to go out to dinner. He joked that he was old enough to be my grandfather but I took his number and phoned him."

On their first date, he took her to see the tree he'd crashed into in 1973 and pointed out the dents it still bore.

Piper Terrett was excited to be in on the ground floor of a new enterprise: "It was a brilliant place to work. Advertising and sponsorship revenues were well ahead of expectations and a potential audience of six million had been identified. We were all young and were learning on the job. It was really buzzy."

But the Money Channel hit a stumbling block soon after it was launched. The executives and producers, it appeared, had made certain assumptions – as it turned out incorrect assumptions – about Adam's day-to-day involvement with the channel.

"He [Adam] had a bit of a falling out with these guys," says David Courtney. "He said, 'I don't want to go on air. I don't want to appear.' And they said, 'If you don't appear then the revenue stream is gonna dry up from the advertising.' Because they want Adam Faith up there on the screen."

Piper Terrett suggested a possible reason was his lack of confidence reading autocue – the device that projects a script onto the camera lens. Eventually he agreed to do bits and bobs – a series of short inserts called *Jargon Busters* in which he'd explain, for instance, what a blue chip stock was, but he saw himself more as a face in the boardroom, leaving the presenting duties to pros like Gavin Campbell and Emma Crosby.

"Adam wasn't there running it 24 hours a day or anything like that," says Piper. "You'd see him around the office from time to time, that's all. He'd come in and perch on the corner of somebody's desk and chat. He was seen as having had a reasonably high profile and he'd been a property developer and a journalist. He'd made money and lost it all and then he lost it all again. He liked chatting up the girls and I think girls quite liked him. It was flattering but, I mean, it was bit like being chatted up by your granddad really. I don't think he was really all that old then – maybe about 60 – but I guess he'd been a smoker all his life. He looked like a smoker to me – so he'd gone off.

"Adam brought Tanya to work at the Channel. He got her a job there. She looked a bit like a deer. She looked even younger than she was. She was lovely – she looked after the Green Room – we had a Green Room where all the guests would come in to be looked after before they went into the studio.

"It's strange, there were a lot of other girls there who were very brassy – all cleavage and all that – but she wasn't like that at all. She was like a child. We'd see her wandering around with Adam and they would maybe leave together and things. She wasn't tall and he was quite little too, so it was sweet to see them together. I must admit I'm totally naive and – ironically being a journalist – I'm always the last person to know about all this naughty stuff. When I heard that they were an item, I was really shocked and I think quite a few people were. The impression that we got was that he saw himself as a Casanova, but we were surprised that he was successful with somebody as young as Tanya."

The Money Channel lasted just over two years. Adam had started out with shares worth about £1.2m for which he appears to have paid £216,000.

The company's value rocketed. At one point it was valued at £240m.

"My shares that I had had for nothing were suddenly worth about £30m," Adam told the *Guardian*. "And, in what seemed a blink of an eye, they were back to wallpaper."

The stock market was partly to blame. Economies were wobbly and the markets depressed at the time of the channel's launch. The anticipated bounce back never came. Not then, anyway. In 2001, France and Germany slid into recession. The USA did the same in 2002. The notion on which the channel and Margaret Thatcher's 'enterprise culture' were predicated – that stocks and shares were a fun way to make a fortune without doing a stroke of work – took a walloping when the dot-com bubble burst and shares tipped as sure-fire winners crashed through the floor and kept going. The administrators moved in to the Money Channel and started flogging off the assets.

Later, Adam acknowledged that the Money Channel was, or should have been, essentially a shopping channel flogging stocks and shares. "QVC was the benchmark," he said. "But financial services are much more difficult to sell than a £3 watch or a bit of jewellery."

"It all went belly up," says Piper Terrett. "I think, by the time I left, I wasn't that surprised that it went bust. By that time we'd had the dot-com crash. The management seemed to disappear into the sunset without having paid people's wages for the last month. They buggered off and all the journalists were up in arms – especially the people who hadn't joined the NUJ. It took the NUJ about a year before they got their money – it's really not a good idea to piss off financial journalists. Anyway, Adam went bankrupt and his shareholding was worthless."

"In a way it was a bit like a death," Adam said. "I felt like I wanted to lie down in a darkened room and forget about everything. I did that for a while but it wears off. It's just like a bereavement. Then you get up and start again."[117]

Adam and Leo. DAVID COURTNEY, PRIVATE COLLECTION

"What you've got to realise is, I was a good looking boy who couldn't sing, but Leo…" IAN DICKSON/REX FEATURES

Convalescing after the accident. TERRY O'NEILL/ICONIC IMAGES LIMITED

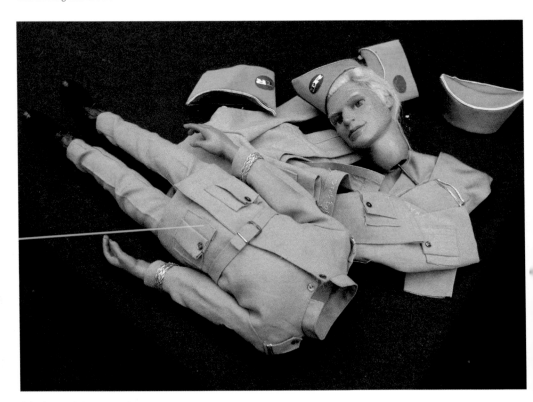

Adam's *Thunderbirds* puppet in a re-enactment. NILS JORGENSEN/REX FEATURES

Adam being no fun with David Essex on the set of *Stardust*. COURTESY OF THE BFI NATIONAL ARCHIVE

John McVicar, Adam, Walter Probyn, Roger Daltrey, 1980. PHOTOSHOT/HULTON ARCHIVE/GETTY IMAGES

Chris Evert and John Lloyd. CHRIS BARHAM/DAILY MAIL/REX FEATURES

Anita Dobson, *Budgie The Musical.*
STEVE POOLE/ASSOCIATED NEWSPAPERS/REX FEATURES

Running with Seb Coe, 1987. MONTY FRESCO/REX FEATURES

Adam. JOHN VOOS/THE INDEPENDENT/REX FEATURES

Adam and Zoë – *Love Hurts*. FREMANTLEMEDIA LTD/REX FEATURES

"You can take the boy out of Acton". TERRY O'NEILL/GETTY IMAGES

Roger Levitt. DAVID O'NEILL/MAIL ON SUNDAY/REX FEATURES

Juggling phones. UPP/TOPFOTO

Building the Money Channel. TOPFOTO/NATIONAL NEWS

Back with Jackie. In France with David Courtney. DAVID COURTNEY, PRIVATE COLLECTION

"It was like carrying a hugely heavy picnic basket." MARK LARGE/DAILY MAIL/REX FEATURES

He did what he always did. He regenerated and went back to work.

"It was a redeeming quality of Adam's," says Keith Altham. "When he fell on his face, he never complained about it. He just got up, dusted himself off and got another job. Going back on the road, doing some acting. He'd start work again and build himself up. He didn't moan about losing all his money – he was never a whiner."

Chapter Thirty-Seven

""All my life I've had one motto in marriage. If you're going to do it, do it and shut up. What the eye doesn't see, the heart doesn't grieve over."
Donald Churchill, *Love And Marriage*

*T*he *House That Jack Built* was a BBC sitcom written by Gary Lawson and John Phelps charting the ups and downs of Jack Squire – played by Adam – a working-class self-made millionaire who lived in a tasteless house with his wife and long-in-the-tooth kids.

Adam was excited to be acting on telly again, and this time he was determined to concentrate his energies on the task in hand: "I've cancelled all business appointments until the last day of filming. In the past I've tried to do too many things. I've learnt that you can't, you have to prioritise."[118]

"I liked *The House That Jack Built* straight away because it locks into the greatest single area of humour, which is class," Adam told the *Radio Times*. "I saw Jack as a class warrior. He doesn't earn money to be flash, he does it to say 'Up yours'!"

Adam may have liked it, but the viewing millions were so-so. The formula was jaded and ratings poor. The critics savaged it. "Beggars belief", "lamentable excuse" and "tripe" were some of the kinder remarks.

Charlie Catchpole, in the *Daily Express*, thought the best joke, in light of Adam's previous – and possibly the only joke in the entire thing – was the opening shot of Jack reading the *Financial Times*. "So what else is funny? Search me. This is a sitcom with one sit and no com."

"Think *2.4 Children*, without the biting satire and the gritty social realism. It's as if *The Young Ones*, *The Royle Family*, *Spaced* and *Black Books* never happened."

The failure of *The House That Jack Built* cannot have been eased by the knowledge that Zoë Wanamaker was enjoying a roaring success with *My Family*, another, vaguely similar, domestic sitcom.

"Unfortunately, *The House That Jack Built* is like tacky melamine next to *My Family*'s swish parquet flooring,"[119] said David Stephenson in the *Sunday Express*.

The good news, reported around the same time as *The House That Jack Built* was aired, was that Adam was back with Jackie, in a new house – a rambling farmhouse with barn and several cottages in the grounds – in Tudeley, a village a few miles outside Tunbridge Wells in Kent.

"It seems that after a bumpy seven years," the *Daily Mail* said, "which have included Faith losing £32 million on digital television failure the Money Channel, the couple are making a fresh start.

"Locals say Faith is a constant presence at his 60-year-old wife's side and they have been spotted out shopping and dining. A family friend at the house said: 'Yes, they do both live here, but he's out at the moment and Jackie's too busy to talk to you.'"[120]

"Everyone who meets Jack knows they are with someone special," said Adam. "She is incredibly artistic; someone who cannot let her eyes fall on an ugly sight. She's given me 35 years of living in beautiful houses.

"As you get older, your priorities change. Some men are great at treating women properly, but most need to put a few miles on the clock before the motor that drives them moves from below to above the belt."

Adam's health wasn't good. He used an amyl nitrate inhaler for his angina. The stents continued to give him trouble and he had operations at the Royal Brompton Hospital and the Cromwell Hospital to improve his circulation. But he was driven by a fierce need to prove himself, and by a desperate and unaccountable fear of loneliness.

He continued to see Tanya.

"Adam Faith is only 42," he said. "It's Terry Nelhams-Wright who's 62. I compartmentalise these things, because you want to keep your sanity, don't you?"

"To be honest with you," said David Courtney, "Tel just didn't like being alone. He always wanted somebody with him, so he always had a sort of companion, you know. That's really what a lot of it was. I don't think it was so much the full on sexual thing with her. She was like his companion."

It was the same when he phoned people and talked about nothing for hours, or nagged them to share a car journey to somewhere he needed to be but they didn't, or popped in unexpectedly.

"Once, we had rented a cottage in a tiny, tiny place outside Chichester," says Zoë Wanamaker, "and he phoned us and said, 'I was just in Brighton and I thought I'd come and visit you.' So he turned up. I don't know how he found us. He came around at 11 or 12 at night and we had a drink and we had a chat about a project he was trying to get my husband, Gawn, to write for him."

He went on tour with a production of Donald Churchill's comedy *Love And Marriage*: 11 venues, starting at the Churchill Theatre, Bromley.

He played the aptly named Bill, a golf-playing dentist whose shenanigans with younger women mean he continually lies to his wife. "All my life I've had one motto in marriage," says Bill. "If you're going to do it, Bill, do it and shut up. What the eye doesn't see, the heart doesn't grieve over."

Sometimes life imitates art and sometimes it's not so much an imitation as a distressing clone.

Adam described Bill as an "emotional culprit and committed crumpet man like every man would like to be" but denied that his decision to do the play was anything to do with an affinity with the character. "It's not a personal thing, a play is either well written, in which case it's easy to perform, or it is badly written, in which case it's difficult."

Not being a whiner, and insisting, as ever, that the ups and down, twists and turns in his career were never the result of chance or circumstance but always of choice – he was in control, got it? – he told the press he was happy to be on tour again. He likened it to a 14-week holiday, staying in nice hotels, eating nice food and getting paid. He said the "buzz of hearing laughs" was like a drug high.

Andrew Tribe wasn't convinced: "He was terribly down. He was depressed and down. He felt he'd come to the end of Adam Faith and there was only Terry Nelhams left."

Things were not going well with Tanya. She suspected he'd been seeing other women. "Babe," he protested, "how's an old git like me going to get girls chasing after him?"

The tour had reached the Regent Theatre in Hanley, Stoke-on-Trent. Tanya, planning a confrontation about his 'philandering', arranged to see him there.

After the show, Adam signed autographs and had a quick drink with the cast and stage staff at the Unicorn Pub, across the street from the theatre. Then he went on to the Moat House Hotel where he was staying. Tanya was waiting for him.

He was tired. The confrontation never happened. They chatted inconsequentially.

"I remember Tanya telling me later what they were talking about," says Laurence Marks. "He told her he'd forgotten to buy his lottery ticket. Then he said, 'Go and put the telly on' and they ordered a sandwich. Then he said, 'There's a lot of crap on Channel Five' and then he died."

Other sources expand the last words to, "Channel 5 is all shit, isn't it? Christ, the crap they put on there. It's a waste of space."

Crimes Of Passion: Sleepwalking, a 1997 made-for-TV movie starring Hilary Swank was on Channel 5 at around the time he was watching. If he'd switched over to BBC 1, he could have seen *The Ipcress File,* starring Michael Caine with music by his old pal John Barry.

★

As Adam was put on the gurney, someone said to Tanya, "Don't worry, your dad's going to be all right."

At the North Staffordshire Royal Infirmary, Adam was pronounced dead. The press were already on to the story. Tanya phoned Adam's agent, Alan Field. He told her to get out of there before the press storm started. She took a £150 cab ride to her parents' home in Sevenoaks.

Jackie was in Spain staying with their old cook, Angelina. Katya had to ring her mother with the bad news. Jackie flew into Manchester airport on the first available flight.

David Courtney spoke to the press: "Jackie is in a terrible state. It was such a shock. She felt as though her right arm had been torn off. She didn't learn about his death until the next day because we had difficulty getting in touch with her. Jackie had been Adam's cornerstone, his grounding, and however he behaved and wherever he wandered, he always came back to her. And she always came back, too. You can only put that down to love."

"He died a broken man because of the last bankruptcy," says Laurence Marks. "It finished him. If you are going to die, Stoke-on-Trent is as bad a place to die as possible. That really summed up the disappointment of his life – that he should have died in a hotel in Stoke and left this poor girl to clean up the pieces."

His funeral attracted friends from all his many lives: Nigel Lawson, ex-Chancellor of the Exchequer, was there, Terry Venables, Michael Parkinson, Roger Daltrey, Leo Sayer...

Jackie's first wish was to cremate him in their back garden, but that wasn't allowed. Instead, she settled on a humanist funeral. Katya wrote the script. He was dressed for the occasion in black polo neck and jeans.

Bob Henrit was one of the pallbearers: "Staggering around with a wicker coffin – it's to be avoided. It was like carrying a hugely heavy picnic basket. It moved around. I couldn't understand why it was so heavy. Afterwards, I asked Jackie why it was so heavy and Jackie said, 'Well, we put two pairs of his Budgie clogs in there and a Budgie jacket and a big box of Maltesers and his mobile phone.' And I said, 'But Tel was cremated, wasn't he?' and she said, 'Yeah, we took them out in the end. We decided that it wasn't a good idea.' Jackie was a lovely person and I liked her. The funeral was wonderful. The only person who wasn't driving home feeling good was Tel. He was gone."

Laurence Marks and Maurice Gran were there: "No one could believe that he could ever die. But it was a fantastic funeral. It was hard to believe that we wouldn't ever see this child man ever again. He could always get away with doing things that children get away with doing."

Zoë Wanamaker (who always called Adam 'Bill') and her husband, Gawn Grainger, remembered: "We went to the funeral and then we went to the do at a hotel afterwards. I remember looking up and noticing that there was a card on the ceiling of the function room, probably from the night before when they'd had a magician on. I looked up and I thought, 'That's Bill. On the ceiling. It's all been a trick.'"

Understandably, Jackie did not want Tanya in attendance.

Tanya was overwhelmed by media attention and later took the ghoulish step of playing Adam's last voicemails to a TV company.

"People loved Terry and he did so much for charity even when he was ill," Jackie said. "But after Tanya sold her story, everyone thought of him as an old chap with a young girl."

"It's what she's done to his memory that hurts. She betrayed him. The Heart Foundation had been considering creating a charity combined with a memorial in his name, but after that they dropped the idea."

The talk show host and journalist Michael Parkinson, who had given the eulogy at the funeral, told reporters at the *Daily Mail* that his friend was in the mould of a true English eccentric: "He was a remarkable human being. He was an extraordinary optimist, a great man to be with. He was always happy. He was a guy who was full of concern for other people. He talked about you, not himself. I don't think there's anyone who didn't like Adam Faith."

The rock writer Charles Shaar Murray wrote: "His unshakeable self-belief led him to reinvent himself countless times; if one venture failed, he would return with another. His ingenuity, energy and tenacity may well have outweighed his talent, but the combination of all of those qualities took him an awful long way from Acton. He was the epitome of the aspirational working class: not a clownish cockney music-hall revivalist like his contemporary Tommy Steele, but a neatly-dressed, businesslike, articulate harbinger of Mod: a stylish, well-groomed bookend to the faux-Elvis rockerisms of Billy Fury and Cliff Richard. He was also a natural Thatcherite, with the classic self-made man's contempt for the lazy and privileged: his ideal was to get on in life, and he used everything he had to further that aim."[121]

After the funeral, Jackie found that Adam's insistence on always living like a millionaire had taken its toll.

She had to leave the farmhouse in Tudeley.

"I cannot afford to stay here because of the money situation and by the time things are finished I won't be able to afford a cardboard box, let alone a house," she told the *Daily Mail*. "The insolvency people want half of everything – even the paltry life insurance policy. I am moving back up north to be with my family. It's such a happy house and we were so happy here that I would not stay here even if I could afford it, because of the memories. I keep expecting him to walk around the kitchen door and say 'all right Jacks?' He was made bankrupt and the insolvency people came and looked at all our things just after Christmas."[122]

There's nothing more to say.

End Notes

1   *The Independent*, February 9, 2003

2   Goldrosen, John J.: *Buddy Holly, His Life And Music,* Spice Box Books Ltd. 1975

3   Fiegel, Eddi: *John Barry: A Sixties Theme,* Faber and Faber 2001

4   ibid

5   http://www.ournottinghamshire.org.uk/page_id__435.aspx

6   Frame, Pete: *The Restless Generation,* Rogan House 2007

7   Walters, Nicholas, quoted in Cohen, Stanley: *Breaking Out, Smashing Up And The Social Context Of Aspiration,* CCCS Selected Working Papers Vol. 2

8   Melly, George: *Revolt Into Style: Pop Arts In Britain,* Penguin Books Ltd. 1972

9   The Jennifer Selway Interview, *Daily Express,* August 1, 2002

10   Cohn, Nick: *Awopbopaloobop Alopbamboom,* Paladin, 1970

11   Hutchins, Chris quoted in Loog Oldham, Andrew: *Stoned,* 2001

12   *The Times,* June 21, 1968

13   *New Musical Express,* July 16, 1965

14   Faith, Adam: *Poor Me,* Four Square 1961 (profusely illustrated)

15   Faith, Adam, *Acts of Faith,* Bantam Press 1996

16   http://www.gillianhills.com/

17   *Cinema Retro,* September 2009

18   Field, Shirley Ann: *A Time For Love,* Bantam 1991.

19   *Nova* magazine in June 1972

20   Faith, Adam: *Adam, His Fabulous Year,* Picture Story Publications, 1960

21   Faith, Adam: *Acts Of Faith,* Bantam Press 1996

22   *Daily Mail,* April 23, 2002

23   Faith, Adam: *Adam, His Fabulous Year,* Picture Story Publications, 1960

24   *Sunday Dispatch,* June 5, 1960

25   ibid

26   *The Times,* letters page, October 20, 1960

27   ibid

28   *Disc,* January 27, 1961

29   *The Evening Standard,* June 9, 1961

30   *Sunday Express,* April 8, 1962

31   *New Record Mirror,* May 19, 1962.

32   *The Times,* Aug 9, 1962

33   *New Record Mirror,* August 25, 1962

34   *New Record Mirror,* July 11, 1964

35   *Daily Herald,* Feb 25, 1963

36   Melly, George: *Revolt Into Style: Pop Arts In Britain,* Penguin Books Ltd. 1972

37   *Daily Express,* Dec 10, 1963

38   Andrew's blog, *Eight Miles Higher,* is at http://andrewdarlington. blogspot.co.uk

39   *The Times,* December 27, 1963

40   Bret, David: *Brit Girls Of The Sixties,* lulu.com, 2010

41   ibid

42   Shaw, Sandie: *The World At My Feet,* Harper Collins, 1991

43   ibid

44   Faith, Adam, *Acts Of Faith,* Bantam Press, 1996

45   *Daily Express,* Jan 15, 1965

46   *Daily Express,* Jan 22, 1965

47   *New Musical Express,* April 2, 1965

48 *Daily Mail,* September 29, 1965
49 *Daily Sketch,* May 24, 1967
50 *Sunday Express,* November 10, 1975
51 *Daily Express,* February 9, 1965
52 Camilla Beach, *Australian Times,* May 18, 1966
53 *Daily Express,* May 7, 1966
54 *The People,* August 11, 1968
55 *The Times,* January 16, 1975
56 *The Observer,* April 4, 1971
57 *Sunday Telegraph,* June 30, 1968
58 ibid
59 *The Times,* November 28, 1968
60 *Glasgow Herald,* April 9, 1969
61 *The Observer,* April 4, 1971
62 *Sunday Mirror,* June 13, 1971
63 *The Times,* April 10, 1971
64 *Daily Telegraph,* July 3, 1971
65 *Daily Express,* June 26, 1971
66 *Sunday Mirror,* June 13, 1971
67 *Daily Mirror,* July 13, 1972
68 *Daily Express,* April 21, 1972
69 *Daily Mirror,* April 21, 1972
70 *Sun,* June 19, 1972
71 Interview with Paul Sinclair, *Super Deluxe Edition,* November 2013.
72 Courtney, David: *The Truth Behind The Music,* Whiteroom 2011
73 *Rolling Stone* magazine, April 1973
74 Courtney, David: *The Truth Behind The Music,* Whiteroom 2011
75 *Daily Mail,* August 11, 1973
76 *Daily Express,* November 10, 1975
77 Interview with Peter Thompson, *Talking Heads,* Australian Broadcasting Corporation, November 1, 2010
78 The Jennifer Selway Interview, *Daily Express,* August 1, 2002
79 Interview with Anthony O'Grady, *RAM,* June, 1975
80 *Time Out,* February 27, 1976
81 Interview with Barbara Charone, *Sounds,* March 13, 1976

82 *Mojo,* May 2013

83 Fletcher, Tony: *Dear Boy – The Life And Times Of Keith Moon,* Omnibus Press, 1998

84 Interview with Anthony O'Grady, *RAM,* June, 1975

85 ibid

86 Interview with Paul Sinclair, *Super Deluxe Edition,* November 2013

87 *Modern Drama,* Vol 27, No. 4.

88 Interview with Barbara Charone, *Sounds,* March 13, 1976

89 ibid

90 Daily Express, March 6, 1976

91 Essex, David: *Over The Moon,* Virgin, 2012

92 http://philip.greenspun.com/flying/helicopters

93 The Jennifer Selway Interview, *Daily Express,* August 1, 2002

94 *Woman,* September 27, 1988

95 Imrie, Celia: *The Happy Hoofer,* Hodder and Stoughton, 2011

96 Interview with Mark Anstead, *The Guardian,* November 20, 2004

97 *The Independent,* October 5, 1988

98 Inverne, James: *Wrestling With Elephants, The Authorised Biography Of Don Black,* Sanctuary Publishing Ltd., 2003

99 *Mail On Sunday,* October 16, 1988

100 *Daily Express,* October 19, 1988

101 *The Times,* January 27, 1991

102 *The Radio Times,* January 4, 1992

103 *Daily Express,* February 19, 1993

104 *Scottish Herald,* July 15, 1993

105 *Mail On Sunday,* February 21, 1993

106 *Daily Express,* January 23, 1993

107 *Daily Express,* February 19, 1993

108 *Daily Express,* December 19, 1992

109 Courtney, David: *The Truth Behind The Music,* Whiteroom 2011

110 *London Review Of Books,* Vol 14, No 19, 1992

111 *The Independent,* July 21, 1995.

112 *Daily Mail,* July 29, 1995

113 *Daily Mail,* August 12, 1995

114 *Sunday Mirror,* 28 July, 1996

115 *Daily Mail,* December 6, 1996

116 ibid

117 The Jennifer Selway Interview, *Daily Express,* August 1, 2002

118 ibid

119 *Sunday Express,* August 4, 2002

120 *Daily Mail,* August 5, 2002

121 *The Independent,* March 11, 2003

122 *Daily Mail,* February 24, 2004

Filmography

Listing major film and TV appearances as an actor.

1959	No Hiding Place (TV)	Vince
1960	Beat Girl	Dave
1960	Never Let Go	Tommy Towers
1961	What A Whopper	Tony Blake
1962	Mix Me A Person	Harry Jukes
1966	Seven Deadly Sins (TV)	Gordon
1971-72	Budgie (TV)	Ronald 'Budgie' Bird
1974	Stardust	Mike
1977	McCloud (TV)	Inspector Craig
1979	Yesterday's Hero	Jake Marsh
1980	McVicar	Walter Probyn
1980	Foxes	Bryan
1984	Just Another Little Blues Song (TV)	Frank
1985	Minder On The Orient Express (TV)	James Crane
1989	Shady Tales (TV)	Gordon Shade
1992-94	Love Hurts (TV)	Frank Carver
2002	The House That Jack Built (TV)	Jack Squire
2003	Murder In Mind (TV)	Terry Cameron

Selected Discography

This includes only major UK releases. For a more complete list including Italian and German language releases and EPs, see:
http://www.adamfaith.org.uk/discog.php
http://www.discogs.com/artist/319135-Adam-Faith
and http://rateyourmusic.com/artist/adam_faith

SINGLES

Release Date	Title	Chart Pos.
January 1958	'(Got A) Heartsick Feeling' / 'Brother Heartache And Sister Tears'	–
November 1958	'High School Confidential' / 'Country Music Holiday'	–
June 1959	'Ah, Poor Little Baby!' / 'Runk Bunk'	–
October 1959	'What Do You Want?' / 'From Now Until Forever'	1
January 1960	'Poor Me' / 'The Reason'	1
April 1960	'Someone Else's Baby' / 'Big Time'	2

June 1960	'Johnny Comes Marching Home' / 'Made You'	5
September 1960	'How About That!' / 'With Open Arms'	4
October 1960	'Lonely Pup (In A Christmas Shop)' / 'Greenfinger'	4
February 1961	'Who Am I?' / 'This Is It'	5
April 1961	'Easy Going Me' / 'Wonderin''	12
July 1961	'Don't You Know It?' / 'My Last Wish'	12
October 1961	'The Time Has Come' / 'A Help-Each-Other Romance'	4
January 1962	'Lonesome' / 'Watch Your Step'	12
April 1962	'As You Like It' / 'Face To Face'	5
August 1962	'Don't That Beat All' / 'Mix Me A Person'	8
December 1962	'Baby Take A Bow' / 'Knocking on Wood'	22
January 1963	'What Now' / 'What Have I Got'	31
July 1963	'Walkin' Tall' / 'Just Mention My Name'	23
September 1963	'The First Time' / 'So Long Baby'	5
December 1963	'We Are In Love' / 'Made For Me'	11
March 1964	'If He Tells You' / 'Talk To Me'	25
May 1964	'I Love Being In Love With You' / 'It's Alright'	33
September 1964	'Only One Such As You' / 'I Just Don't Know'	-
November 1964	'Message To Martha (Kentucky Bluebird)' / 'It Sounds Good To Me'	12
February 1965	'Stop Feeling Sorry For Yourself' / 'I've Gotta See My Baby'	23
April 1965	'Hand Me Down Things' / 'Talk About Love'	-
June 1965	'Someone's Taken Maria Away' / 'I Can't Think Of Anyone Else'	34
September 1965	'I Don't Need That Kind Of Lovin'' / 'I'm Used To Losing You'	-
January 1966	'Idle Gossip' / 'If Ever You Need Me'	-

March 1966	'To Make A Big Man Cry' / 'Here's Another Day'	–
October 1966	'Cheryl's Goin' Home' / 'Funny Kind Of Love'	42
February 1967	'What More Can Anyone Do?' / 'You've Got A Way With Me'	–
September 1967	'Cowman Milk Your Cow' / 'Daddy What'll Happen To Me'	–
November 1967	'To Hell With Love' / 'Close The Door'	–
September 1974	'I Survived' / 'In Your Life'	–
December 1974	'Maybe' / 'Star Song'	–
November 1993	(CD SINGLE) 'Stuck In The Middle' / 'Not Without You' / 'The Promise'	–

ALBUMS

This list excludes 'Greatest Hits' compilations, 'various artists' compilations and re-releases.

1960	*Beat Girl* (didn't chart until the film's release in 1961)	11
1960	*Adam*	6
1962	*Adam Faith*	20
1962	*From Adam With Love*	–
1963	*For You*	–
1964	*On The Move*	–
1965	*Faith Alive*	19
1974	*I Survive*	–
1988	*Budgie – The Musical*	–
1993	*Midnight Postcards*	43

Acknowledgements

We are grateful for the many absorbing hours we spent at the British Library and the BBC Written Archives Centre and to the many people who gave us far more of their time than we had any right to expect and/or generous permission to quote from their work.

They include (in alphabetical order): Keith Altham, Daniel Anderson, Russ Ballard, Louis Barfe, David Barraclough, David Bays (Acton History Group), Raechel Beardwood, Bullseye Bob, Robert Bowman, David Brunt, Pete Butler, Chris Charlesworth, Maureen Colledge (Acton History Group), David Courtney, Andrew Darlngton, Andrew Drummond, Robert Elms, Martin Fenton, John Fiske, Trevor Frecknall, Gawn Grainger, Maurice Gran, Vanessa Green, Roberta Green, Roy Hawkesford, Bob Henrit, Ruth Keating, Cheryl Kennedy, Ray Langstone, Julian Littman, Dirk Maggs, Laurence Marks, Claire McKendrick (Scottish Theatre Archive, University of Glasgow), Robin Morgan, Jim Nelhams, Terry O'Neill, William Orenstein, Nigel Planer, Nicholas Powell, David Prest, Linda Sayle, Warren Sherman, Piper Terrett, Peter Thorp, Andrew Tribe, Jeff Walden (BBC Written Archives), Zoë Wanamaker CBE.

Apologies in advance to anyone we've missed out.

Wherever possible we have sought permission for lengthy quotations, but in cases where we have failed to do this and have exceeded the limits of 'Fair Usage' we would be grateful if the copyright holders could contact us.

Index

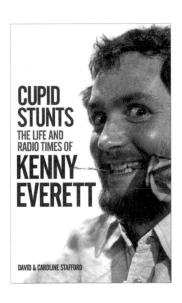

CUPID STUNTS
THE LIFE AND RADIO TIMES OF KENNY EVERETT
by David & Caroline Stafford

Cupid Stunts is the unique chronicle of a self-made media genius who triumphed in the image-free landscape of radio and, improbably enough, repeated the trick on television when he had finally exhausted the collective patience of the radio bosses.

Kenny Everett was a wireless wizard. His passion for the medium and his genius for making magic emerge from the tiny tinny speaker of a transistor has never been equalled. He was in at the birth of no less than four major radio stations but his compulsion to outrage usually resulted in summary dismissal. Then he took his fevered imagination to television, introducing the world to Sid Snot, Captain Kremmen, Cupid Stunt and Brother Lee Love to become one of the nation's best-loved entertainers and the scourge of uptight moralists.

Happily and heterosexually married for 11 years, he eventually came out and had the best of times in the best of clubs – ironically at the exact moment that HIV/AIDS reached epidemic proportions.

David and Caroline Stafford's hugely entertaining book is, in the spirit of the man himself, an exuberant celebration of radio, of genius and of passion.

Available from all good book shops & **www.omnibuspress.com**

ISBN: 978.1.78038.708.6
Order No: OP54945

FINGS AIN'T WOT THEY USED T'BE
THE LIFE OF LIONEL BART

by David & Caroline Stafford

Fings Ain't Wot They Used T'Be presents a vivid picture of the unique musical talent that was Lionel Bart. For ten years in the Fifties and Sixties he was a hit-making machine. He witnessed the birth of British rock'n'roll, gave Cliff Richard his first number one and the James Bond movie franchise its first song. He wrote hit musicals, advised The Beatles and The Rolling Stones and helped Judy Garland in her final drug-addled years. He mixed with serious artists and showbiz celebrities, hosted wild parties and could infuriate or inspire love in equal parts. After things finally started to go wrong in the Seventies, his downfall was as spectacular as his triumphs.

Based on exclusive first-time access to Lionel Bart's private archives and interviews with those who knew him best, Caroline and David Stafford's remarkable biography covers the glory years, the decline and the modest rehabilitation of a great songwriter and quite extraordinary human being.

Caroline and David Stafford have written extensively for newspapers, radio, TV and stand-up. They live in North London with their three children.

Available from all good book shops & **www.omnibuspress.com**

ISBN: 978.1.84938.661.6
Order No: OP53823